QUIET RUMOURS

AN ANARCHA-FEMINIST READER

Quiet Rumours: An Anarcha-Feminist Reader

ISBN: 978-1-84935-103-4 (print)
Library of Congress Control Number: 2012937708

AK Press
674-A 23rd Street
Oakland, CA 94612
USA
www.akpress.org
akpress@akpress.org

AK Press UK
PO Box 12766
Edinburgh EH8 9YE
Scotland
www.akuk.com
ak@akedin.demon.co.uk

The above addresses would be delighted to provide you with the latest AK Press distribution catalog, which features several thousand books, pamphlets, zines, audio and video recordings, and gear, all published or distributed by AK Press. Alternately, visit our websites to browse the catalog and find out the latest news from the world of anarchist publishing:
www.akpress.org | www.akuk.com
revolutionbythebook.akpress.org

Printed in the United States on acid-free recycled paper with union labor.

Design by Maisy's Dad
Illustrations and typeface by Miriam Klein Stahl

CONTENTS

PREFACE TO THE THIRD EDITION

The AK Press Collective

THE MOST ENDURING ANARCHIST RESOURCES ARE THE ONES that withstand the test of time—the ones that continuously change hands, that travel from place to place, across the boundaries of geography and history, that grow and develop a little every time they come into contact with a new generation of readers and writers. *Quiet Rumours* is one of those resources. Originally published as a collection of pamphlets printed in the late '70s by the Black Bear collective, this volume you hold in your hands today is the third incarnation of *Quiet Rumours*, and like its two progenitors, it preserves the original, while adding to it, and updating it for a new generation of anarchist readers and writers.

This book is the product of four different anarchist publishing projects. Black Bear was a London-based anarchist feminist group responsible for the six pamphlets that made up the first edition of this book. Typeset and printed, and in some cases written, by Black Bear throughout the 1970s, those pamphlets—essays numbered 1, 2, 3 and 6, 7, 8 in this edition—spoke to the important overlap at the intersection of anarchism and the women's liberation movement, an overlap that would, over time, begin to form itself into what we now call anarcha-feminism.

Though Black Bear itself would largely disband by the end of the decade, in favor of directing collective energy to the increasing pressures of the anti-nuke movement in the UK, the pamphlets continued to find their way into movement circles. In 1984, the Dark Star collective, a group of anarchist booksellers working in collaboration with Rebel Press, decided that the demand was great enough to issue a collection of the six pamphlets in book form—the original *Quiet Rumours* anthology.

In 2002, Dark Star collaborated with the AK Press collective to release an updated and expanded *Quiet Rumours*, pairing the six original Black Bear pamphlets with Dark Star's own "Untying the Knot" pamphlet, which printed Jo Freeman's infamous "Tyranny of Structurelessness" together with Cathy Levine's pointed response, "The Tyranny of Tyranny." Though these texts grew out of the women's liberation movement and are, in some ways, contradictory to anarchist principles and practice, Dark Star argued that the women's movement had provided an important and concrete glimpse into the revolutionary politics of equality that ultimately defines the anarchist vision of society. The debate over how to organize (rather than why) that "Untying the Knot" confronted is as critically important today as it was in 1984, even as the terms and the stakes have changed.

Thus, as has now become a tradition, the third edition of *Quiet Rumours* has grown in size, and includes three new essays that reflect a small portion of the contemporary conversations and investigations of the anarchist movement. What does it mean to talk about feminism in a social and political context that has begun—finally—to question the logic of the gender binary? In the ten years since the second edition of this book appeared, the struggle for queer and trans rights has taken center ring in the fight for the right to claim our own identities in the ways that seem most fitting to us as individuals. What does it mean to queer feminism? What do we do when these concepts intersect, and intertwine, as has happened more and more over the course of the past decade of anarchist activism and development in the English-speaking world? In their contributions to the third edition of this collection (essays number 4 and 5 in this edition), Sally Darity (editor and creator of the Anarcha Library) and J. Rogue and Abbey Volcano (editors of the AK Press collection *Queering Anarchism*) explore these new intersections of identity, pointing toward a new anarchist intersectionality that stands before us.

At the same time, while anarcha-feminism may have shifted and changed over the years since this book was originally compiled and published, the concept remains a vital one, as Dublin's Revolutionary Anarcha-Feminist Group points out in their contribution to this volume. "Our struggle," they write, "needs to be fought alongside the struggle against other forms of oppression, not treated as an afterthought or as a distraction." The re-publication of this volume speaks to that need, celebrates how far we have come as a movement, and points toward the years of struggle yet to come. It is our hope that future generations of anarchist, of feminists, of queer-liberation organizers, of racial justice activists, and of young folks around the world will add their own stories and strategies to the essays collected here, continuing to grow this book as a critical and lasting movement resource. For our part, we are proud to have been a part of the life of this important project.

AK Press Collective
September 2012

FOREWORD

Dark Star Collective

WITH THE PUBLICATION OF *BENEATH THE PAVING STONES* DARK Star brought together various Situationist pamphlets it had reprinted with Rebel Press into a book format. We are now pleased to be able to produce our second anthology which brings together the feminist and anarcha-feminist pamphlets which we reprinted with Rebel press. We would like to take this opportunity to assert that we still think that pamphlets have an important role to play in the dissemination of Anarchist ideas and hopefully we will go on producing them, and we encourage and support other groups to continue this practice. However as a group of people who have wide experience of working both in the radical and commercial publishing/bookselling arena our decision to produce these anthologies is also eminently practical. We have spent years tracking down pamphlets, articles etc. and we wish to make these as accessible as possible. While libraries are happy to keep books in specialist libraries, which are difficult for 'ordinary' people to access, they are unlikely to keep pamphlets. All of the pamphlets reprinted in this anthology were once readily available in your 'local friendly radical bookshop' or widely available through mail order via radical publications, and had a wide circulation. Regrettably, with the decline of radical bookshops/spaces, one-off publications etc, and the increasing consolidation and money-driven commercial bookshops, these outlets are becoming fewer and fewer, and the chances of placing a book in the commercial domain are far higher than the chances of placing a pamphlet.

Although we know that the criticism *"why reprint old pamphlets?"* will be levelled against us, we have no doubt that these pamphlets have both a historical and continuing significance. Also we feel no need to apologise for seeking to preserve and pass on significant works to younger/newer comrades. Despite the fact that anarchism comes in and goes out of fashion, to leave this task to commercial publishers seems to us a gross irresponsibility. As one-time participants in, and regular visitors to the Anarchist Bookfair, the number of times we have heard the question *"Have you anything on anarcha-feminism?"* would in itself justify our reprinting these pamphlets. Obviously we hope that the re-publication of these pamphlets will also stimulate debate about anarcha-feminism, and encourage a more widespread distribution of the issues that it raised. The first pamphlet that Dark Star reprinted was *The Tyranny Of Structurelessness* shortly followed by *The Tyranny of Tyranny*. Originally reprinted by Dark Star as two separate pamphlets they were reissued together as *Untying The Knot: Feminism, Anarchism & Organisation* (co-published with Rebel Press). At that time most of Dark Star were members of a Bookshop Collective undergoing numerous problems that other collectives and small groups were encountering. *The Tyranny of Structurelessness,* although originating from the Womens Liberation Movement and its associated period of consciousness-raising (and we should emphasise that we have no desire to seek to appropriate it as a work of anarchism), was immediately recognised as relevant to us as a group seeking to formulate non-hierarchical working methods, and by extension, relevant to many libertarian groups around the country. We reprinted it as much as a discussion document for those groups as a pamphlet in its own right. To cite the continued relevance of this pamphlet consider:

> "The many and various people who did Angry Brigade things were not very comfortable with clandestinity, which is inevitably elitist when it doesn't come out of a mass movement. Looked at now this conclusion seems inescapable. One of the most important texts of the time was The Tyranny of Structurelessness which showed how informal leaderships were especially undemocratic AND IT REMAINS ESPECIALLY RELEVANT NOW WHEN IDEOLOGUES OF THE INTERNET DISTORT ITS DEMOCRATIC POTENTIAL WITH THEIR HOLISTIC FLIM-FLAM" (our caps).
> *John Barker, review of Tom Vague's Anarchy in the U.K. (Transgression No4)*

> "I'd like to take up some of your points about structures. In certain specific arenas, such as when organising actions, such a (de-centralised, non-hierarchical) structure is useful in terms of not having leaders of demos etc, but in terms of organisation it's not. I would definitely recommend you read (if you haven't)The Tyranny of Structurelessness in Untying the Knot.
>
> In practice, the sort of movement you're advocating is dominated by informal leaders who thrive on the lack of a structure (which could shut them up and bring more hesitant people, unconfident about their ideas, more to the fore). Such groups preclude the involvement of most working class people as they represent friendship cliques which are created usually in middle class circles and, crucially, OUTSIDE of the meeting/action basis of the group movement..."
> *AF member replying to a letter in Organise 51*

It seemed to us at the time, and it still seems to be the case, that the issues raised in *Untying the Knot* are essential reading for anarchists in the understanding of organisational practice. (We also advocate that people study *Worker's Councils, The Miner's Next Step*, the experiments in Spain etc). The pamphlets contained in *Untying the Knot* had a direct practical impact upon us.They were addressing problems that we were attempting to deal with daily. Our nightly fantasies of International Anarcho-Syndicalist Unions seizing the means of production, Workers Councils arising, tenants taking over etc. were crushed against the daily reality of trying to run a bookshop!

The issues these pamphlets raised and the recognition they evoked in certain sections of the radical movements of that period would seem to suggest that there was a certain area of possible dialogue between the discourse of certain strands of the Womens Liberation Movement and the Anarchist movement. A position made explicit by Cathy Levine:

> "Like masturbation, anarchism is something we have been brought up to fear, irrationally and unquestioningly, because not to fear it might lead us to probe it, learn it and like it. For anyone who has ever considered the possibility that masturbation might provide more benefits than madness, a study of anarchism is highly recommended—all the way back to the time of Marx, when Bakunin was his most radical socialist adversary..."

A strand, a tendency, whatever you wish to call it began to emerge, eventually defining itself as anarcha-feminism. It would be dishonest to assert that anarcha-feminism was welcomed with open arms by the anarchist movement: consider the following report from *Zero No 5* Feb/March 78:

> "The South East and London Anarchist Libertarian conference, the first to be held since Warwick three years ago, took place over January 27/28/29 at Essex University. Organised on sexual politics and communication, around 150 people took part. We hope it will prove to be a watershed in the Anarchist movement's history.
>
> On the Friday night a planning meeting took place to finalise workshops and other conference details. From the hostility with which the already scheduled all-women's and all-men's workshops were challenged it became clear that confrontation over the issue of sexual politics was likely to dominate the entire weekend. This was borne out as the workshops got underway; workshops not on sexual politics rarely got

> beyond hostile conflict over sexism, while workshops on sexual politics were of necessity taken up with discussing what was happening in the conference itself.
>
> The women's workshop began with a coherent supportive discussion in which we tried to clarify the links between our anarchism and our feminism. On the whole we were in agreement on the need both for an autonomous women's movement and to develop feminism within the Anarchist movement. These feelings were not shared by some of the men in the conference who saw no evidence of sexism in the anarchist movement and attached little importance to patriarchal oppression. At times throughout the conference women were belittled and even insulted, and their ideas trivialised—often by men who claimed to be 'insulted' by our allegations of sexism...
>
> Some of us came away depressed although others of us saw what happened as more constructive. This was, after all, the conference at which feminist and homosexual politics raised their angry beautiful heads and refused to go away. Essex could have been the first conference of a new, sexpol-conscious, anarchist politics, but left us instead determined that it should be the last of the old. The anarchist movement will fail to accomplish anything until it has come to terms with the oppression of men over women..."

We have no wish to dwell upon the reception that anarcha- feminism received from certain sections of the anarchist movement, but merely to remind ourselves as anarchists that we have not been as receptive to new challenges as we might hope to be. Retrospectively certain of the ideas of anarcha-feminism seem to fall coherently into ideas that were current at the time. The slogan 'The personal is political' can be seen in Breton's "Transform the world, said Marx, change life said Rimbaud...," seen in the Situationist demand for the revolution of everyday life, and seen in the rather more prosaic tradition of "How come we always make the tea and do the typing?"

Fortunately the Black Bear anarcha-feminist imprint produced six pamphlets which constituted the original *Quiet Rumours* and we would like to take this opportunity to commend their commitment to their publishing project without which anarcha-feminist ideas would never have had the impact which they did. Between them these pamphlets offer not only an overview of anarcha-feminism but an excellent and lucid exposition of both the Womens Liberation Movement and anarchism.

As Peggy Kornegger observes in *Anarchism: the Feminist Connection*:

> "The current women's movement and a radical feminist analysis of society have contributed much to libertarian thought. In fact, it is my contention that feminists have been unconscious anarchists in both theory and practice for years. We now need to become consciously aware of the connections between anarchism and feminism and use that framework for our thoughts and actions."

A review of *Quiet Rumours* in *The Anarchist Feminist Magazine* Winter 1985 reads "I hope this outline inspires you to read this collection and move on. What happened to anarcha-feminist writings since the seventies?"

We are pleased to offer this retrospective anthology in the hope that it works not only as an essential collection of texts past but offers inspiration for future discussion and debate.

Dark Star Collective

QUIET RUMOURS
AN INTRODUCTION TO THIS ANTHOLOGY

Roxanne Dunbar-Ortiz

UP UNTIL RECENTLY THE TERMS ANARCHISM AND FEMINISM were rarely found in the same sentence, much less interpreted as integrally related. Indeed 'anarcha-feminist' would appear almost as an oxymoron, Emma Goldman being the single example most people could identify as such.

With this important collection of and about anarcha-feminists over more than a century, stunning female anarchist heroes are restored to our collective memory. And this collection is only a sampling that should lead readers to other foremothers of anarcha-feminism, such as Lucy Parsons, Mother Jones, Jessie Bross Lloyd, Hortensia Black, Sarah Ames, Lizzie Swank Holmes, Johanna Greie, Kate Austin, Helen Keller, Louise Michel, Azecena Fernandez Barba, and thousands of other historical figures and contemporary feminist anarchists.

The historical amnesia we suffer serves well the state authorities, military-industrial civilization, and capitalist thieves that control our lives and destinies. The Sixties liberation movements broke through the chains that bound us, thinking we were the first generation to do so, only to discover we had true rebel heroes we could and must learn from and be inspired by. Most of the current younger generation is ignorant of past struggles unless they happen upon some of the small press publications such as this one. Bombarded as we are by the obvious fakery of the mainstream press and textbooks, we often become nihilistic rather than pro-active.

Young working class women, in particular, being prisoners of the beauty myth and consumer culture, have been short-changed. For in the piecing together of a usable radical past in recent years, women have hardly been present in terms of liberating role models, rather only as an icon or two, or a Florence Nightingale kind of nurturing woman. Women like Voltairine de Cleyre, Emma Goldman, and Charlotte Wilson were something else, being independent, pro-birth control, and anti-marriage before women had even the right to vote. They were lifelong agitators, on the move, speaking to large and small gatherings, writing calls to action and social/political critiques. They were far ahead of anarchist men in their vision of freedom.

Just like today, men find it difficult or unthinkable to not only give up their male privileges but also their sense of supremacy. Independent radical women often live lonely lives if they expect equality. Our task as anarcha-feminists can be nothing less than changing the world and to do that we need to consult our heroic predecessors.

WHY ANARCHA-FEMINISM?

Revolutionary Anarcha-Feminist Group Dublin

Why Anarcha-feminism?

RAG IS A GROUP OF ANARCHA-FEMINIST WOMEN IN DUBLIN, Ireland. We are all feminists, united in our recognition that women's subordination exists. Our struggle needs to be fought alongside the struggle against other forms of oppression, not treated as an afterthought or as a distraction. We are all anarchists, united in our belief for the need to create alternatives to this capitalist, patriarchal society wherein all are dominated and exploited. RAG meets weekly as a group to discuss topics which are important to us. We have produced five issues of a magazine, *The Rag*, and we hold occasional open meetings. The article below was written from notes on an open discussion we held called "Why Anarcha-feminism?" It touches briefly upon a lot of topics in a short article, so to read a more in-depth analysis of the issues raised please refer to the *Rag* magazine.

What is Anarchism?

Sometimes defined as libertarian socialism, the ultimate aim of anarchism is total democracy—for each person to have a direct say in issues that affect their lives, not rely on government to represent them. This requires the destruction of state, hierarchy and class society, and the construction of non-hierarchical bottom-up systems of organisations such as local councils and unions to replace these. There is the need for strong grassroots action and organisation in to prepare for radical change. As many people as possible need to be personally invested in organising to take control of our own resources and interests and to defend our right to do so.

Class and Feminism

Anarcha-feminists have tried to develop an understanding of class, race, ability and LGBTQ issues, paying attention to the fact that all women do not have the same experiences in their oppression as women. We try to be aware of privilege and to make ourselves aware of and learn from women's struggles globally.

From an anarchist perspective, some anarchists see feminism as a divisive issue, distracting from the "real" issue of class struggle. Thanks to anarcha-feminism, the anarchist approach increasingly accepts that sexism does exist, and is not just a minor side issue which will fade away with the end of capitalism. When anarchists constantly stress that all experience of patriarchy is linked to class, they can gloss over another truth: the experience of class is differentiated by gender.

In traditional anarchist dialogue the site for revolution has been the workplace; from a feminist perspective the family and the body are additional sites of conflict. This is our literal "means of production," which we should be determined to seize.

Anarcha-feminist Identity

Anarcha-feminists often find it easier to publicly label themselves as feminist than as anarchist. This is because many people who have not considered either concept are more willing to accept the premise that women and men should have equality than to question the core of the current economic and political systems. Many people who profess to believe in equality have not even considered life without capitalism, or that economic systems affect equality. Anarchism also suffers from negative connotations, for example the misassociation with chaos and violence. Ironically, some anarchists are unwilling to identify as feminist due to the negative connotations associated with the feminist label. The capitalist system is very effective in muddying the meaning of concepts which pose a clear threat to that system. It is important to us to be clear that we are feminists and anarchists, and that we see this as a pathway to freedom.

Equality not Sameness

We believe that true equality can never be achieved within any capitalist system. Capitalism will only concede enough to give a convincing illusion of equality. The ideals that early feminists courageously fought for have now been entirely diluted and sold back to us as pink and sterile girl power. We can be whatever we want to be as long as it's sexy—politician, athlete, scientist or "housewife." We need to be clear that when feminist gains are won, it is in the name of true equality for all people, not as a concession or privilege. Real feminism requires complete social restructuring which can essentially be equated with true anarchism.

One of the misconceptions of the feminist movement has been that for women to be equal to men, we have to be the same. Women joined the rush into the modern workplace to have equal access to exploitation. Many women find they experience a double shift of work ñ both outside and inside the home. Capitalism has made effective use of patriarchy and in many ways is reliant on it—for example on the nuclear family as the unit of effective consumption and control. The work that women do in producing and caring for children, in keeping the home and in caring for the sick and the old is not valued under capitalism. The value system of capitalism is profit-driven; only that which produces profit is seen as productive.

Queer Feminism

There are overlaps between feminism and queer theory (queerness might be roughly defined as gender or sexuality non-conformism). Anarcha-feminism recognises the fluidity of gender and its construction from birth as a way of acting/talking/thinking. While recognising gender binaries as socially constructed, anarcha-feminism sees that society divides people into "male" and "female," oppressing women and those that don't fit into strict gender roles.

Although there is some acceptance by wealthy capitalist countries of difference with regard to gender and sexuality, ultimately it is acceptable only as a lifestyle choice, not as a revolutionary force, which it should ultimately be. The destruction of the systems of capitalism, state and patriarchy would lead to an explosion in different ways of being—sexualities, gender identities, family structures, etc.

Patriarchy and Men

The fight for women's equality has been framed as a "battle of the sexes." However, feminism has led to a growing consciousness of male oppression under patriarchy, such as strict adherence to masculine gender roles, duty to "provide" in the realm of work and lack of equal rights to active parenthood. Male oppression has been misconstrued as either a product of the feminist movement, or an oversight of it. Yet it is often through feminist dialogue that a space has opened up for discussing these aspects of men's lives and experiences. Pro-feminist solidarity between men and women can make meaningful inroads into these issues.

Meaningful Reform

Many very real changes have been made in women's lives due to feminist efforts. These include suffrage, the right to work outside the home, equal pay legislation, domestic violence legislation, etc. Unlike anarchism, feminist ideology can and has been accepted into capitalist reform. Yet it is socialists and anarchists who have mainly been behind meaningful reform—through the trade union movements, anti-racism work, community work and women's liberation movements. Unfortunately, many of the ultimate aims of those who struggled to create these reforms have now been lost. Their achievements have been co-opted into seeming like the achievements of "democracy" when in fact they were concessions hard won by activists condemned as radicals of their time.

While continuing to fight for meaningful reform (for example, abortion rights and free childcare), we also want to remain completely clear about what we are fighting for: not just women's equality, but absolute equality. The ultimate endpoint of feminism is anarchism.

1

ANARCHA-FEMINISM: TWO STATEMENTS

Red Rosa and Black Maria
Black Rose Anarcho-Feminists

Who we are: An Anarcho-Feminist Manifesto

WE CONSIDER ANARCHO-FEMINISM TO BE THE ULTIMATE AND necessary radical stance at this time in world history, far more radical than any form of Marxism.

We believe that a Women's Revolutionary Movement must not mimic, but destroy, all vestiges of the male-dominated power structure, the State itself—with its whole ancient and dismal apparatus of jails, armies, and armed robbery (taxation); with all its murder; with all of its grotesque and repressive legislation and military attempts, internal and external, to interfere with people's private lives and freely-chosen co-operative ventures.

The world obviously cannot survive many more decades of rule by gangs of armed males calling themselves governments. The situation is insane, ridiculous and even suicidal. Whatever its varying forms of justifications, the armed State is what is threatening all of our lives at present. The State, by its inherent nature, is really incapable of reform. True socialism, peace and plenty for all, can be achieved only by people themselves, not by representatives ready and able to turn guns on all who do not comply with State directives. As to how we proceed against the pathological State structure, perhaps the best word is to outgrow rather than overthrow. This process entails, among other things, a tremendous thrust of education and communication among all peoples. The intelligence of womankind has at last been brought to bear on such oppressive male inventions as the church and the legal family; it must now be brought to re-evaluate the ultimate stronghold of male domination, the State.

While we recognise important differences in the rival systems, our analysis of the evils of the State must extend to both its communist and capitalist versions.

We intend to put to the test the concept of freedom of expression, which we trust will be incorporated in the ideology of the coming socialist Sisterhood which is destined to play a determining role in the future of the race, if there really is to be a future.

We are all socialists. We refuse to give up this pre-Marxist term which has been used as a synonym by many anarchist thinkers. Another synonym for anarchism is libertarian socialism, as opposed to Statist and authoritarian varieties. Anarchism (from the Greek *anarchos*—without ruler) is the affirmation of human freedom and dignity expressed in a negative, cautionary term signifying that no person should rule or dominate another person by force or threat of force. Anarchism indicates what people should not do to one another. Socialism, on the other hand, means all the groovy things people can do and build together, once they are able to combine efforts and resources on the basis of common interest, rationality and creativity.

We love our Marxist sisters and all our sisters everywhere, and have no interest in disassociating ourselves from their constructive struggles. However, we reserve the right to criticise their politics when we feel that they are obsolete or irrelevant or inimical to the welfare of womankind.

As Anarcho-Feminists, we aspire to have the courage to question and challenge absolutely everything—including, when it proves necessary, our own assumptions.

Blood of the Flower: An Anarcha-Feminist Statement

We are an independent collective of women who feel that anarchism is the logically consistent expression of feminism.

We believe that each woman is the only legitimate articulator of her own oppression. Any woman, regardless of previous political involvement knows only too intimately her own oppression, and hence, can and must define what form her liberation will take.

Why are many women sick and tired of 'movements'? Our answer is that the fault lies with the nature of movements, not with the individual women. Political movements, as we have known them, have separated our political activities from our personal dreams of liberation, until either we are made to abandon our dreams as impossible or we are forced to drop out of the movement because we hold steadfastly to our dreams. As true anarchists and as true feminists, we say *dare to dream the impossible, and never settle for less than total translation of the impossible into reality.*

There have been two principle forms of action in the women's liberation movement. One has been the small, local, volitionally organised consciousness-raising group, which at best has been a very meaningful mode of dealing with oppression from a personal level and, at worst, never evolved beyond the level of a therapy group.

The other principle mode of participation has been large, bureaucratized groups which have focused their activities along specific policy lines, taking great pains to translate women's oppression into concrete, single-issue programmes. Women in this type of group often have been involved in formal leftist politics for some time, but could not stomach the sexism within other leftist groups. However, after reacting against the above-mentioned attitude of leftist males, many women with formal political orientations could not accept the validity of what they felt were the 'therapy groups' of their suburban sisters; yet they themselves still remained within the realm of male-originated Marxist-Leninist, Trotskyist, Maoist rhetoric, and continued to use forms of political organisation employed by the male leftist groups they were reacting against. The elitism and centralisation of the old male left thereby has found, and already poisoned parts of the women's movement with the attitude that political sophistication must mean 'building' a movement around single issue programmes, thereby implying that 'we must be patient until the masses' consciousness is raised to our level.' How condescending to assume that an oppressed person must be told that she is oppressed! How condescending to assume that her consciousness will grow only by plodding along, from single-issue to next single issue.

In the past decade or more, women of the left were consistently intimidated out of fighting for our own liberation, avoiding the obvious fact that all women are an oppressed group. We are so numerous and dispersed that we have identified ourselves erroneously as members of particular classes on the basis of the class of 'our men', our fathers or our husbands. So women of the left regarding ourselves as middle-class more than oppressed women, have been led to neglect engaging in our own struggle as our primary struggle. Instead, we have dedicated ourselves to fight on behalf of other oppressed peoples, thus alienating ourselves from our own plight. Many say that this attitude no longer exists in the women's movement, that it originated only from the guilt trip of the white middle class male, but even today women in autonomous women's movements speak of the need to organise working class women, without concentrating on the need to organise ourselves—as if we were already beyond that level. This does not mean (if we insist first and foremost on freeing ourselves) that we love our oppressed sisters any the less; on the contrary, we feel that the best way for us to be true to all liberation struggles is to accept and deal directly with our own oppression.

Why Anarchism?

We do not believe that rejection of Marxist-Leninist analysis and strategy is by definition political naiveté. We do not believe it is politically naive to maintain the attitude that even a 'democratically centralised' group could be considered the 'vanguard' spokeswoman for us. The nature of groups concerned with 'building' movements is: 1) to water down the 'more extreme' dreams into 'realistic' demands, and 2) to eventually become an organ of tyranny itself. No thanks!

There is another entire radical tradition which has run counter to Marxist-Leninist theory and practice through all of modern radical history—from Bakunin to Kropotkin to Sophie

Perovskaya to Emma Goldman to Errico Malatesta to Murray Bookchin—and that is anarchism. It is a tradition less familiar to most radicals because it has consistently been distorted and misrepresented by the more highly organised State organisations and Marxist-Leninist organisations.

Anarchism is not synonymous with irresponsibility and chaos. Indeed, it offers meaningful alternatives to the outdated organisational and policy-making practices of the rest of the left. The basic anarchist form of organisation is a small group, volitionally organised and maintained, which must work toward defining the oppression of its members and what form their struggle for liberation must take.

Organising women, in the New Left and Marxist left, is viewed as amassing troops for the Revolution But we affirm that each woman joining in struggle is the Revolution. WE ARE THE REVOLUTION!

We must learn to act on impulse, to abandon the restrictions on behaviour that society has taught us to place on ourselves. The 'movement' has been, for most of us, a thing removed from ourselves. We must no longer think of ourselves as members of a movement, but as *individual* revolutionaries, co-operating. Two, three, five or ten such individual revolutionaries who know and trust each other intimately can carry out revolutionary acts and make our own policy. As members of a leaderless affinity group, each member participates on an equal level of power, thus negating the hierarchical function of power. DOWN WITH ALL BOSSES! Then we will not be lost in a movement where leadership determines for us the path the movement will take—we are our own movement, we determine our own movement's direction. We have refused to allow ourselves to be directed, spoken for, and eventually cooled off.

We do not believe, as some now affirm, that the splintering of the Women's Movement means the end to all of our revolutionary effectiveness. No! The spirit of the women is just too large to be guided and manipulated by 'a movement'. Small groups, acting on their own and deciding upon their own actions, are the logical expression of revolutionary women. This, of course, does not preclude various groups working together on various projects or conferences.

To these ends, and because we do not wish to he out of touch with other women, we have organised as an autonomous collective within the Women's Centre in Cambridge, Mass. The Women's Centre functions as a federation; that is, not as a policy-making group, but as a centre for various women's groups to meet. We will also continue to write statements like this one as we feel moved to. We would really like to hear from all and sundry!

ALL POWER TO THE IMAGINATION!

2

FEMINISM AS ANARCHISM

Lynne Farrow

FEMINISM PRACTICES WHAT ANARCHISM PREACHES. ONE MIGHT go as far as to claim feminists are the only existing protest groups that can honestly be called practicing Anarchists; first because women apply themselves to specific projects like abortion clinics and day-care centres; second, because as essentially apolitical women for the most part refuse to engage in the political combat terms of the right or the left, reformism or revolution, respectively.

But women's concern for specific projects and their a-political activities constitute too great a threat to both the right and the left, and feminist history demonstrates how women have been lured away from their interests, co-opted on a legislative level by the established parties and co-opted on a theoretical level by the Left. This co-option has often kept us from asking exactly what is the Feminist situation? What's the best strategy for change?

The first impulse toward female liberation came in the 1840's when liberals were in the midst of a stormy abolition campaign. A number of eloquent Quaker women actively made speeches to liberate the slaveholding system of the South and soon realized that the basic rights they argued for Blacks were also denied women. Lucy Stone and Lucretia Mott, two of the braver women abolitionists, would occasionally tack some feminism ideas on the end of the abolition speeches, annoying to an unusual degree their fellow liberals. But the women were no threat so long as they knew their place and remembered which cause was the more serious.

Then in 1842 the World anti-slave convention was held in London and some American women crossed the Atlantic along with other Abolition delegates to find that not only were women denied a part in the proceedings, but worse, they were forced to sit behind a curtain. Lucretia Mott and Elizabeth Cade Stanton, enraged at the hypocrisy of the liberal's anti-slavery gathering denying women participation, then and there determined to return to America and organise on behalf of liberating women.

The first Women's Rights Convention was held at Seneca Falls, New York, in 1848, attracting with only three days' notice in a local newspaper a huge number of women filling the church in which they met. At the end of the very moving convention the gathering drew up a Declaration of Rights and Sentiments based on the Declaration of Independence only directed at men rather than England's King George. After this convention which is identified as the formal beginning of the Women's Rights Movement in America, feminism picked up quickly aiming at women's property laws and other grievances.

As American Feminism gathered a small measure of support, liberals became nervous that these women were spending energy on the woman issue rather than the real issue of the time: abolition. After all, they insisted, this is "the negroes' hour" and women shouldn't be so petty as to think of themselves at a time like this. When the Civil War became imminent this rhetoric grew from subtlety to righteous indignation. How could women be so unpatriotic as to devote themselves to feminism during a *national* crisis. Virtually every feminist in America suspended her feminist consciousness and gave support to the liberal interests at this point, assured that when the war was over and Blacks were given equal rights under the Constitution women would be included.

Susan B. Anthony, an ardent Abolitionist, was the only known feminist at the time that refused to buy the liberals' proposal. She continued appealing for the rights of women despite the gradual disintegration of her following who had been coopted by the Abolitionists into joining their ranks. She insisted that both struggles could be run simultaneously and if they didn't women would be forgotten after the war. She was right. When the 14th Amendment was introduced in Congress after the war, not only were women omitted, they were specifically excluded. For the first time the word "male" was written into the Constitution making it clear that when it referred to a person that was the equivalent to male person.

This substantial blow to organised feminism hindered further legal advance for women. Then around 1913 when British women launched their militant tactics bombing buildings and starting fires, Alice Paul, an enthusiastic young American woman of Quaker stock, traveled to England to study and ended up working with the notorious Pankhursts. She returned to the States determined to rejuvenate the cause of suffrage and soon had persuaded the practically non-functioning National Woman's Suffrage Association to re-open the federal campaign for suffrage in Washington.

In a very short time and due to nothing but her sheer genius for organising and strategy Alice Paul created a multifactional movement to be reckoned with. Her most effective tactic was picketing the White House with embarrassing placards denouncing President Wilson's authoritarian stand on Woman Suffrage while he preached democracy abroad. World War I approached steadily and the stage was again set for the feminists' co-option.

The pacifists appealed to the women to suspend their cause temporarily and join the peace effort while at the same time the majority, the war hawks, were scandalized that the women abandoned their country at a time like this. Again the women were coopted as thousands left the feminist cause to go to the aid of their parties, but nevertheless a small efficient group, the National Woman's Party, stayed intact to fight suffrage through.

It is difficult to ascertain which side, the right or the left, has been more responsible for co-opting the feminist efforts at change. History assures us their methods have been identical and their unquestioning confidence in the priority of "the larger struggle" inevitably leads to a dismissal of feminist issues as tangential. The analysis of the current Black Movement and the Marxist dominated left squeezes women into their plans symptomatically, i.e. when the essential struggle is fought and won women then will come into their own. Women must wait. Women must help the *larger* cause.

The poetry of Black women identifies intensely with building the egos of the Black male in the conventional way egos are built, by self-depreciation. The theme heard over and over again tells of the Black woman's proud suffering at the hands of the Black man who has been emasculated by his white boss and so needs his woman to at least feel superior to. She does her part. Her suffering is a direct contribution to the Black (Male) struggle which she considers a noble sacrifice. (As Germaine Greer has suggested, since women have no power to threaten, they cannot be castrated and therefore no one sees their powerlessness as anything but natural and no one's going to lie down for women to kick.) Whereas the Black male's powerlessness is only temporary, since he is male and has the potential power of the white male. All he needs is a woman to dominate the way the white man has dominated him and his stature will be restored. Blacks have challenged white supremacy by realizing Black is beautiful. They have yet to challenge the white family model, the patriarchal family as something to be desired and therefore still uphold male supremacy.

Juliet Mitchell is a Marxist feminist whose ideas, as in *Woman's Estate*[1], typifies the conceptual style of interpreting a group's very concrete grievances, like those of the feminists, as basically irrelevant to or symptomatic of the larger struggle where all groups participate in abstractions called ideologies. Predictably, if contradictions are found in the theory, Mitchell calls for an "overview," an abstraction that will enlarge itself to accommodate them. When interest groups such as students, women, Blacks or homosexuals formulate their priorities stemming directly from their situation, Mitchell accuses them of being helplessly short-sighted in refusing to see their needs as a symptom. What they need to understand, she continues, is the "totalism," the analysis to end all analyses.

The fully developed political consciousness of an exploited class or an oppressed group cannot come from within itself, but only from a knowledge of the interrelationships (and domination structures) of all the classes in society . . . This does not mean an immediate comprehension of the ways in which other groups and classes were exploited or oppressed, but it does mean what one could call a "totalist" attack on capitalism which can come to realize the need for solidarity with all other oppressed groups.

Mitchell might easily be accused of conceptual imperialism considering the "totalist" terms she uses serve to gobble up lesser terms reducing them to subsidiary categories under the authority of her original Marxist idea. According to Mitchell individual groups responding in their own way to their own interests must learn to see the way and sacrifice. Her idea that they must renounce their individual concern for the good of the total is an abstraction that has ceased to represent any interests at all, since it has come to be so large it cannot relate to diverse interests in any way.

The totalist position is a precondition for this realization, but it must diversify its awareness or get stuck in the mud of Black chauvinism, which is the racial and cultural equivalent of working class economism, seeing no further than one's own badly out of joint nose.

Mitchell's ideas invalidate all forms of individualism in the same way the organised left and organised right have historically co-opted women from working in their own interests. Women are asked to be "totalist' in the same way citizens are asked to be "patriotic." We are being asked to switch one kind of paternalism for another. We are asked to comply with an hierarchical meta-analysis which we cannot assume with the even most remote faith has any connection with our immediate grievance. What is good for all is supposed to he good for one.

With the spectre of totalism looming intimidatingly over us we are called upon to *justify* and rationalize the authenticity of our interests, i.e., stop *pursuing* our cause and be drawn into the diversionary web of *defending* it. We are so accustomed to thinking in terms of one group's interests being more significant, more basic, than another's that we are baited into self-rationalisation rather than question the value of pitting one group against another in the first place.

Not only does the "totalistic" approach make for much scrambling as to which cause is prior, it suggests that *when the nature of the problem is totalistic so then the solution must be*, which brings us to the place women have always been shafted. Groups may function under the illusion they are "all in it together" for just so long, usually as long as they are theorizing, e.g., like the promises made to the feminists before the Civil War. When it comes to doing something specific about this abstractly designed situation, one cannot so easily search and destroy the totalistic enemy. Solutions, in short, necessarily imply specific choices to be made about what will be done first and for whom. Thus the cause most efficient at coercing the others will be given priority and the others will wait. Either that or the totalistic solution will be so diffuse as to mobilize energies that will help noone. Women lose either way when they see their struggle against sexism in the context of any larger struggle.

If the feminist struggle is not tangential or subsidiary to other political movements then how can it be characterized?

Because most women live or work with men for at least part of their lives they have a radically different approach from others to the problems they face with what would ordinarily be called "the oppressor." Since a woman generally has an interest in maintaining a relationship with men for personal or professional reasons the problem cannot only be reduced to or located with men. First, that would imply removal of them from the situation as a solution which is of course against her interests. Second, focusing on the source of the problem is not necessarily the problem. It is a mistake to locate a conflict with certain people rather than the kind of *behaviour* that takes place between them.

It seems to follow then that women because of their interest in preserving a relationship with men must relate to their own condition in an entirely different, necessarily situationist basis. It follows that the energies of feminism will be problem-centred rather than people (or struggle) centred. The emphasis will not be directed at competing us-against-them style with mythological oppressor for certain privileges but rather an avoidance of any pitting of sides against each other. E.g., if a competitive situation already exists between the sexes, learning Karate will only reinforce the stockpiling of arms, on both sides; the terms of the struggle don't change the balance of power on both sides.

Feminism as situationism means that elaborate social analysis and first causes a la Marx would be superfluous because changes will be rooted in situations from which the problems stem; instead change will be idiosyncratic to the people, the time and the place. This approach has generally been seen as unpopular because we do not respect person to person problem-solving or are embarrassed by it or both. We characterize these concerns as petty if they cannot immediately seem to identify with any large scale interests or if those concerns cannot be universalised to a "symptom of some larger condition." Discussing "male chauvinism" is as fruitless as discussing "capitalism" in that, safely reduced to an explanation, we have efficiently distanced ourselves from a problem and the necessity to immediately interact with it or respond to other people. *Such theoretical over-articulation gives one the illusion of responding to a critical situation without ever really coming to grips with one's own participation in it.*

Originally the feminists were accused of not having one comprehensive theory but a lot of little gripes. This made for much amusement in the media because there was no broad-based theoretical connection made between things like married women taking their husband's names, inadequate day care facilities, the persistent use of 'girl' for woman and women wanting to work on equal basis with men. Rather than this diversity being seen as a strength it was seen as a weakness. Predictably a few Marxist feminists rose to the occasion, becoming apologists for the cause and made feminism theoretically respectable, centreing women's problems around the 'ideology of reproduction' and other such vague notions.

Feminism has traditionally tried to find ad hoc solutions appropriate to needs at the time, i.e., centreed around the family or community of friends. However, certain unscrupulous, legal, well-publicised (as well as theoretical) attempts have been made to bring women's liberation into the big time.

For example, some friends and I were recently involved in setting up a feminist conference on divorce. We found some speakers who would describe how to go about getting a divorce and some attorneys who would give free legal advice to women who wanted it. Various workshops were organised around topics that interested those involved or concerned with divorce. A huge number of women from the community came, attracted because of the problem-centred topic, women who would probably not have identified themselves with the mystifying concept of feminism. Everyone participated enthusiastically exchanging advice, phone numbers, lawyers names. Some women cried in the workshops, overwhelmed at the supportiveness of women in similar predicaments.

The conference was running smoothly when a speaker from the National Organisation for Women made a presentation of the official national position on divorce and the organisation's plans for the future. Included was a proposal that couples should be able to pass a test before they married so only qualified people could participate in this kind of legal arrangement. Presumably those who could not pass the test created by the law makers would be discouraged, thus preventing any future divorces.

Aside from the obvious fallacy of believing more laws will change what existing laws have created and thereby save people from themselves, the N.O.W. proposal exemplifies the attempt to solve the problem of women's liberation by high-handed monolithic means very similar to the Marxist Branka Magas' ambition of 'seizing the culture.' The impulse to coerce people by national laws is similar to the impulse to create a revolution to change the balance of power. Each kind of grand scale change will find reasons to service its own magnanimous authoritarianism. Moreover each side claims what's good for all is good for one and therefore any means can be used to advance the ambitions of the revolution, in model of the corporation.

These occasional large scale proposals lead people to believe such a thing as a non-situationist Women's Liberation Movement exists, a veritable army clamouring in unison for national reforms. The media perpetuated it. But there is no feminist movement per se. Feminists have been too busy working at their community based projects within families, communes, working places, to focus on building an image or identity for themselves. Further, a single movement image or principle would be counterproductive and have women constantly comparing their lives with the image, monitoring life styles and their work to see if it was in *compliance* with the MOVEMENT.'

The 'movement' at the same time has been criticised for not being cohesive and for not having a programme. Exactly. That's the point. The diversity in which feminists implement and practice change is its strength. Feminism has no leaders in the lieutenant sense for the same reason. There is nothing to lead. We plan no revolution. Women are doing what they can where they can. We are not unified because women do not see themselves as one class struggling against another. We do not envision a women's liberation army mobilized against male tyranny. Solidarity for its own sake is the stuff governments are made of and adapting these methods only reinforces the perspective of us against them sex-class antagonism. Identifying with other strugglers in such paranoid fashion encourages brutal competition and keeps the contest going. What's more, stressing solidarity can only lead to a self-consciousness about what we are doing as personalities, thereby accentuating our individual differences and causing conflicts before we even begin to apply ourselves to the practical problems of sexism.

The National Organisation for Women notwithstanding, feminism begins at home and it generally doesn't go a whole lot further than the community.

Midwives and witches practising their herbals and healing arts figure prominently in our individualist tradition. Women in families passed on information on how to diagnose pregnancy, prevent conception, cure infections, stop bleeding, prevent cramping and alleviate pain. Quietly, sometimes mysteriously, women have ministered to children and friends without elaborating on the policy of it. Their effectiveness inspired awe and fear and risked ridicule but they did not stop to explain or mystify what they were doing, they merely did it. What mysterious description remains of midwife methods, a female lore passed along from mother to daughter, has been deprecated as 'old wives tales.'

The current feminist wave maintains this individualist tradition in that women's health problems have surfaced as the principle concern. Small projects have sprung up all over the country for the purpose of meeting local needs for adequate abortions, birth control, pregnancy-testing and general medical care. Previously women had limited facilities or had to rely on the paternalism of doctors. New women's groups discovered there are many routine examinations and services that can be performed safely at little or no cost by women themselves.

Just such a group has organised around these interests at our local women's centre, providing various services, i.e., abortion referrals and information to the community on a daily basis, as the demands arise. Those involved see their function as community action problem-solving, assessing the needs of women and coming up with the most efficient way of dealing with that problem with the resources available. Of course, there are things we've learned are within our ability to do and things we must refer. Pregnancy tests are done quite simply and for free by volunteers at the centre. Abortion cases are referred to a competent carefully checked out physician who charges a minimum fee. A list of the cheapest and best venereal disease clinics has been completed and distributed by flyers. The scope and ambition of our project is dictated entirely by the interests of the people nearby. We enthusiastically co-operate with other groups on the mutual exchange of information but have no intention of expanding. We have too much to do to create an analysis or policy, and we haven't the time to stop and observe what's going on.

Where Do We Move From Here?

Where do we move from here? Feminists have always possessed an exuberant disregard for the 'why?' questions, the theoretical mainstay of our menfolk. Kate Millet's *Sexual Politics* for one was severely attacked by reviewers for spending all those pages *not* formulating a theory on why sexism existed. Our disinterest in theoretical speculation has been construed as a peculiar deficiency. Of course. Similarly our distrust for logic and that which has been unscrupulously passed off as the Known in the situation. We can't 'argue rationally' we are told and it probably is true that we avoid this kind of verbal jigging. But the fact is we haven't any real stake in the game. KNOWLEDGE and ARGUMENT as it relates to women is so conspicuously alien to our interests that female irreverence for the intellectual arts is rarely concealed. In fact, women seem to regard male faith in these processes as a form of superstition because there appears no apparent connection between these arts and the maintenance of life, the principle female concern.

Women's occupation centres basically around survival processes, the gathering of resources, the feeding, clothing and sheltering of children and meeting the necessities of life on a day to day basis. Our energies must necessarily be applied to 'how to' questions rooted in our practical responsibilities. Observing and evaluating life routines must be the occupation of the comparatively idle, those with less responsibilities, i.e., men. Similarly, an old joke points at the delusionary importance men invest their work with: the head of the family reports to his friends, "I make the big decisions in the family like whether Red China should he admitted to the UN and my wife makes the small ones like if we need a new car and what school the kids should go to."

Because women have no vested interest in theoretical assumptions and their implications and hence no practice in the arts of verbal domination they will not easily be drawn into its intricate mechanics. Instead, even young girl children, appraising their lot, acquire an almost automatic distrust (like Lucy of *Peanuts* fame) for the theoretical in the situation and rely on their wits and instincts of the moment to solve pressing practical problems. Women are suspicious of logic and its rituals the same way the poor are suspicious of our legal labyrinths. Veiled in mystification both institutions function against their interests.

The province of our interests, the ministering of practical needs as women, has been so seriously and consistently devalued that there is scarcely anything we do that is regarded as significant. Where our conversation is about people and problems it is pejoratively referred to as gossip; our work, because it is necessarily repetitive and home-centred, is not considered work, but when we ask for help with it is called nagging. When we won't argue logically it is the source of great amusement and it never occurs to anyone to ask us if we wanted to pursue such competitive fancy in the first place.

We must learn to see our so-called defects as advantages, as a problem-to-problem, person-to-person approach to Living rooted in the individual situation. We must learn to value other than the traditional ways of 'knowing' and instead smarten our senses and quicken our responses to the situations in which we find ourselves.

Feminism means finding new terms to deal with traditional situations, not traditional terms to deal with what has been called a new movement. It is a mistake for us to argue the validity of our cause; that would imply we wanted in. It would suggest there was a contest going on that we consented to enter, and there would be a dominating winner and a dominated loser.

Arguing a case for feminism is a form of appeal, like a powerless class asking for power or a PR enterprise attempting to sell something to a potential buyer. Feminism means rejecting all the terms we are offered to gain legitimacy as a respectable social movement and redefining our real interests as we meet them. So when our disinterest in aggression is called 'passivity' and our avoidance of systematic organisation called 'naive', we must heartily agree. How else can you get anything done?

1. Juliet Mitchell, Woman's Estate, Pantheon books, 1971, p. 23

ANARCHISM: THE FEMINIST CONNECTION

Peggy Kornegger

ELEVEN YEARS AGO, WHEN I WAS IN A SMALL-TOWN ILLINOIS high school, I had never heard of the word "anarchism"—at all. The closest I came to it was knowing that anarchy meant "chaos." As for socialism and communism, my history classes somehow conveyed the message that there was no difference between them and fascism, a word that brought to mind Hitler, concentration camps, and all kinds of horrible things which never happened in a free country like ours. I was subtly being taught to swallow the bland pablum of traditional American politics: moderation, compromise, fence-straddling, Chuck Percy as wonder boy. I learned the lesson well: it took me years to recognise the bias and distortion which had shaped my entire "education." The "history" of mankind (white) had meant just that; as a woman I was relegated to a vicarious existence. As an anarchist I had no existence at all. A whole chunk of the past (and thus possibilities for the future) had been kept from me. Only recently did I discover that many of my disconnected political impulses and inclinations shared a common framework—that is, the anarchist or libertarian tradition of thought. It was like suddenly seeing red after years of colourblind greys.

Emma Goldman furnished me with my first definition of anarchism:

> Anarchism, then, really stands for the liberation of the human mind from the dominion of religion; the liberation of the human body from the dominion of property; liberation from the shackles and restraint of government. Anarchism stands for a social order based on the free grouping of individuals for the purpose of producing real social wealth, an order that will guarantee to every human being free access to the earth and full enjoyment of the necessities of life, according to individual desires, tastes, and inclinations.[1]

Soon, I started making mental connections between anarchism and radical feminism. It became very important to me to write down some of the perceptions in this area as a way of communicating to others the excitement I felt about anarcha-feminism. It seems crucial that we share our visions with one another in order to break down some of the barriers that misunderstanding and splinterism raise between us. Although I call myself an anarcha-feminist, this definition can easily include socialism, communism, cultural feminism, lesbian separatism, or any of a dozen other political labels. As Su Negrin writes: "No political umbrella can cover all my needs."[2] We may have more in common than we think we do. While I am writing here about my own reactions and perceptions, I don't see either my life or thoughts as separate from those of other women. In fact, one of my strongest convictions regarding the Women's Movement is that we do share an incredible commonality of vision. My own participation in this vision is not to offer definitive statements or rigid answers but rather possibilities and changeable connections which I hope will bounce around among us and contribute to a continual process of individual and collective growth and evolution/revolution.

What Does Anarchism Really Mean?

Anarchism has been maligned and misinterpreted for so long that maybe the most important thing to begin with is an explanation of what it is and isn't. Probably the most prevalent stereotype of the anarchist is a malevolent-looking man hiding a lighted bomb beneath a black cape, ready to destroy or assassinate everything and everybody in his path. This image engenders fear and revulsion in most people, regardless of their politics; consequently, anarchism is dismissed as ugly, violent, and extreme. Another misconception is the anarchist as impractical idealist, dealing in useless, Utopian abstractions and out of touch with concrete reality. The result: anarchism is once again dismissed, this time as an "impossible dream."

Neither of these images is accurate (though there have been both anarchist assassins and idealists—as is the case in many political movements, left and right). What is accurate depends, of course, on one's frame of reference. There are different kinds of anarchist, just as there are different kinds of socialists. What I will talk about here is communist anarchism, which I see as virtually identical to libertarian (i.e. nonauthoritarian) socialism. Labels can be terribly confusing, so in hopes of clarifying the term, I'll define anarchism using three major principles (each of which I believe is related to a radical feminist analysis of society—more on that later):

> (1) Belief in the abolition of authority, hierarchy, government. Anarchists call for the dissolution (rather than the seizure) of power—of human over human, of state over community. Whereas many socialists call for a working class government and an eventual "withering away of the state," anarchists believe that the means create the ends, that a strong State becomes self-perpetuating. The only way to achieve anarchism (according to anarchist theory) is through the creation of co-operative, anti-authoritarian forms. To separate the process from the goals of revolution is to ensure the perpetuation of oppressive structure and style.
>
> (2) Belief in both individuality and collectivity. Individuality is not incompatible with communist thought. A distinction must be made though, between "rugged individualism," which fosters competition and a disregard for the needs of others, and true individuality, which implies freedom without infringement on others' freedom. Specifically, in terms of social and political organisation, this means balancing individual initiative with collective action through the creation of structures which enable decision-making to rest in the hands of all those in a group, community, or factory, not in the hands of "representatives" or "leaders." It means coordination and action via a non-hierarchical network (overlapping circles rather than a pyramid) of small groups or communities. (See descriptions of Spanish anarchist collectives in next section.) Finally, it means that successful revolution involves unmanipulated, autonomous individuals and groups working together to take "direct, unmediated control of society and of their own lives." [3]
>
> (3) Belief in both spontaneity and organisation. Anarchists have long been accused of advocating chaos. Most people in fact believe that anarchism is a synonym for disorder, confusion, violence. This is a total misrepresentation of what anarchism stands for. Anarchists don't deny the necessity of organisation; they only claim that it must come from below, not above, from within rather than from without. Externally imposed structure or rigid rules which foster manipulation and passivity are the most dangerous forms a socialist "revolution" can take. No one can dictate the exact shape of the future. Spontaneous action within the context of a specific situation is necessary if we are going to create a society which responds to the changing needs of individuals and groups. Anarchists believe in fluid

forms: small-scale participatory democracy in conjunction with large-scale collective cooperation and coordination (without loss of individual initiative).

So anarchism sounds great, but how could it possibly work? That kind of Utopian romanticism couldn't have any relation to the real world... right? Wrong. Anarchists have actually been successful (if only temporarily) in a number of instances (none of which is very well known). Spain and France, in particular, have long histories of anarchist activity, and it was in these two countries that I found the most exciting concretisations of theoretical anarchism.

Beyond Theory—Spain 1936-39, France 1968

"The revolution is a thing of the people, a popular creation; the counter-revolution is a thing of the State. It has always been so, and must always be so, whether in Russia, Spain, or China."[4]
Anarchist Federation of Iberia (FAI), Tierra y Libertad, July 3, 1936

The so-called Spanish Civil War is popularly believed to have been a simple battle between Franco's fascist forces and those committed to liberal democracy. What has been overlooked, or ignored, is that much more was happening in Spain than civil war. A broadly-based social revolution adhering to anarchist principles was taking firm, concrete form in many areas of the country. The gradual curtailment and eventual destruction of this libertarian movement is less important to discuss here than what was actually achieved by the women and men who were part of it. Against tremendous odds, they made anarchism work.

The realization of anarchist collectivisation and workers' self-management during the Spanish Revolution provides a classic example of organisation-plus-spontaneity. In both rural and industrial Spain, anarchism had been a part of the popular consciousness for many years. In the countryside, the people had a long tradition of communalism; many villages still shared common property or gave plots of land to those without any. Decades of rural collectivism and cooperation laid the foundation for theoretical anarchism, which came to Spain in the 1870s (via the Italian revolutionary, Fanelli, a friend of Bakunin) and eventually gave rise to anarcho-syndicalism, the application of anarchist principles to industrial trade unionism. The Confederacion National del Trebajo, founded in 1910, was the anarcho-syndicalist union (working closely with the militant Federacion Anarquista Iberica) which provided instruction and preparation for workers' self-management and collectivization. Tens of thousands of books, newspapers, and pamphlets reaching almost every part of Spain contributed to an even greater general knowledge of anarchist thought.[5] The anarchist principles of non-hierarchical cooperation and individual initiative combined with anarcho-syndicalist tactics of sabotage, boycott and general strike, and training in production and economics, gave the workers background in both theory and practice. This led to a successful spontaneous appropriation of both factories and land after July 1936.

When the Spanish right responded to the electoral victory of the Popular Front with an attempted military takeover, on July 19, 1936, the people fought back with a fury which checked the coup within 24 hours. At this point, ballot box success became incidental; total social revolution had begun. While the industrial workers either went on strike or actually began to run the factories themselves, the agricultural workers ignored landlords and started to cultivate the land on their own. Within a short time, over 60% of the land in Spain was worked collectively—without landlords, bosses, or competitive incentive. Industrial collectivization took place mainly in the province of Catalonia, where anarcho-syndicalist influence was strongest. Since 75% of Spain's industry was located in Catalonia, this was no small achievement.[6] So, after 75 years of preparation and struggle, collectivization was achieved, through the spontaneous collective action of individuals dedicated to libertarian principles.

What, though, did collectivization actually mean, and how did it work? In general, the anarchist collectives functioned on two levels: (1) small-scale participatory democracy and (2) large-scale coordination with control at the bottom. At each level, the main concern was decentralisation and individual initiative. In the factories and villages, representatives were chosen to councils which operated as administrative or coordinating bodies. Decisions always came from more general membership meetings, which all workers attended. To guard against the dangers of representation, representatives were workers themselves, and at all times subject to immediate, as well as periodic, replacement. These councils or committees were the basic units of self-management. From there, they could be expanded by further coordination into loose federations which would link together workers and operations over an entire industry or geographical area. In this way, distribution and sharing of goods could be performed, as well as implementation of programmes of wide-spread concern, such as irrigation, transportation, and communication. Once again, the emphasis was on the bottom-to-top process. This very tricky balance between individuality and collectivism was most successfully accomplished by the Peasant Federation of Levant, which included 900 collectives, and the Aragon Federation of Collectives, composed of about 500 collectives.

Probably the most important aspect of self-management was the equalization of wages. This took many forms, but frequently the "family wage" system was used, wages being paid to each worker in money or coupons according to her/his needs and those of dependants. Goods in abundance were distributed freely, while others were obtainable with "money."

The benefits which came from wage equalization were tremendous. After huge profits in the hands of a few men were eliminated, the excess money was used both to modernize industry (purchase of new equipment, better working conditions) and to improve the land (irrigation, dams, purchase of tractors, etc.). Not only were better products turned out more efficiently, but consumer prices were lowered as well. This was true in such varied industries as: textiles, metal and munitions, gas, water, electricity, baking, fishing, municipal transportation, railroads, telephone services, optical products, health services, etc. The workers themselves benefited from a shortened work week, better working conditions, free health care, unemployment pay, and a new pride in their work. Creativity was fostered by self-management and the spirit of mutual aid; workers were concerned with turning out products which were better than those turned out under conditions of labour exploitation. They wanted to demonstrate that socialism works, that competition and greed motives are unnecessary. Within months, the standard of living had been raised by anywhere from 50-100% in many areas of Spain.

The achievements of the Spanish anarchists go beyond a higher standard of living and economic equality; they involve the realization of basic human ideals: freedom, individual creativity, and collective cooperation. The Spanish anarchist collectives did not fail; they were destroyed from without. Those (of the right and left) who believed in a strong State worked to wipe them out—of Spain and history. The successful anarchism of roughly eight million Spanish people is only now beginning to be uncovered.

"C'est pour toi que tu fais la revolution."[7]
[It is for yourself that you make the revolution.]
Daniel and Gabriel Cohn-Bendit

Anarchism has played an important part in French history, but rather than delve into the past, I want to focus on a contemporary event—May-June, 1968. The May-June events have particular significance because they proved that a general strike and takeover of the factories by the workers, and the universities by the students, could happen in a modern, capitalistic, consumption-oriented country. In addition, the issues raised by the students and workers in France (e.g. self-determination, the quality of life) cut across class lines and have tremendous implications for the possibility of revolutionary change in a post-scarcity society.[8]

On March 22, 1968, students at the University of Nanterre, among them anarchist Daniel Cohn-Bendit, occupied administrative buildings at their school, calling for an end to both the Vietnam war and their own oppression as students. (Their demands were similar in content to those of students from Columbia to Berlin protesting in loco parentis.) The University was closed down, and the demonstrations spread to the Sorbonne. The SNESUP (the union of secondary school and university teachers) called for a strike, and the students' union, the UNEF, organised a demonstration for May 6. That day, students and police clashed in the Latin Quarter in Paris; the demonstrators built barricades in the streets, and many were brutally beaten by the riot police. By the 7th, the number of protesters had grown to between twenty and fifty thousand people, marching toward the Etoile singing the Internationale. During the next few days, skirmishes between demonstrators and police in the Latin Quarter became increasingly violent, and the public was generally outraged at the police repression. Talks between labour unions and teachers' and students' unions began, and the UNEF and the FEN (a teachers' union) called for an unlimited strike and demonstration. On May 13, around six hundred thousand people—students, teachers, and workers—marched through Paris in protest.

On the same day, the workers at the Sud-Aviation plant in Nantes (a city with the strongest anarcho-syndicalist tendencies in France[9]) went out on strike. It was this action that touched off the general strike, the largest in history, including ten million workers—"professionals and labourers, intellectuals and football players."[10] Banks, post offices, gas stations, and department stores closed; the subway and busses stopped running; and trash piled up as the garbage collectors joined the strike. The Sorbonne was occupied by students, teachers, and anyone who wanted to come and participate in discussions there. Political dialogues which questioned the vary basis of French capitalist society went on for days. All over Paris posters and graffiti appeared: It is forbidden to forbid. Life without dead times. All power to the Imagination. The more you consume, the less you live. May-June became both an "assault on the established order" and a "festival of the streets."[11] Old lines between the middle and working classes often became meaningless as the younger workers and the students found themselves making similar demands: liberation from an oppressive authoritarian system (university or factory) and the right to make decisions about their own lives.

The people of France stood at the brink of total revolution. A general strike had paralysed the country. The students occupied the universities and the workers, the factories. What remained to be done was for the workers actually to work the factories, to take direct unmediated action and settle for nothing less than total self-management. Unfortunately, this did not occur. Authoritarian politics and bureaucratic methods die hard, and most of the major French workers' unions were saddled with both. As in Spain, the Communist Party worked against the direct, spontaneous actions of the people in the streets: the Revolution must be dictated from above. Leaders of the CGT (the Communist workers' union) tried to prevent contacts between the students and workers, and a united left soon became an impossibility. As de Gaulle and the police mobilized their forces and even greater violence broke out, many strikers accepted limited demands (better pay, shorter hours, etc.) and returned to work. Students continued their increasingly bloody confrontations with police, but the moment had passed. By the end of June, France had returned to "normality" under the same old Gaullist regime.

What happened in France in 1968 is vitally connected to the Spanish Revolution of 1936; in both cases anarchist principles were not only discussed but implemented. The fact that the French workers never did achieve working self-management may be because anarcho-syndicalism was not as prevalent in France in the years prior to 1968 as it was in Spain before 1936. Of course, this is an over-simplification; explanation for a "failed" revolution can run on into infinity. What is crucial here, once again, is the fact that it happened at all. May-June, 1968, disproves the common belief that revolution is impossible in an advanced capitalist country. The children of the French middle and working classes, bred to passivity, mindless consumerism, and/or alienated labor, were rejecting much more than capitalism. They were questioning authority itself, demanding the right to a free and meaningful existence. The reasons for revolution in modern industrial society are thus no longer limited to hunger and material scarcity; they include the desire for human liberation from all forms of domination, in essence a radical change in the very "quality of everyday life."[12] They assume the necessity of a libertarian society. Anarchism can no longer be considered an anachronism.

"It is often said that anarchists live in a world of dreams to come and do not see things which happen today. We see them only too well, and in their true colours, and that is what makes us carry the hatchet into the forest of prejudices that besets us."[13]
Peter Kropotkin

There are two main reasons why revolution was aborted in France: (1) inadequate preparation in the theory and practice of anarchism and (2) the vast power of the State coupled with authoritarianism and bureaucracy in potentially sympathetic left-wing groups. In Spain, the revolution was more widespread and tenacious because of the extensive preparation. Yet it was still eventually crushed by a fascist State and authoritarian leftists. It is important to consider these two factors in relation to the situation in the United States today. We are not only facing a powerful State whose armed forces, police, and nuclear weapons could instantly destroy the entire human race, but we also find ourselves confronting a pervasive reverence for authority and hierarchical forms whose continuance is ensured daily through the kind of home-grown passivity bred by family, school, church, and TV screen. In addition, the U.S. is a huge country, with only a small, sporadic history of anarchist activity. It would seem that not only are we unprepared, we are literally dwarfed by a State more powerful than those of France and Spain combined. To say we are up against tremendous odds is an understatement.

But where does defining the Enemy as a ruthless, unconquerable giant lead us? If we don't allow ourselves to be paralysed by fatalism and futility, it could force us to redefine revolution in a way that would focus on anarcha-feminism as the framework in which to view the struggle for human liberation. It is women who now hold the key to new conceptions of revolution, women who realize that revolution can no longer mean the seizure of power or the domination of one group by another—under any circumstances, for any length of time. It is domination itself that must be abolished. The very survival of the planet depends on it. Men can no longer be allowed to wantonly manipulate the environment for their own self-interest, just as they can no longer be allowed to systematically destroy whole races of human beings. The presence of hierarchy and authoritarian mindset threaten our human and our planetary existence. Global liberation and libertarian politics have become necessary, not just utopian pipe dreams. We must "acquire the conditions of life in order to survive."[14]

To focus on anarcha-feminism as the necessary revolutionary framework for our struggle is not to deny the immensity of the task before us. We do see "only too well" the root causes of our oppression and the tremendous power of the Enemy. But we also see that the way out of the deadly historical cycle of incomplete or aborted revolutions requires of us new definitions and new tactics—ones which point to the kind of "hollowing out"[15] process described later in the "Making Utopia Real" section. As women, we are particularly well-suited for participation in this process. Underground for ages, we have learned to be covert, subtle, sly, silent, tenacious, acutely sensitive, and expert at communication skills.

For our own survival, we learned to weave webs of rebellion which were invisible to the "masterful" eye.

> We know what a boot looks like
> when seen from underneath,
> we know the philosophy of boots...
>
> Soon we will invade like weeds,
> everywhere but slowly;
> the captive plants will rebel
> with us, fences will topple,
> brick walls ripple and fall,
>
> there will be no more boots.
> Meanwhile we eat dirt
> and sleep; we are waiting
> under your feet.
> When we say Attack
> you will hear nothing
> at first.[16]

Anarchistic preparation is not non-existent in this country. It exists in the minds and actions of women readying themselves (often unknowingly) for a revolution whose forms will shatter historical inevitability and the very process of history itself.

Anarchism and the Women's Movement

> The development of sisterhood is a unique threat, for it is directed against the basic social and psychic model of hierarchy and domination...[17]
> *Mary Daly*

> All across the country, independent groups of women began functioning without the structure, leaders, and other factotums of the male left, creating independently and simultaneously, organisations similar to those of anarchists of many decades and locales. No accident, either.[18]
> *Cathy Levine*

I have not touched upon the matter of woman's role in Spain and France, as it can be summed up in one word—unchanged. Anarchist men have been little better than males everywhere in their subjection of women.[19] Thus the absolute necessity of a feminist anarchist revolution. Otherwise the very principles on which anarchism is based become utter hypocrisy.

The current women's movement and a radical feminist analysis of society have contributed much to libertarian thought. In fact, it is my contention that feminists have been unconscious anarchists in both theory and practice for years. We now need to become consciously aware of the connections between anarchism and feminism and use that framework for our thoughts and actions. We have to be able to see very clearly where we want to go and how to get there. In order to be more effective, in order to create the future we sense is possible, we must realise that what we want is not change but total transformation.

The radical feminist perspective is almost pure anarchism. The basic theory postulates the nuclear family as the basis for all authoritarian systems. The lesson the child learns, from father to teacher to boss to God, is to OBEY the great anonymous voice of Authority. To graduate from childhood to adulthood is to become a full-fledged automaton, incapable of questioning or even thinking clearly. We pass into middle-America, believing everything we are told and numbly accepting the destruction of life all around us.

What feminists are dealing with is a mind-fucking process—the male domineering attitude toward the external world, allowing only subject/object relationships. Traditional male politics reduces humans to object status and then dominates and manipulates them for abstract "goals." Women, on the other hand, are trying to develop a consciousness of "Other" in all areas. We see subject-to-subject relationships as not only desirable but necessary. (Many of us have chosen to work with and love only women for just this reason—those kinds of relationships are so much more possible.) Together we are working to expand our empathy and understanding of other living things and to identify with those entities outside of ourselves, rather than objectifying and manipulating them. At this point, a respect for all life is a prerequisite for our very survival.

Radical feminist theory also criticises male hierarchical thought patterns—in which rationality dominates sensuality, mind dominates intuition, and persistent splits and polarities (active/passive, child/adult, sane/insane, work/play, spontaneity/organisation) alienate us from the mind-body experience as a Whole and from the Continuum of human experience. Women are attempting to get rid of these splits, to live in harmony with the universe as whole, integrated humans dedicated to the collective healing of our individual wounds and schisms.

In actual practice within the Women's Movement, feminists have had both success and failure in abolishing hierarchy and domination. I believe that women frequently speak and act as "intuitive" anarchists, that is, we approach, or verge on, a complete denial of all patriarchal thought and organisation. That approach, however, is blocked by the powerful and insidious forms which patriarchy takes—in our minds and in our relationships with one another. Living within and being conditioned by an authoritarian society often prevents us from making that all-important connection between feminism and anarchism. When we say we are fighting the patriarchy, it isn't always clear to all of us that that means fighting all hierarchy, all leadership, all government, and the very idea of authority itself. Our impulses toward collective work and small leaderless groups have been anarchistic, but in most cases we haven't called them by that name. And that is important, because an understanding of feminism as anarchism could springboard women out of reformism and stop-gap measures into a revolutionary confrontation with the basic nature of authoritarian politics.

If we want to "bring down the patriarchy," we need to talk about anarchism, to know exactly what it means, and to use that framework to transform ourselves and the structure of our daily lives. Feminism doesn't mean female corporate power or a woman President; it means no corporate power and no Presidents. The Equal Rights Amendment will not transform society; it only gives women the "right" to plug into a hierarchical economy. Challenging sexism means challenging all hierarchy—economic, political, and personal. And that means an anarcha-feminist revolution.

Specifically, when have feminists been anarchistic, and when have we stopped short? As the second wave of feminism spread across the country in the late '60s, the forms which women's groups took frequently reflected an unspoken libertarian consciousness. In rebellion against the competitive power games, impersonal hierarchy, and mass organisation tactics of male politics, women broke off into small, leaderless, consciousness-raising groups, which dealt with personal issues in our daily lives. Face-to-face, we attempted to get at the root cause of our oppression by sharing our hitherto unvalued perceptions and experiences. We learned from each other that politics is not "out there" but in our minds and bodies and between individuals. Personal relationships could and did oppress us as a political class. Our misery and self-hatred were a direct result of male domination—in home, street, job, and political organisation.

So, in many unconnected areas of the U.S., C-R groups developed as a spontaneous, direct (re)action to patriarchal forms. The emphasis on the small group as a basic organisational unit, on the personal and political, on anti-authoritarianism, and on spontaneous direct action was essentially anarchistic. But, where were the years and years of preparation which sparked the Spanish revolutionary activities? The structure of women's groups bore a striking resemblance to that of anarchist affinity groups within anarcho-syndicalist unions in Spain, France, and many other countries. Yet, we had not called ourselves anarchists and consciously organised around anarchist principles. At the time, we did not even have an underground network of communication and idea-and-skill sharing. Before the women's movement was more than a handful of isolated groups groping in the dark toward answers, anarchism as an unspecified ideal existed in our minds.

I believe that this puts women in the unique position of being the bearers of a subsurface anarchist consciousness which, if articulated and concretized can take us further than any previous group toward the achievement of total revolution. Women's intuitive anarchism, if sharpened and clarified, is an incredible leap forward (or beyond) in the struggle for human liberation. Radical feminist theory hails feminism as the Ultimate Revolution. This is true if, and only if, we recognise and claim our anarchist roots. At the point where we fail to see the feminist connection to anarchism, we stop short of revolution and become trapped in "ye olde male political rut." It is time to stop groping in the darkness and see what we have done and are doing in the context of where we want to ultimately be.

C-R groups were a good beginning, but they often got so bogged down in talking about personal problems that they failed to make the jump to direct action and political confrontation. Groups that did organise around a specific issue or project sometimes found that the "tyranny of structurelessness" could be as destructive as the "tyranny of tyranny."[20] The failure to blend organisation with spontaneity frequently caused the emergence of those with more skills or personal charisma as leaders. The resentment and frustration felt by those who found themselves following sparked in-fighting, guilt-tripping, and power struggles. Too often this ended in either total ineffectiveness or a backlash adherence to "what we need is more structure" (in the old male up/down sense of the word).

Once again, I think that what was missing was a verbalized anarchist analysis. Organisation does not have to stifle spontaneity or follow hierarchical patterns. The women's groups or projects which have been the most successful are those which experimented with various fluid structures: the rotation of tasks and chairpersons, sharing of all skills, equal access to information and resources, non-monopolised decision-making, and time slots for discussion of group dynamics. This latter structural element is important because it involves a continued effort on the part of group members to watch for "creeping power politics." If women are verbally committing themselves to collective work, this requires a real struggle to unlearn passivity (to eliminate "followers") and to share special skills or knowledge (to avoid "leaders"). This doesn't mean that we cannot be inspired by one another's words and lives; strong actions by strong individuals can be contagious and thus important. But we must be careful not to slip into old behaviour patterns.

On the positive side, the emerging structure of the women's movement in the last few years has generally followed an anarchistic pattern of small project-oriented groups continually weaving an underground network of communication and collective action around specific issues. Partial success at leader/"star" avoidance and the diffusion of small action projects (Rape Crisis Centres, Women's Health Collectives) across the country have made it extremely difficult for the women's movement to be pinned down to one person or group. Feminism is a many-headed monster which cannot be destroyed by singular decapitation. We spread and grow in ways that are incomprehensible to a hierarchical mentality.

This is not, however, to underestimate the immense power of the Enemy. The most treacherous form this power can take is cooptation, which feeds on any short-sighted unanarchistic view of feminism as mere "social change." To think of sexism as an evil which can be eradicated by female participation in the way things are is to ensure the continuation of domination and oppression. "Feminist" capitalism is a contradiction in terms. When we establish women's credit unions, restaurants, bookstores, etc., we must be clear that we are doing so for our own survival, for the purpose of creating a counter-system whose processes contradict and challenge competition, profit-making, and all forms of economic oppression. We must be committed to "living on the boundaries,"[21] to anti-capitalist, non-consumption values. What we want is neither integration nor a coup d'etat which would "transfer power from one set of boys to another set of boys."[22] What we ask is nothing less than total revolution, revolution whose forms invent a future untainted by inequity, domination, or disrespect for individual variation—in short, feminist-anarchist revolution. I believe that women have known all along how to move in the direction of human liberation; we only need to shake off lingering male political forms and dictums and focus on our own anarchistic female analysis.

Where Do We Go From Here? Making Utopia Real

> "Ah, your vision is romantic bullshit, soppy religiousity, flimsy idealism." "You're into poetry because you can't deliver concrete details." So says the little voice in the back of my (your?) head. But the front of my head knows that if you were here next to me, we could talk. And that in our talk would come (concrete, detailed) descriptions of how such and such might happen, how this or that would be resolved. What my vision really lacks is concrete, detailed human bodies. Then it wouldn't be a flimsy vision, it would be a fleshy reality.[23]
> *Su Negrin*

> Instead of getting discouraged and isolated now, we should be in our small groups—discussing, planning, creating, and making trouble... we should always be actively engaging in and creating feminist activity, because we all thrive on it; in the absence of [it], women take tranquilizers, go insane, and commit suicide.[24]
> *Cathy Levine*

Those of us who lived through the excitement of sit-ins, marches, student strikes, demonstrations, and REVOLUTION NOW in the '60s may find ourselves disillusioned and downright cynical about anything happening in the '70s. Giving up or in ("open" marriage? hip capitalism? the Guru Maharaji?) seems easier than facing the prospect of decades of struggle and maybe even ultimate failure. At this point, we lack an overall framework to see the process of revolution in. Without it, we are doomed to dead-ended, isolated struggle or the individual solution. The kind of framework, or coming-together-point, that anarcha-feminism provides would appear to be a prerequisite for any sustained effort to reach Utopian goals. By looking at Spain and France, we can see that true revolution is "neither an accidental happening nor a coup d'etat artificially engineered from above."[25] It takes years of preparation: sharing of ideas and information, changes in consciousness and behaviour, and the creation of political and economic alternatives to capitalist, hierarchical structures. It takes spontaneous direct action on the part of autonomous individuals through collective political confrontation. It is important to "free your mind" and your personal life, but it is not sufficient. Liberation is not an insular experience; it occurs in conjunction with other human beings. There are no individual "liberated women."

So, what I'm talking about is a long-term process, a series of actions in which we unlearn passivity and learn to take control over our own lives. I am talking about a "hollowing out" of the present system through the formation of mental and physical (concrete) alternatives to the way things are. The romantic image of a small band of armed guerrillas overthrowing the U.S. government is obsolete (as is all male politics) and basically irrelevant to this conception of revolution. We would be squashed if we tried it. Besides, as the poster says, "What we want is not the overthrow of the government, but a situation in which it gets lost in the shuffle." This is what happened (temporarily) in Spain, and almost happened in France. Whether armed resistance will be necessary at some point is open to debate. The anarchist principle of "means create ends" seems to imply pacifism, but the power of the State is so great that it is difficult to be absolute about non-violence. (Armed resistance was crucial in the Spanish Revolution, and seemed important in France 1968 as well.) The question of pacifism, however, would entail another discussion, and what I'm concerned with here is emphasizing the preparation needed to transform society, a preparation which includes an anarcha-feminist framework, long-range revolutionary patience, and continual active confrontation with entrenched patriarchal attitudes.

The actual tactics of preparation are things that we have been involved with for a long time. We need to continue and develop them further. I see them as functioning on three levels: (1) "educational" (sharing of ideas, experiences), (2) economic/political, and (3) personal/political.

"Education" has a rather condescending ring to it, but I don't mean "bringing the word to the masses" or guilt-tripping. individuals into prescribed ways of being. I'm talking about the many methods we have developed for sharing our lives with one another—from writing (our network of feminist publications), study groups, and women's radio and TV shows to demonstrations, marches, and street theatre. The mass media would seem to be a particularly important area for revolutionary communication and influence—just think of how our own lives were misshaped by radio and TV.[26] Seen in isolation, these things might seem ineffectual, but people do change from writing, reading, talking, and listening to each other, as well as from active participation in political movements. Going out into the streets together shatters passivity and creates a spirit of communal effort and life energy which can help sustain and transform us. My own transformation from all-American girl to anarcha-feminist was brought about by a decade of reading, discussion, and involvement with many kinds of people and politics—from the Midwest to the West and East Coasts. My experiences may in some ways be unique, but they are not, I think, extraordinary. In many, many places in this country, people are slowly beginning to question the way they were conditioned to acceptance and passivity. God and Government are not the ultimate authorities they once were. This is not to minimize the extent of the power of Church and State, but rather to emphasize that seemingly inconsequential changes in thought and behaviour, when solidified in collective action, constitute a real challenge to the patriarchy.

Economic/political tactics fall into the realm of direct action and "purposeful illegality" (Daniel Guerin's term). Anarcho-syndicalism specifies three major modes of direct action: sabotage, strike, and boycott. Sabotage means "obstructing by every possible method, the regular process of production."[27] More and more frequently, sabotage is practised by people unconsciously influenced by changing societal values. For example, systematic absenteeism is carried out by both blue and white collar workers. Defying employers can be done as subtly as the "slow-down" or as blatantly as the "fuck-up." Doing as little work as possible as slowly as possible is common employee practice, as is messing up the actual work process (often as a union tactic during a strike). Witness habitual misfiling or loss of "important papers" by secretaries, or the continual switching of destination placards on trains during the 1967 railroad strike in Italy.

Sabotage tactics can be used to make strikes much more effective. The strike itself is the workers' most important weapon. Any individual strike has the potential of paralysing the system if it spreads to other industries and becomes a general strike. Total social revolution is then only a step away. Of course, the general strike must have as its ultimate goal worker's self-management (as well as a clear sense of how to achieve and hold on to it), or else the revolution will be still-born (as in France, 1968).

The boycott can also be a powerful strike or union strategy (e.g., the boycott of non-union grapes, lettuce, and wines, and of Farah pants). In addition, it can be used to force economic and social changes. Refusal to vote, to pay war taxes, or to participate in capitalist competition and over-consumption are all important actions when coupled with support of alternative, non-profit structures (food co-ops, health and law collectives, recycled clothing and book stores, free schools, etc.). Consumerism is one of the main strongholds of capitalism. To boycott buying itself (especially products geared to obsolescence and those offensively advertised) is a tactic that has the power to change the "quality of everyday life." Refusal to vote is often practised out of despair or passivity rather than as a conscious political statement against a pseudo-democracy where power and money elect a political elite. Non-voting can mean something other than silent consent if we are simultaneously participating in the creation of genuine democratic forms in an alternative network of anarchist affinity groups.

This takes us to the third area—personal/political, which is of course vitally connected to the other two. The anarchist affinity group has long been a revolutionary organisational structure. In anarcho-syndicalist unions, they functioned as training grounds for workers' self-management. They can be temporary groupings of individuals for a specific short-term goal, more "permanent" work collectives (as an alternative to professionalism and career elitism), or living collectives where individuals learn how to rid themselves of domination or possessiveness in their one-to-one relationships. Potentially, anarchist affinity groups are the base on which we can build a new libertarian, non-hierarchical society. The way we live and work changes the way we think and perceive (and vice versa), and when changes in consciousness become changes in action and behaviour, the revolution has begun.

Making Utopia real involves many levels of struggle. In addition to specific tactics which can be constantly developed and changed, we need political tenacity: the strength and ability to see beyond the present to a joyous, revolutionary future. To get from here to there requires more than a leap of faith. It demands of each of us a day-to-day, long-range commitment to possibility and direct action.

The Transformation of the Future

> The creation of female culture is as pervasive a process as we can imagine, for it is participation in a VISION which is continually unfolding anew in everything from our talks with friends, to meat boycotts, to taking over storefronts for child care centres, to making love with a sister. It is revelatory, undefinable, except as a process of change. Women's culture is all of us exorcising, naming, creating toward the vision of harmony with ourselves, each other, and our sister earth. In the last ten years our having come faster and closer than ever before in the history of the patriarchy to overturning its power... is cause of exhilarant hope—wild, contagious, unconquerable, crazy HOPE!... The hope, the winning of life over death, despair and meaninglessness is everywhere I look now—like taliswomen of the faith in WOMANVISION...[28]
> *Laurel*

I used to think that if the revolution didn't happen tomorrow, we would all be doomed to a catastrophic (or at least, catatonic) fate. I don't believe anymore that kind of before-and-after revolution, and I think we set ourselves up for failure and despair by thinking of it in those terms. I do believe that what we all need, what we absolutely require, in order to continue struggling (in spite of oppression of our daily lives) is HOPE, that is, a vision of the future so beautiful and so powerful that it pulls us steadily forward in a bottom-up creation of an inner and outer world both habitable and self-fulfilling for all*. I believe that hope exists—that it is in Laurel's "womanvision," in Mary Daly's "existential courage"[29] and in anarcha-feminism. Our different voices describe the same dream, and "only the dream can shatter stone that blocks our mouths."[30] As we speak, we change, and as we change, we transform ourselves and the future simultaneously.

It is true that there is no solution, individual or otherwise, in our society.[31] But if we can only balance this rather depressing knowledge with an awareness of the radical metamorphoses we have experienced—in our consciousness and in our lives—the perhaps we can have the courage to continue to create what we DREAM is possible. Obviously, it is not easy to face daily oppression and still continue to hope. But it is our only chance. If we abandon hope (the ability to see connections, to dream the present into the future), then we have already lost. Hope is woman's most powerful revolutionary tool; it is what we give each other every time we share our lives, our work, and our love. It pulls us forward out of self-hatred, self-blame, and the fatalism which keeps us prisoners in separate cells. If we surrender to depression and despair now, we are accepting the inevitability of authoritarian politics and patriarchal domination ("Despair is the worst betrayal, the coldest seduction: to believe at last that the enemy will prevail."[32] Marge Piercy). We must not let our pain and anger fade into hopelessness or short-sighted semi-"solutions." Nothing we can do is enough, but on the other hand, those "small changes" we make in our minds, in our lives, in one another's lives, are not totally futile and ineffectual. It takes a long time to make a revolution: it is something that one both prepares for and lives now. The transformation of the future will not be instantaneous, but it can be total... a continuum of thought and action, individuality and collectivity, spontaneity and organisation, stretching from what is to what can be.

Anarchism provides a framework for this transformation. It is a vision, a dream, a possibility which becomes "real" as we live it. Feminism is the connection that links anarchism to the future. When we finally see that connection clearly, when we hold to that vision, when we refuse to be raped of that HOPE, we will be stepping over the edge of nothingness into a being now just barely imaginable. The womanvision that is anarcha-feminism has been carried inside our women's bodies for centuries. "It will be an ongoing struggle in each of us, to birth this vision"[33] but we must do it. We must "ride our anger like elephants into battle."

We are sleepwalkers troubled by nightmare flashes,
In locked wards we closet our vision, renouncing ...
Only when we break the mirror and climb into our vision,
Only when we are the wind together streaming and singing,
Only in the dream we become with our bones for spears,
we are real at last
and wake.[34]

*And by self-fulfilling I mean not only in terms of survival needs (sufficient food, clothing, shelter, etc) but psychological needs as well I (e.g., a non-oppressive environment which fosters total freedom of choice before specific, concretely possible alternatives).

Notes

1. Emma Goldman, "Anarchism: What It Really Stands For," *Red Emma Speaks* (Vintage Books, 1972), p.59.
2. Su Negrin, *Begin at Start* (Times Change Press, 1972), p. 128.
3. Murray Bookchin, "On Spontaneity and Organisation," *Liberation*, March, 1972, p.6.
4. Paul Berman, *Quotations from the Anarchists* (Praeger Publishers, 1972), p. 68.
5. Sam Dolgoff, *The Anarchist Collectives* (Free Life Editions, 1974), p. 27.
6. Ibid, pp.6, 7, 85.
7. Daniel and Gabriel Cohn-Bendit, *Obsolete Communism—The Left Wing Alternative* (McGraw-Hill, 1968), p.256.
8. See Murrey Bookchin's *Post-Scarcity Anarchism* (Ramparts Press, 1974) for both an insightful analysis of the May-June events and a discussion of revolutionary potential in a technological society.
9. Ibid, p.262.
10. Ibid, p.250.
11. Bookchin, "On Spontaneity and Organisation," pp. 11-12.
12. Bookchin, *Post-Scarcity Anarchism*, p.249.
13. Berman, p.146.
14. Bookchin, *Post-Scarcity Anarchism*, p.40.
15. Bookchin, "On Spontaneity and Organisation," p.10.
16. Margaret Atwood, "Song of the Worms," *You Are Happy* (Harper & Row, 1974), p.35.
17. Mary Daly, *Beyond God the Father* (Beacon Press, 1973), p. 133.
18. Cathy Levine, "The Tyranny of Tyranny," *Black Rose* 1, p.56.
19. Temma Kaplan of the UCLA history department has done considerable research on women's anarchist groups (esp. "Mujeres Liberes") in the Spanish Revolution. See also Liz Willis, *Women in the Spanish Revolution*, Solidarity Pamphlet No. 48.
20. See Joreen's "The Tyranny of Structurelessness," *Second Wave*, Vol. 2, No. 1, and Cathy Levine's "The Tyranny of Tyranny," *Black Rose* 1.
21. Daly, p.55.
22. Robin Morgan, speech at Boston College, Boston, Mass., Nov., 1973.
23. Negrin, p.171.
24. Levine, p.50.
25. Dolgoff, p. 19.
26. The Cohn-Bendits state that one major mistake in Paris 1968 was the failure to take complete control of the media, especially the radio and TV.
27. Goldman, "Syndicalism: Its Theory and Practice," *Red Emma Speaks*, p.71.
28. Laurel, "Towards a Woman Vision," *Amazon Quarterly*, Vol. 1, Issue 2, p.40.
29. Daly, p.23.
30. Marge Piercy, "Provocation of the Dream."
31. Fran Taylor, "A Depressing Discourse on Romance, the Individual Solution, and Related Misfortunes," *Second Wave*, Vol. 3, No. 4.
32. Marge Piercy, "Laying Down the Tower," *To Be of Use* (Doubleday, 1973), p.88.
33. Laurel, p.40.
34. Piercy, "Provocation of the Dream."

ANARCHA-FEMINISM AND THE NEWER "WOMAN QUESTION"

Stacy/Sally Darity

GONE ARE THE DAYS WHEN ANARCHA-FEMINISTS NURTURED visions of revolution brought on by a unity of women. While we may have found the following quote in a nineteen-seventies essay "Anarchism and the Feminist Connection," "The development of sisterhood is a unique threat, for it is directed against the basic social and psychic model of hierarchy and domination..."[1] it has become clear that sisterhood alone is not a threat to hierarchy and domination. The logical conclusion of any type of feminism should not be to simply seek equality between each woman to her race/class male counterpart, leaving other inequalities in place. More explicit in anarcha-feminism is that a focus on gender oppression is not at the expense of attention to other systems of power. While some of this is addressed by intersectionality, I am also interested in further questioning this concept of sisterhood, or more specifically, expanding what I will call the newer "woman question:" are we to continue to orient around an identity called "woman," or should we instead oppose the power structures that have created this category to oppress us?

While many agree that anarchism opposes all hierarchy and oppression and therefore is against sexism and such, still necessary is a tendency in which gendered concerns are central. I propose that anarcha-feminism has two main and related principles specific to its emphasis on feminism: Everyone should have freedom from all that is coercive about gender (or *gender stratum*, see below), and everyone should have bodily autonomy—freedom from bodily harm, and the freedom to do, or not do, what they want with their bodies.

Rather than referring to patriarchy, I address coercion related to gender because gender oppression works in multi-dimensional and complex ways. Individuals may have a variety of experiences based on their body parts and functions, what gender they're perceived to be (gender attribution), their gender presentation, their sexuality, and/or how well they conform to their imposed gender box—either based on their gender assignment or their gender inclination. Now of course this oppression is structured in this way primarily because of the gendered order in which men are deemed superior and women inferior, while enforcing this order maintains its strength.

The principle relating to bodily autonomy is multi-dimensional as well. It relates primarily though not always to a gendered manifestation of oppression. Not only does it refer to sexuality, consent, reproductive freedom, etc., but also to an ideal society in which we can make truly free choices, e.g. we should have the freedom to get liposuction, but we would ideally be free of any pressure to do so. Of course on a practical level the latter principle is incredibly complex as it relates to power dynamics, what justice looks like, and issues around technology, etc. The principle of bodily autonomy requires a bit more consideration of the balance of individual freedom with collective freedom, as is important in the context of heated debates about such things as sex work, which I will not be addressing here. This balance should also apply to the debate on the ways defining "woman" impacts others' freedom. These working principles ought to inform these debates.

Although I am not arguing that we must abandon concepts that refer to the real effects of gender oppression, I argue that the above working principles are preferable to identity politics. Identity politics tend to prioritize one particular type of oppression and harden the boundaries around the identity related to that oppression[2] most often in the interest of gaining equal representation and participation in the system.[3] As many have argued, this creates alliances where they shouldn't be (e.g. cross-class), marginalizes intersections and complexities of identities, reinforces the identities and perhaps therefore the oppression, and strengthens loyalty to the system when assimilation is a strategy. The type of power sought to balance out inequalities is often not questioned.

Anarcha-feminism—or perhaps it is a queer anarcha-feminism—is not identity politics as long as its aim is to destroy the gender categories rather than perpetuate them. I argue that we can center the above principles, and oppose gender oppression without getting caught up in boundaries of identity. The point is to oppose and acknowledge the power structures and their very real effects, but to not create or reinforce our identities around our oppressions.

Anarcha-Feminism and Gender: New Ideas

As safer spaces and separatism have been discussed as responses to sexism and sexual violence, it has become clear that these issues are not so clear-cut. We know that abuse can occur between two women for example. We know that women's groups or spaces are not necessarily free from hierarchy simply because they are free of men (as discussed by various feminists of color, as well as Jo Freeman's "The Tyranny of Structurelessness"). Spaces created by feminists to be safer or simply to allow better focus on gender oppression, have increasingly encountered the difficulty with where, if anywhere, to draw a line between the gender categories. More importantly are the implications of drawing that line if it means excluding trans people and ignoring our common struggles. The Michigan Women's Music Festival has been a classic contemporary example of the controversy around spaces only for "womyn-born-womyn." This became a topic in zines and online forums, something I encountered on a radical cheer listserv around 2001. Whether because of the increased visibility and presence of trans people in anarchist and feminist spaces, the influence of queer theory, or other reasons, it has become more common in these spaces over the past few years in the U.S. and elsewhere for trans people to be included in this grouping, even though some involvement by trans folks in anarcha-feminism in the 1970's has been documented.[4] Currently, it is simply assumed in most cases, along with the expectation of respecting one's gender pronouns, that women's spaces are for women—in which trans women are included, or there are spaces for women and all trans folks, although the process of defining these can be problematic as well.

In terms of theory, anarchist feminists have not until more recently addressed the gender binary as such. They have addressed gender roles and biological determinism, but have not criticized the concept of the sexes as binary, mutually-exclusive political/social categories whose meanings have been made significant over time. This is changing.[5]

One need not read Judith Butler's *Gender Trouble* to understand the concerns with politically orienting around the identity of woman, although her influence cannot be denied. Among the questions raised by Butler, we might gain from asking: "Is the construction of the category of women as a coherent and stable subject an unwitting regulation and reification of gender relations? And is not such a reification precisely contrary to feminist aims?... The identity of the feminist subject ought not to be the foundation of feminist politics, if the formation of the subject takes place within a field of power regularly buried through the assertion of that foundation."[6]

Within feminism, "women" sometimes refers to those whose sex is female, although confusion can somewhat be allayed by using the term "woman" to refer to gender, while "female" refers to sex. However, distinguishing gender from sex tends to establish sex as an actuality on which the construct is based. I believe it is about time we incorporate into our understanding the ways in which sex is gendered. In the absence of anarcha-feminist theory about the origins of gender oppression, I pull some ideas together from various perspectives. Although I have qualms about the approach and am not interested in limiting analysis to materialism, I find it useful to understand construction of gender categories to an extent from that of French Materialist Feminists Christine Delphy, Monique Wittig and Collette Guillaumin.[7] Although Delphy acknowledges that there's only so much we can know, she writes,

> "For most people... anatomical sex (and its physical implications) creates, or at least permits, gender—the technical division of labour. This in turn creates, or at least permits, the domination

of one group by another. We believe, however, that it is oppression which creates gender; that logically the hierarchy of the division of labour is prior to the technical division of labour and created the latter, i.e. created sex roles, which we call gender. Gender in its turn created anatomical sex, in the sense that the hierarchical division of humanity into two transforms an anatomical difference (which is in itself devoid of social implications) into a relevant distinction for social practice. Social practice, and social practice alone, transforms a physical fact (which is in itself devoid of meaning, like all physical facts) into a category of thought."[8]

Delphy and others suggested that the concept of woman only exists within a power relationship. Sex differences are not natural but *naturalized*. This diverges greatly from theories that maintain sex as a given. Some theorize that sex led to gender roles and/or that gender/sex oppression was the first form of hierarchy. But if we don't take sex as a natural category, as a given, but instead a naturalized category, we can understand gender oppression and all that comes with it in a different light, and as something much more unstable.

Feminists understand gender as a social construct. But perceiving sex-as-gendered is a step beyond that, and has implications for how we should orient politically around an identity such as woman or female. Some may find it hard to argue with tangible differences; sex being considered the biological/anatomical/hormonal/genetic difference between humans, generally primarily corresponding to reproduction of the species. Yet rarely is it acknowledged that these do not always align (e.g. genetics and anatomy may not "match") nor fall in only one of two categories. Examination of non-Western cultures and the rest of the animal kingdom also reveals many exceptions to Western thought's dualistic concepts.[9] While the reality of a general organization into two categories of different bodies and their reproductive function can be acknowledged, I believe that the significance and polarization of these differences is gendered; the categories naturalized out of political interests. For this reason, I often include sex with gender as a social construct—writing it as sex/gender, even though I see gender and sex as referring to different aspects of gender.

Whether the first form of hierarchy had anything to do with gender, that naturalization of gender hierarchy has had a cascade effect. Andrea Smith wrote, "...Heteropatriarchy[10] is essential for the building of US empire. Patriarchy is the logic that naturalizes social hierarchy. Just as men are supposed to naturally dominate women on the basis of biology, so too should the social elites of a society naturally rule everyone else through the nation-state form of governance that is constructed through domination, violence and control."[11] In a speech, she said, "This is why in the history of Indian genocide the first task that colonizers took on was to integrate patriarchy into native communities. The primary tool used by colonists is sexual violence. What sexual violence does for colonialism and white supremacy is render women of color inherently rape-able, our lands inherently invadable, and our resources inherently extractable."[12]

In a sense, we can see this logic of conquest in the history of the construction of gender that was occurring during the witch hunts that essentially spelled out the defeat of women (European women, and then nearly all women through colonization/imperialism), as Silvia Federici describes in *Caliban and the Witch*. To summarize what I got out of the book, the witch hunts played a significant role in naturalizing gender/sex hierarchy by reinforcing divisions along lines of sex; functioned as counter-insurgency measures by breaking down solidarity along those lines among serfs/proletariat (in the transition to capitalism); justified exploitation (unpaid work in the home); increased dependence of women on men; and sought to control reproduction to increase the workforce by enforcing monogamy/marriage, heterosexuality, anti-abortion/birth control (accusations of causing infertility, infant death, impotence, etc.), and burning of queer folks ("faggots"/kindling). Women's bodies were to some degree the new commons (for men) as enclosures increased. As such, women continued to lose bodily autonomy, and in the process were further coerced into specific gender roles (roles varied based on race and class). Although not the beginning nor the end of the naturalization process of gender oppression, this served as a sort of conquest over women, trans, queer people, and European peasantry in general (and then far beyond) as part of the transition to capitalism.[13] It is inextricable from colonization of the "new world," as well as the construction of whiteness.

In this context, we can see how important eradicating gender oppression is. If it is the case that without hierarchy bodily differences would have no meaning, then we would not want to reinforce these categories, but destroy them. Before we discuss this, I want to point out the implications of not specifying what we mean by "gender."

Upon reflection, there appears to be a contradiction in seeking the destruction or abolition of gender, meanwhile building a culture of respecting everyone's gender, pronouns, etc. Indeed, there are some radical feminists who advocate the former but, not seeing a place for trans people's liberation (and in fact often finding it a threat), oppose the latter. I have determined that the problem lies in the ways in which gender is defined and understood. To many radical and materialist feminists, gender is only a relationship of power, therefore it must be destroyed. However, the concept of gender was borrowed by feminists from a psychologist who, in the late 1960's, wrote about the phenomenon of transsexuals feeling "trapped in the wrong body."[14] Not to imply that one meaning is unrelated to the other, but it would seem that "gender" came to refer to different concepts while not seeming to.

Perceiving gender as only related to power as the French Materialist Feminists and other radical feminists do can and has led to some transphobic bias.[15] For this reason, I would like to propose two different terms for gender as a way to make sense of the vastly different concepts of gender. *Gender stratum* refers to the binary hierarchically-defined socially constructed categories—that which is coercive and related to power. Sex, being gendered, would be included by this term, as are *gender assignment* (or designation), *gender roles*, and to some degree *gender attribution*, some of the terms that Kate Bornstein has used to identify the multiple aspects of gender.[16] *Gender inclination* is another term for what is generally referred to as gender identity but since identity is in question, I prefer this different term. I believe gender inclination would have different meaning in the absence of gender stratum, but I believe it is something distinct enough that it should not be lumped in with the other concept. Although the "trapped in the wrong body" concept has its problems, it shows that from its first use in relation to people, the term "gender" did not necessarily have anything to do with power other than the fact that the concept comes from a gendered order of which the power-based naturalization process was concealed. After all, there are various ways of defining one's gender which may be multi-layered, non-binary, and/or shifting through time. This is not to mention, as I discuss elsewhere,[17] that the concepts "masculinity" and "femininity" have different meanings and can be understood to be separate from power relationships.[18]

Using these terms, we can talk about the destruction or abolition of gender stratum, and promote the freedom of people to live out their gender inclination and have it respected. This is important when it comes to determining solutions for the problem of gender stratum—such proposals being androgyny, a proliferation of genders, and/or a negation of gender. But there is a potential for these to be coercive if the target of destruction is not specifically gender stratum. A truly liberatory position on gender/sex requires self-determination of gender inclination.[19] Everyone's experiences and sense of identity should be incorporated into an idea of what gender means.

More Than Just Theory

Anarcha-feminism, in seeking an end to all domination with an emphasis on freedom of bodily autonomy and freedom from gender stratum demands a newer "woman question." While some of this may seem rather theoretical, it can and should inform the way we approach gender oppression. We must fight for each person to be able to be who they are and to be able to participate equally in struggle, in decision-making, etc.. Using the working principles of bodily autonomy and freedom from gender stratum is a way to address gendered (but not always gendered) oppression without reinforcing boundaries around imposed categories and other problems of identity politics.

While I do not see a lot of utility in putting to much of an emphasis on language alone, it makes more sense to address issues within each context and use language that reflects the situation. For example, when referring to an issue that directly relates to pregnancy, one may refer to "people who are, will be, or were capable of becoming pregnant" rather than "women," because of course not all women can or do get pregnant, and not only people who identify as women can or do get pregnant. Of course, as many women of color and others have discussed, assuming that something like pregnancy or having a uterus creates unity or "sisterhood" among those who share that, is inaccurate, essentialist, if not at times racist in practice. Rather than the typical white middle-class-centered approach of mainstream feminism, the working principles I discuss also allow for an approach to a wide range of factors relating to such things as pregnancy—one's age, race, or citizenship/immigration status, whether one lives or works in areas where one is exposed to toxic chemicals (which is more likely in poor communities of color) which affects fertility and survival of the fetus or child, whether one lives in the context of war, whether one is on welfare, whether one is living as their assigned or designated sex, whether they're partnered and with whom and how. All of this factors into whether someone is encouraged or discouraged from having a child, and whether they are even capable of choosing one way or the other, not to mention the actual experiences—sometimes trauma—of birth, sterilization, abortion, or taking birth control, depending on the context. In the face of this, the standard feminist demand for access to birth control and abortion falls flat. Of course what I'm getting at is not that fertility, pregnancy, and reproduction are the prime example around which bodily autonomy revolves, but that we can see how those which aren't automatically considered feminist issues, such as the health problems related to exposure to toxins also have to do with bodily autonomy whether they affect fertility or not. While approaching issues this way seems much more difficult than the simplicity provided by identity politics, using the working principles discussed above allows for us to see the ways that capitalism, the state, and the very real effects of the social constructs of race and gender intersect or share similarities.

Beyond drawing together similar struggles based on these working principles, it is necessary to recognize the significance of this construct called "woman" that was created in many ways as a cage.

Plainly, as long as we understand sex as two natural categories, there remains little to no room for intesex, transgender, and all other people who don't fit neatly into those categories. And while feminists have found it useful to call gender what it is, a social construct, gender is considered to generally correlate with sex, and as long as the sex is seen as one of two mutually exclusive rigid categories and the legitimate counterpart to gender the construct, we may never be released from the confines of gender.

Now, to what extent is increased freedom in terms of gender transgression and sexuality accommodated because of the shifting needs of capitalism and the state rather than the struggles of feminists, queers, and trans people over the years? And to what extent are the efforts of the latter on the part of predominantly white and middle-class people? These questions should be considered as we move forward.

"What about teh menz?" is a relevant question in the following context. The gender roles assigned to men are important for maintaining a culture of domination. For any anarchist to believe that we could live free of hierarchy requires the belief that there isn't anything intrinsic in men that makes them the natural oppressor. This differs from some other feminisms which refer to essentialized male ways of being or thinking which are seemingly incorrigible. Anarchists and others such as prison-abolitionists believe that there is nothing natural to one group or another (such as men of color) that makes them more inclined to violence, otherwise state-based forms of "justice" may seem necessary and justified. bell hooks argues that it might be counterproductive to refer to men having privilege—that not being able to be in touch with one's emotions and not being able to have equal relationships (something that has been imposed, not natural) is not liberatory,[20] therefore men must also see the struggle against gender oppression as theirs as well. It is not that they don't benefit, but the benefits come with costs even while it is significant that they are able to ignore the costs. This is not to say that we should have sympathy with men who choose to continue to play out the role of domination. However, the rejection on the part of many women of color of separatism and misandry (not to imply that there is a consensus on this) speaks to a need for other understandings of possibility.

The belief that men are natural oppressors also legitimizes women's participation in domination (e.g. white supremacy). On the flipside, militant resistance to the state and capital is in some cases characterized as belonging to man the oppressor, and therefore condemned, even if a woman participates in it. [21]

Anarcha-feminism is a specific type of feminism and a specific type of anarchism that is critical of power relationships, particularly those that are gendered. Take or leave the term "feminism" with all its baggage and relationship to identity politics. It seems useful however to use a term that points to gender oppression as something that anarchism doesn't tend to address in practice. We are in a new position, compared to the anarcha-feminists like Peggy Kornegger before us, to move beyond the idea that sex is a given—that it's women against men. What is necessary now for anarcha-feminism is the destruction of gender stratum while recognizing the real and complex effects of the gender construct, along with the opposition to state and capitalism.

Notes

1. Mary Daly quoted in Peggy Kornegger, "Anarchism and the Feminist Connection" (1975).
   From anarchalibrary.blogspot.com/2010/09/anarchism-feminist-connection-1975.html (accessed February 6, 2012). Somehow Daly did not see transphobia as incompatible with hierarchy and domination. In "Politicizing Gender: Moving toward revolutionary gender politics," Carolyn writes, "In *Gyn/Ecology*, Mary Daly reasons that transsexuals want to destroy the burgeoning women's community, stating, 'their whole presence becomes a member invading women's presence and dividing us once more from each other.' Daly also supported Janice Raymond's anti-trans book "Transsexual Empire": http://anarchalibrary.blogspot.com/2010/09/politicizing-gender-moving-toward.html.
2. I would note that "bisexual" often denotes a binary, and thus does not necessarily upset gender, but pointing to the recuperative nature of the power structure, Paula Rust wrote, "Thus lesbianism was initially constructed as a challenge to gender. But once 'woman' was reconstructed to include 'lesbian', lesbians became part of the prevailing gender structure. In effect, lesbianism was co-opted into gender and ceased to be a challenge to it. Furthermore, the rise of cultural feminism reified rather than challenged gender, maximized rather than minimized the differences between women and men, and created a concept of lesbianism that was dependent on the preservation of gender... Given lesbians' initial challenge to gender, one might expect bisexuals' efforts to break down gender to be well received among lesbians. But because of the change in the relationship of lesbianism to gender..., bisexuals' contemporary challenge to gender is also a threat to lesbianism." Paula Rust, "Bisexual

Politics," reprinted in Judith Lorber, *Gender Inequality, Feminist Theories and Politics* (Roxbury Publishing Co., 1998), 93-94.

3. See also the following essays printed in *Pink and Black Attack*: "Identity, Politics, and Anti-politics: A critical perspective" (2010) http://anarchalibrary.blogspot.com/2011/09/identity-politics-and-anti-politics.html; "No Gods, No Sponsors: Pride and the problem of assimilation" (2009) http://anarchalibrary.blogspot.com/2011/09/no-gods-no-sponsors-pride-and-problem.html.
4. "On the Edge of All Dichotomies: Anarch@-Feminist Thought, Process and Action, 1970-1983" (2009) http://wesscholar.wesleyan.edu/cgi/viewcontent.cgi?article=1355&context=etd_hon_theses 80-81. See also http://anarchalibrary.blogspot.com/2010/09/on-edge-of-all-dichotomies-anarch.html.
5. See "Politicizing Gender: Moving toward revolutionary gender politics" (circa 1993) http://anarchalibrary.blogspot.com/2010/09/politicizing-gender-moving-toward.html; "The Anarchy of Queer (2006)" http://anarchalibrary.blogspot.com/2010/10/anarchy-of-queer-2006-zine.html; "Strengthening Anarchism's Gender Analysis" (2009) http://anarchalibrary.blogspot.com/2010/10/strengthening-anarchisms-gender.html; "Thoughts on Developing Anarchist Queer Theory" (2010) http://anarchalibrary.blogspot.com/2011/03/thoughts-on-developing-anarchist-queer.html; "Towards An Insurrectionary Transfeminism" (2010) http://anarchalibrary.blogspot.com/2010/10/towards-insurrectionary-transfeminism.html.
6. Judith Butler. *Gender Trouble* (1990): 6.
7. See Namascar Shaktini, *On Monique Wittig* (2005); Christine Delphy, *Close to Home* (1984); Monique Wittig, "One is Not Born a Woman" (1981), printed in *The Straight Mind* (1992) http://zinelibrary.info/one-not-born-woman-monique-wittig; Christine Delphy, "Rethinking Sex and Gender" (1993); Stevi Jackson, *Christine Delphy* (1996), Colette Guillaumin, *Racism, sexism, power, and ideology* (1995).
8. Christine Delphy, *Close to Home* (1984): 144
9. See Bruce Bagemihl, *Biological Exuberance* (1999); and Joan Roughgarden, *Evolution's Rainbow* (2004).
10. "By heteropatriarchy, I mean the way our society is fundamentally based on male dominance—dominance inherently built on a gender binary system that presumes heterosexuality as a social norm." Andrea Smith, "Dismantling Hierarchy, Queering Society," *Tikkun* Magazine (July/August 2010). From www.tikkun.org/article.php/july2010smith (accessed February 6, 2012).
11. Andrea Smith, "Indigenous Feminism without Apology" (2006) http://www.awid.org/eng/Issues-and-Analysis/Library/Indigenous-feminism-without-apology-Decentering-white-feminism.
12. US Social Forum 2007, Liberating Gender and Sexuality Plenary, http://www.youtube.com/watch?v=x5crWlrksZs (accessed January 28, 2012).
13. Silvia Federici, *Caliban and the Witch* (2004).
14. http://plato.stanford.edu/entries/feminism-gender/.
15. I examine this more thoroughly in "When Feminism is Revolting" (2012) http://anarchalibrary.blogspot.com/2012/02/when-feminism-is-revolting-initial.html.
16. "In hir book, *My Gender Workbook*, Kate Bornstein characterizes gender's components as fourfold: gender assignment, gender role, gender identity, and gender attribution. Gender assignment is what the doctor calls you at birth, so it can be written off as a description of sex (Bornstein reserves the word sex for sex acts so as to circumvent Essentialist argumentation). Gender role is described as what culture thinks your niche should be, while gender identity is totally subjective. Gender attribution refers to how another person might interpret your gender cues." Stephe Feldmen, "Components of Gender" http://androgyne.ocatch.com/components.htm (accessed January 28, 2012). I find Bornstein's terms useful, but not adequate for dealing with issues of power.
17. "When Feminism is Revolting" (2012).
18. For example, bell hooks distinguishes "patriarchal masculinity" from other forms of masculinity. See also "When Feminism is Revolting" (2012) http://anarchalibrary.blogspot.com/2012/02/when-feminism-is-revolting-initial.html.
19. See Emi Koyama, "Transfeminist Manifesto" (2000). From eminism.org/readings/pdf-rdg/tfmanifesto.pdf (accessed February 6, 2012); Michelle O'Brien, "Trans Liberation and Feminism: Self-Determination, Healthcare, and Revolutionary Struggle" (2003). From anarchalibrary.blogspot.com/2010/09/trans-liberation-and-feminism-self.html (accessed February 6, 2012); and Carolyn, "Politicizing Gender: Moving toward Revolutionary Gender Politics." From www.spunk.org/texts/pubs/lr/sp001714/gender.html (accessed February 6, 2012).
20. bell hooks, *Feminist Theory: From Margin to Center* (1984): 73-75.
21. I discuss this further in "Gender Sabotage," in *Queering Anarchism* (2012).

INSURRECTION AT THE INTERSECTIONS
FEMINISM, INTERSECTIONALITY, AND ANARCHISM

J. Rogue and Abbey Volcano

> We need to understand the body not as bound to the private or to the self—the western idea of the autonomous individual—but as being linked integrally to material expressions of community and public space. In this sense there is no neat divide between the corporeal and the social; there is instead what has been called a "social flesh."
>
> —*Wendy Harcourt and Arturo Escobar*[1]

The Birth of Intersectionality

In response to various U.S. feminisms and feminist organizing efforts,[2] the Combahee River Collective,[3] an organization of black lesbian socialist-feminists, wrote a statement that became the midwife of *intersectionality*. Intersectionality sprang from black feminist politics near the end of the 1970s and beginning of the 1980s and is often understood as a response to mainstream feminism's construction around the erroneous idea of a "universal woman" or "sisterhood."[4] At the heart of intersectionality lies the desire to highlight the myriad ways that categories and social locations such as race, gender, and class intersect, interact, and overlap to produce systemic social inequalities; given this reality, talk of a universal women's experience was obviously based on false premises (and typically mirrored the most privileged categories of women—i.e. white, non-disabled, "middle class," heterosexual, and so on). Initially conceived around the triad of "race/class/gender," intersectionality was later expanded by Patricia Hill Collins to include social locations such as nation, ability, sexuality, age, and ethnicity.[5] Rather than being conceptualized as an additive model, intersectionality offers us a lens through which to view race, class, gender, sexuality, etc. as mutually-constituting processes (that is, these categories do not exist independently from one another; rather, they mutually reinforce one another) and social relations that materially play out in people's everyday lives in complex ways. Rather than distinct categories, intersectionality theorizes social positions as overlapping, complex, interacting, intersecting, and often contradictory configurations.

Toward an Anarchist Critique of Liberal Intersectionality

Intersectionality has been, and often still is, centered on identity. Although the theory suggests that hierarchies and systems of oppression are interlocking, mutually constituting, and sometimes even contradictory, intersectionality has often been used in a way that *levels* structural hierarchies and oppressions. For instance, "race, class, and gender" are often viewed as oppressions that are experienced in a variety of ways/degrees by everyone—that is, no one is free of the forced assignations of identity. This concept can be useful, especially when it comes to struggle, but the three "categories" are often treated solely as identities, and as though they are similar because they are "oppressions." For instance, it is put forward that we all have a race, a gender, and a class. Since everyone experiences these identities differently, many theorists writing on intersectionality have referred to something called "classism" to complement racism and sexism. This can lead to the gravely confused notion that class oppression needs to be rectified by rich people treating poor people "nicer" while still maintaining class society. This analysis treats class differences as though they are simply cultural differences. In turn, this leads toward the limited strategy of "respecting diversity" rather than addressing the root of the problem. This argument precludes a class struggle analysis which views capitalism and class society as institutions and enemies of freedom. We don't wish to "get along" under capitalism by abolishing snobbery and class elitism. Rather, we wish to overthrow capitalism and end class society all together. We do recognize that there are some relevant points raised by the folks who are talking about classism—we do not mean to gloss over the stratification of income within the working class. Organizing within the extremely diverse working class of the United States requires that we acknowledge and have consciousness of that diversity. However, we feel it is inaccurate to conflate this with holding systemic power over others—much of the so-called middle class may have relative financial advantage over their more poorly-waged peers, but that is not the same as exploiting or being in a position of power over them. This sociologically-based class analysis further confuses people by mistakenly leading them to believe their "identity" as a member of the "middle class" (a term which has so many definitions as to make it irrelevant) puts them in league with the ruling class/oppressors, contributing to the lack of class consciousness in the United States. Capitalism is a system of exploitation where the vast majority work for a living while very few own (i.e.: rob) for a living. The term classism does not explain exploitation, which makes it a flawed concept. We want an end to class society, not a society where classes "respect" each other. It is impossible to eradicate exploitation while class society still exists. To end exploitation we must also end class society (and all other institutionalized hierarchies). This critical issue is frequently overlooked by theorists who use intersectionality to call for an end to "classism." Rather, as anarchists, we call for an end to all exploitation and oppression and this includes an end to class society. Liberal interpretations of intersectionality miss the uniqueness of class by viewing it as an identity and treating it as though it is the same as racism or sexism by tacking an "ism" onto the end. Eradicating capitalism means an end to class society; it means class war. Likewise, race, gender, sexuality, dis/ability, age—the gamut of hierarchically-arranged social relations—are in their own ways unique. As anarchists, we might point those unique qualities out rather than leveling all of these social relations into a single framework.

By viewing class as "just another identity" that should be considered in the attempt to understand others' (and one's own) "identities," traditional conceptions of intersectionality do a disservice to liberatory processes and struggle. While intersectionality illustrates the ways in which relations of domination interact with and prop up each other, this does not mean that these systems are identical or can be conflated. They are unique and function differently. These systems also reproduce one another. White supremacy is sexualized and gendered, heteronormativity is racialized and classed. Oppressive and exploitative institutions and structures are tightly woven together and hold one another up. Highlighting their intersections—their seams—gives us useful angles from which to tear them down and construct more liberatory, more desirable, and more sustainable relations with which to begin fashioning our futures.

An Anarchist Intersectionality of Our Own

Despite having noted this particularly common mistake by theorists and activists writing under the label of intersectionality, the theory does have a lot to offer that shouldn't be ignored. For instance, intersectionality rejects the idea of a central or primary oppression. Rather, as previously noted, all oppressions overlap and often mutually constitute each other. Interpreted on the structural and institutional levels, this means that the struggle against capitalism must also be the struggle against heterosexism, patriarchy, white supremacy, etc. Too often intersectionality is used solely as a tool to understand how these oppressions overlap in the everyday lives of people to produce an *identity* that is unique to them in degree and composition. What is more useful to us as anarchists is using intersectionality to understand how the daily lives of people can be used to talk about the ways in which *structures* and *institutions* intersect and interact. This project can inform our analyses, strategies, and struggles against all forms of domination. That is, anarchists might use lived reality to draw connections to institutional processes that create, reproduce, and maintain social relations of domination. Unfortunately, a liberal interpretation of intersectionality precludes this kind of institutional analysis, so while we might borrow from intersectionality, we also need to *critique* it from a distinctly anarchist perspective.

It is worth noting that there really is no universally-accepted interpretation of intersectionality. Like feminism, it requires a modifier in order to be truly descriptive, which is why we'll use the term "anarchist intersectionality" to describe our perspective in this essay. We believe that an anti-state and anti-capitalist perspective (as well as a revolutionary stance regarding white supremacy and heteropatriarchy) is the logical conclusion of intersectionality. However, there are many who draw from intersectionality, yet take a more liberal approach. Again, this can be seen in the criticisms of "classism" rather than capitalism and class society, and the frequent absence of an analysis of the state.[6] Additionally, there is also at times a tendency to focus almost solely on individual experiences rather than systems and institutions. While all these points of struggle are relevant, it is also true that people raised in the United States, socialized in a deeply self-centered culture, have a tendency to focus on the oppression and repression of individuals, oftentimes to the detriment of a broader, more systemic perspective. Our interest lies with how institutions function and how institutions are reproduced through our daily lives and patterns of social relations. How can we trace our "individual experiences" back to the systems that (re)produce them (and vice versa)? How can we trace the ways that these systems (re)produce one another? How can we smash them and create new social relations that foster freedom?

With an institutional and systemic analysis of intersectionality, anarchists are afforded the possibility of highlighting the *social flesh* mentioned in the opening quote. And if we are to give a full account of this social flesh—the ways that hierarchies and inequalities are woven into our social fabric—we'd be remiss if we failed to highlight a glaring omission in nearly everything ever written in intersectional theories: the state. We don't exist in a society of political equals, but in a complex system of domination where some are *governed* and *controlled* and ruled in institutional processes that anarchists describe as the state. Gustav Landauer, who discussed this hierarchical arrangement of humanity where some rule over others in a political body above and beyond the control of the people, saw the state as a social relationship.[7] We are not just bodies that exist in assigned identities such as race, class, gender, ability, and the rest of the usual laundry list. We are also political subjects in a society ruled by politicians, judges, police, and bureaucrats of all manner. An intersectional analysis that accounts for the social flesh might be extended by anarchists, then, for insurrectionary ends, as our misery is embedded within institutions like capitalism and the state that produce, and are (re)produced, by the web of identities used to arrange humanity into neat groupings of oppressors and oppressed.

As anarchists, we have found that intersectionality is useful to the degree that it can inform our struggles. Intersectionality has been helpful for understanding the ways that oppressions overlap and play out in people's everyday lives. However, when interpreted through liberal frameworks, typical intersectional analyses often assume myriad oppressions to function identically, which can preclude a class analysis, an analysis of the state, and analyses of our ruling institutions. Our assessment is that everyday experiences of oppressions and exploitation are important and useful for struggle *if* we utilize intersectionality in a way that can encompass the different methods through which white supremacy, heteronormativity, patriarchy, class society, etc. function in people's lives, rather than simply listing them as though they all operate in similar fashions. Truth is, the histories of heteronormativity, of white supremacy, of class society need to be understood for their similarities and differences. Moreover, they need to be understood for how they've each functioned to (re)shape one another, and vice versa. This level of analysis lends itself to a more holistic view of how our ruling institutions function and how that informs the everyday lives of people. It would be an oversight to not utilize intersectionality in this way.

From Abstraction to Organizing: Reproductive Freedom and Anarchist Intersectionality

The ways in which capitalism, white supremacy, and heteropatriarchy—and disciplinary society more generally—have required control over bodies has been greatly detailed elsewhere,[8] but we would like to offer a bit of that history in order to help build an argument that organizing for reproductive freedom would benefit from an anarchist intersectional analysis. Reproductive freedom, which we use as an explicitly anti-state, anti-capitalist interpretation of reproductive justice, argues that a simple "pro-choice" position is not sufficient for a revolutionary approach to reproductive "rights." Tracing how race, class, sexuality, nationality, and ability intersect and shape a woman's access to reproductive health requires a deeper understanding of systems of oppression, which Andrea Smith outlines in her book *Conquest*.[9] Looking at the history of colonialism in the Americas helps us understand the complexities of reproductive freedom in the current context. The state as an institution has always had a vested interest in maintaining control over social reproduction and in particular, the ways in which colonized peoples did and did not reproduce. Given the history of forced sterilization of Native Americans, as well as African-Americans, Latinos, and even poor white women,[10] we can see that simple access to abortion does not address the complete issue of reproductive freedom.[11] In order to have a comprehensive, revolutionary movement, we need to address all aspects of the issue: being able to have and support children, access to health care, housing, education, and transportation, adoption, non-traditional families, and so on. In order for a movement to be truly revolutionary it must be inclusive; the pro-choice movement has frequently neglected to address the needs of those at the margins. Does Roe *v.* Wade cover the complexities of the lives of women and mothers in prison? What about the experiences of people who are undocumented? Trans* folks have long been fighting for healthcare that is inclusive.[12] Simply defending the right to legal abortion does not bring together all those affected by heteropatriarchy. Similarly, legal "choice" where abortions are expensive procedures does nothing to help poor women and highlights the need to smash capitalism in order to access positive freedoms. Reproductive justice advocates have argued for an intersectional approach to these issues, and an anarchist feminist analysis of reproductive freedom could benefit by utilizing an anarchist intersectional analysis.

An anarchist intersectional analysis of reproductive freedom shows us that when a community begins to struggle together, they require an understanding of the ways that relations of ruling operate together in order to have a holistic sense of what they are fighting for. If we can figure out the ways that oppressive and exploitative social relations work together—and form the tapestry that is daily life—we are better equipped to tear them apart. For instance, to analyze the ways that women of color have been particularly and historically targeted for forced sterilizations requires an understanding of how heteropatriarchy, capitalism, the state, and white supremacy have worked together to create a situation where women of color are targeted bodily through social programs such as welfare, medical experiments, and eugenics. How has racism and white supremacy functioned to support heteropatriarchy? How has sexuality been racialized in ways that have facilitated colonizers to remain without guilt about rape, genocide, and slavery, both historically and contemporarily? How has white supremacy been gendered with images such as the Mammy and the Jezebel?[13] How has the welfare state been racialized and gendered with an agenda for killing the black body?[14] Systemic oppressions such as white supremacy cannot be understood without an analysis of how those systems are gendered, sexualized, classed, etc. Similarly, this kind of analysis can be extended to understanding how heteropatriarchy, heteronormativity, capitalism, the state—all human relations of domination function. This is the weight behind an anarchist intersectional analysis. An anarchist intersectional analysis, at least the way we are utilizing the standpoint, does not centralize any structure or institution over another, except by context. Rather, these structures and institutions operate to (re)produce one another. They are one another. Understood in this way, a central or primary oppressive or exploitative structure simply makes no sense. Rather, these social relations cannot be picked apart and one declared "central" and the others "peripheral." And they *are* intersectional. After all, what good is an insurrection if some of us are left behind?

Notes

1. Harcourt, Wendy, and Arturo Escobar. 2002. "Women and the politics of place." *Development* 45 (1): 7-14.
2. "Refusing to Wait: Anarchism and Intersectionality." http://theanarchistlibrary.org/HTML/Deric_Shannon_and_J._Rogue__Refusing_to_Wait__Anarchism_and_Intersectionality.html (last accessed 5/10/2012).
3. Combahee River Collective Statement. 1977. In Anzalduza, Gloria, and Cherrie Moraga (Eds). 1981. *This Bridge Called My Back: Writings by Radical Women of Color*. Watertown, Mass: Persephone Press. Available at http://circuitous.org/scraps/combahee.html (last accessed 5/10/2012).
4. For example: Crenshaw, Kimberlé W. 1991. "Mapping the Margins: Intersectionality, Identity Politics, and Violence against Women of Color." *Stanford Law Review*, 43 (6): 1241–1299.
5. See: Purkayastha, Bandana. 2012. "Intersectionality in a Transnational World." Gender & Society 26: 55-66.
6. "Refusing to Wait: Anarchism and Intersectionality."
7. Landauer, Gustav. 2010. *Revolution and Other Writings*, translated by Gabriel Kuhn. Oakland: PM Press.
8. For more analysis on how race, gender and sexuality shaped capitalism and colonialism in the U.S., see: Smith, Andrea. 2005. *Conquest: Sexual Violence and American Indian Genocide*. Cambridge, MA: South End Press.
9. Smith, Andrea. 2005. *Conquest: Sexual Violence and American Indian Genocide*. Cambridge, MA: South End Press.
10. For example: http://rockcenter.msnbc.msn.com/_news/2011/11/07/8640744-victims-speak-out-about-north-carolina-sterilization-program-which-targeted-women-young-girls-and-blacks?lite (last accessed 5/30/2012).
11. For a good book that shows examples and the history of reproductive justice, see: Silliman, Jael M. 2004. *Undivided Rights: Women of Color Organize for Reproductive Justice*. Cambridge, Mass: South End Press.
12. Trans* is taken generally to mean: Transgender, Transsexual, genderqueer, Non-Binary, Genderfluid, Genderfuck, Intersex, Third gender, Transvestite, Cross-dresser, Bi-gender, Trans man, Trans woman, Agender.
13. Hill Collins, Patricia. 1991. *Black Feminist Thought: Knowledge, Consciousness, and the Politics of Empowerment*. New York: Routledge.
14. Roberts, Dorothy E. 1999. *Killing the Black Body: Race, Reproduction, and the Meaning of Liberty*. New York: Vintage.

6

VOLTAIRINE deCLEYRE

AN INTRODUCTION

Marian Leighton

THE HISTORY OF AMERICAN RADICALISM REQUIRES MUCH FURther in-depth exploration. This is particularly true of the American anarchist tradition. Ask an anarchist of today who he-she claims as radical intellectual forebears and, depending upon if he-she is of the left-wing or right-wing, they will reply Bakunin—Emma Goldman—Kropotkin or Benjamin Tucker—Josiah Warren—Lysander Spooner, respectively.

Interestingly, this reply would lead one to believe that right-wing anarchism is more indigenous a part of the American radical experience than left-wing anarchism which, based on the work of Bakunin, Goldman, Kropotkin, Berkman would seem more rooted in the nineteenth century European urban insurrectionary tradition. Is this in any way a fair distinction? Is it at all significant that the left-wing anarchist tradition intellectually seems to rely so heavily upon an imported radicalism that largely grew out of a European background? If this in true, does it matter in any way? Of course, it also remains to be seen just how much more "American" the right-wing or laissez-faire anarchist tradition is.

Motivation for interest in the above relationships has greater significance than an esoteric quibbling over historical antecedents. Nor do I pose the above questions on any chauvinistic assumption that a radical tradition that is "truly American" is superior to the "imported immigrant variety." However, more legitimately, the relationship of contemporary left-wing anarchism to an ongoing American radical historical experience could be important for sorting out the bases for appeal that may or may not exist between anarchism and various American subcultures other than those of anarchism's usual constituency of counterculture youth and fairly sophisticated intellectual radicals. In addition to concern with "to whom and for what reasons does anarchism appeal," there is the larger question of accounting for the experiential roots of American anarchism.

Just how much is glib historical simplification in streaming the relationship between left-wing anarchism and European anarchism and right-wing anarchism and American indigenous radicalism? After all the right-wing anarchists also emphasise their intellectual legacy from Adam Smith, Max Stirner, Nietzsche (as did Emma Goldman). and contemporarily the Russian-born Ayn Rand. Left-wing anarchists affirm their interest in the home-grown radicalism of Thoreau, Eugene Debs, Big Bill Haywood, and other Wobblies. The point remains, however, that the anarcho-capitalists can legitimately "capitalise" on the strain of individualism in native American radicalism. The left-wing anarchists, in contrast, were most active and perhaps most effective in this country during a period when the Marxist-scientific socialist analysis and organisational policies had obvious relevance to urban immigrants faced with the horrors of the expanding factory system.

The comparatively greater knowledge of left-wing anarchism during this particular period, the labour and unemployment agitation of the 1880's through the First World War, should be no surprise. This was also probably the period when anarchism reached the greatest number of Americans. The principal anarchist agitators of that time are those still most well-known to us today. However, this association of left-wing anarchism at its height to scientific socialism should not preclude investigation by contemporary anarchists into left-wing anarchist antecedents in America prior to the 1880's. Nor should we, as has so often been the case. allow the judgements of European socialists to distort our vision of many of the radical scenes in this country prior to the European socialist impact here, particularly the socialist anti-clericalism in looking at American religious radicalism, the oldest radical tradition in this country

Although I do not concur with the author in all of her evaluations, a good basic work to read on anarchism prior to the period of anarcho-communist activity is Eunice Schuster's *Native American Anarchism: A Study of Left-wing Anarchist Individualism*. Schuster's main point, with which I agree, is that the demise of the left-wing anarchist individualist tradition is in large part owing to its non-class-conscious appeal at a time when the industrial-labour situation increasingly required self-conscious immigrant labour spokespeople and organisations. In spite of this limitation, native American anarchists, like the anarcho-communists of European background, "assailed the same evils, but in a different manner, and aimed at the same theoretical objective, but proposed to arrive there by different routes," according to Schuster. She further believes there is a valid analogy to he made between Anne Hutchinsons's judgement and expulsion at the hands of her Massachusetts Bay Colony inquisitors and the treatment which Emma Goldman suffered from the US government nearly three hundred years later.

The crucial period to consider in the relationship of the two main strands which create American anarchism, native American left-wing individualism and anarcho-communism (later anarcho-syndicalism), is the 1860's through the First World War. Not only was this the time of greatest immigrant labour activity and anarcho-communist growth and agitation, but was also the scene of the left-wing anarchist individualist demise. Benjamin Tucker, probably the most important populariser of the tradition, left America in 1908 and never returned. The style of protest which he had known and many before him, that of stern ethical judgement and verbal protest and a course of withdrawal from and passive non-resistance to the unethical government, had been replaced by more active forms of protest, larger organised resistance, and direct actionism as a form of protest.

Certainly not all American left-wing anarchists left their homeland. Among those who stayed was Voltairine de Cleyre. As a native American anarchist, her politics and ethical choices had been for the most part typical of those held by left-wing individualist anarchists of the period preceding great influence by European socialism. She was in her early anarchism both a pacifist and non-resistant, favouring individual solutions to social problems.

During her early radical days she was a Free Thought lecturer stressing the rights of the individual against encroachment by larger social/political units. She relied for inspiration upon and was widely acquainted with the earlier American Republican ideals and their possible radical implications. Thomas Paine and Thomas Jefferson and their ideals furnished subjects for her free thought lecture.

She was thoroughly acquainted with notions of the rugged individualism of the American frontiersman and of the indomitable will of the individualist who would "move on" rather than allow his rights to be encroached upon by neighbours or politicians who didn't mind their own business. She was susceptible to the force of this image as part of the early American experience.

Even after her rejection of religion and her turning to free thought, her view of life was strongly tinged with a basic religious idealism, a belief that the long-suffering and compassionate individuals "will win out," having been supported against the evils of materialism, conformity, and apathy by the march of history. Consequently, a narrowly materialistic determination of the individual could never be compatible with Voltairine de Cleyre's temperament and politics. Mere desire for material betterment would never be sufficient motivation for the revolutionary, who must also basically be motivated by a devotion to a vision of life beyond the self.

Her choice of non-resistance as a form of protest is thoroughly American and very rooted in her religious ideology. "Non-resistance," refusal to pay unjust taxes, refusal to military induction, refusal to participate in electoral practices of corrupt governments is as American as apple pie and has been a traditional form of protest adopted by such native American radicals as Quakers, antinomians, transcendentalists, abolitionists, Shakers, and so many others. Underlying this stance is the belief that the Good Man is he who waits, who is passive, who will not respond in kind to the wickedness and tyranny of the Malevolent Man. Goodness is manifested in passivity.

Voltairine de Cleyre's ideas on how radical social change can be effected were altered drastically during her lifetime, just as the "American System" itself was undergoing drastic transformation.

The Haymarket Square legal atrocities and subsequent martyrdom of several anarchists not only outraged members of the immigrant labour population like Emma Goldman and Alexander Berkman, but also outraged native American radicals who, as regards the needs of labour, had been bred in another age. Thus, as a result of the Haymarket incident, Voltairine de Cleyre records her first recollection of total disillusionment with the "justice" of the American legal system.

With the passage of time, she came to feel that her emphasis upon the virtues of Americans bred in isolated, self-sustaining, independent pioneer communities had little relevance to an America whose trends in labour were directed toward construction of huge manufacturing conglomerates. This trend made evident the need for new radical solutions to the needs of labour. Concomitantly, she ceased to believe in the effectiveness of lecturing, as she had in her Free Thought days, on the virtues of the American Revolutionaries of 1776. In summary, she felt that during the American colonial and pioneer period, the harshness of making a life in a new land had fostered a kind of sectarian independence jealously guarded, that being thrown upon their own resources the settlers had been made into well-rounded and well-balanced individuals, and that this experience had also made strong such social bonds as existed in the comparative simplicity of their small communities.

But this old Golden Age had virtually disappeared and the new reality of America, she felt, was its huge manufacturing plants, and the terrifying and depersonalising experience of urban poverty and isolation. With good reason Voltairine de Cleyre could testify to the latter realities in her role as English teacher among the urban immigrant poor of Philadelphia. Amid material conditions of utter deprivation, she was forced to choose teaching as her only means of subsistence. (Goldman, *Living My Life*, vol. 2, p. 504).

In her social activist vision of a transformed future, there was a constructive transition made in her thinking that mirrored her analysis of her country's changes. Voltairine de Cleyre did not—as many individualist anarchists did and continue to do posit as a solution the restoration of that state of pioneer sovereign individuality. (Modern anarcho-capitalists behave as if they believed money, "running your own little capitalist enterprise," has the power of bringing back the golden days of the Great American Individual, as if the frontier had never disappeared.) Instead, she felt .."..the great manufacturing plants will break up, population will go after the fragments, and there will be seen not indeed the hard self-sustaining, isolated pioneer communities of early America, but thousands of small communities stretching along the lines of transportation, each producing very largely for its own needs, able to rely upon itself, and therefore able to be independent." (p. 134. *Selected Writings of Voltairine de Cleyre*). Is this not similar in some respects to what many anarchists are now attempting by decentralising new technologies, alternate energy and food production systems to make smaller neighbourhood areas more nearly autonomous by means of co-operation among the neighbourhood residents? The result of her thinking, thus, pointed neither to resurrection of the ideal of isolated frontier individualism, nor to the faceless bureaucracy of State socialism.

Toward the end of her life, Voltairine de Cleyre came to accept "direct actionism" as a form of public protest, thus obviously revising her earlier stance of pacifist non-resistance. Even after her acceptance of direct actionism, Voltairine de Cleyre, unlike Emma Goldman, could not approve of advising anyone to do anything "involving a risk to herself, " since each individual can only assume such great responsibility over their own lives ultimately; she nonetheless declared that the "spirit which animates Emma Goldman is the only one which will emancipate the slave from his slavery, the tyrant from his tyranny—the spirit which is willing to dare and suffer." (pp. 9-10, Hippolyte Havel's introduction to *Selected Writings of Voltairine de Cleyre*.) In 1894, with such words as the above, she greeted the unemployed of Philadelphia as stand-in for Emma Goldman who had been arrested a few hours earlier for her expropriation speech to unemployed New York workers the previous night. Thus, Voltairine de Cleyre lent her support to the expropriation of private property, a far cry from the traditional individualist anarchist stance on the sanctity of private property.

In her ideals at least, Voltairine de Cleyre made a constructive transition from a style of fairly narrow left-wing individualist anarchism to an anarchism more attuned to the evolving economic realities of an expanding industrial age. However, it would be false to assume that she made her way to an acceptance of what in her time was called Anarchist Communism, Bakuninist Anarchism.

Faith in individual awareness as the crucial factor in the moulding of the social/political/economic environment is, and always has been, a major emphasis in native American radicalism Voltairine de Cleyre was able to make the cognitive leap from the narrow, frontierist conception of individuality to an understanding of the breadth of individuality in its more complex social context, and thence to direct actionism and expropriative rights and their implications. However, it is significant that in her essay on her close friend and co-worker, Dyer D. Lum, who was largely responsible for convincing her of the correctness of direct actionism, she stresses his belief in transcendence as the most basic positive force in individual development, rather than his labour agitational activities. Her insistence that individual consciousness must accompany social development and change is a synthesis with no less validity for anarchists today. As Voltairine de Cleyre affirmed:

> The free and spontaneous inner life of the individual the anarchists have regarded as the source of greatest pleasure and also of progress itself, or as some would prefer to say, social change.
> *Selected Writings of Voltairine de Cleyre*

THE MAKING OF AN ANARCHIST

Voltairine de Cleyre

> "Here was one guard, and here was the other at this end; I was here opposite the gate. You know those problems in geometry of the hare and the hounds—they never run straight, but always in a curve, so, see? And the guard was no smarter than the dogs; if he had run straight he would have caught me."

It was Peter Kropotkin telling of his escape from the Petro-Paulovsky fortress. Three crumbs on the table marked the relative position of the outwitted guards and the fugitive prisoner; the speaker had broken them from the bread on which he was lunching and dropped them on the table with an amused grin. The suggested triangle had been the starting-point of the life-long exile of the greatest man, save Tolstoy alone, that Russia has produced: from that moment began the many foreign wanderings and the taking of the simple, love-given title "Comrade," for which he had abandoned the "Prince," which he despises.

We were three together in the plain little home of a London workingman—Will Wess, a one-time shoemaker—Kropotkin, and I. We had our "tea" in homely English fashion, with thin slices of buttered bread; and we talked of things nearest our hearts, which, whenever two or three anarchists are gathered together, means present evidences of the growth of liberty and what our comrades are doing in all lands. And as what they do and say often leads them into prisons, the talk had naturally fallen upon Kropotkin's experience and his daring escape, for which the Russian government is chagrined unto this day

Presently the old man glanced at the time and jumped briskly to his feat: "I am late. Good-by, Voltairine; good-by, Will. Is this the way to the kitchen? I must say good-by to Mrs. Turner and Lizzie." And out to the kitchen he went, unwilling, late though he was, to leave without a hand-clasp to those who had so much as washed a dish for him. Such is Kropotkin, a man whose personality is felt more than any other in the anarchist movement—at once the gentlest, the most kindly, and the most invincible of men. Communist as well as anarchist, his very heart-beats are rhythmic with the great common pulse of work and life.

Communist am not I, though my father was, and his father before him during the stirring times of '48, which is probably the remote reason for my opposition to things as they are: at bottom convictions are mostly temperamental. And if I sought to explain myself on other grounds, I should be a bewildering error in logic; for by early influences and education I should have been a nun, and spent my life glorifying Authority in its most concentrated form, as some of my schoolmates are doing at this hour within the mission houses of the Order of the Holy Names of Jesus and Mary. But the old ancestral spirit of rebellion asserted itself while I was yet fourteen, a schoolgirl at the Convent of Our Lady of Lake Huron, at Sarnis, Ontario. How I pity myself now, when I remember it, poor lonesome little soul, battling solitary in the murk of religious superstition, unable to believe and yet in hourly fear of damnation, hot, savage, and eternal, if I do not instantly confess and profess! How well I recall the bitter energy with which I repelled my teacher's enjoinder, when I told her that I did not wish to apologise for an adjudged fault, as I could not see that I had been wrong, and would not feel my words. "It is not necessary," said she, "that we should feel what we say, but it is always necessary that we obey our superiors." "I will not lie," I answered hotly, and at the same time trembled lest my disobedience had finally consigned me to torment!

I struggled my way out at last, and was a freethinker when I left the institution, three years later, though I had never seen a book or heard a word to help me in my loneliness. It had been like the Valley of the Shadow of Death, and there are white scars on my soul yet, where Ignorance and Superstition burnt me with their hell-fire in those stifling days. Am I blasphemous? It is their word, not mine. Beside that battle of my young days all others have been easy, for whatever was without, within my own Will was supreme. It has owed no allegiance, and never shall; it has moved steadily in one direction, the knowledge and the assertion of its own liberty, with all the responsibility falling thereon.

This, I am sure, is the ultimate reason for my acceptance of anarchism, though the specific occasion which ripened tendencies to definition was the affair of 1886-87, when five innocent men were hanged in Chicago for the act of one guilty who still remains unknown. Till then I believed in the essential justice of the American law and trial by jury. After that I never could. The infamy of that trial has passed into history, and the question it awakened as to the possibility of justice under law has passed into clamorous crying across the world. With this question fighting for a hearing at a time when, young and ardent, all questions were pressing with a force which later life would in vain hear again, I chanced to hear a Paine Memorial Convention in an out-of-the-way corner of the earth among the mountains and the snow-drifts of Pennsylvania. I was a freethought lecturer at the time, and had spoken in the afternoon on the lifework of Paine; in the evening I sat in the audience to hear Clarence Darrow deliver an address on socialism. It was my first introduction to any plan for bettering the condition of the working-classes which furnished some explanation of the course of economic development, I ran to it as one who has been turning about in darkness runs to the light. I smile now at how quickly I adopted the label "socialist" and how quickly I cast it aside. Let no one follow my example; but I was young. Six weeks later I was punished for my rashness, when I attempted to argue for my faith with a little Russian Jew named Mozersky, at a debating club in Pittsburgh. He was an anarchist, and a bit of a Socrates. He questioned me into all kinds of holes, from which I extricated myself most awkwardly, only to flounder into others he had smilingly dug while I was getting out of the first ones. The necessity of a better foundation became apparent: hence began a course of study in the principles of sociology and of modern socialism and anarchism as presented in their regular journals. It was Benjamin Tucker's *Liberty*, the exponent of Individualist anarchism, which finally convinced me that "Liberty is not the Daughter but the Mother of Order." And though I no longer hold the particular economic gospel advocated by Tucker, the doctrine of anarchism itself, as then conceived, has but broadened, deepened, and intensified itself with years.

To those unfamiliar with the movement, the various terms are confusing. Anarchism is, in truth, a sort of Protestantism, whose adherents are a unit in the great essential belief that all forms of external authority must disappear to be replaced by self-control only, but variously divided in our conception of the form of future society. Individualism supposes private property to be the cornerstone of personal freedom; asserts that such property should consist in the absolute possession of one's own product and of such share of the natural heritage of all as one may actually use. Communist-anarchism, on the other hand, declares that such property is both unrealisable and undesirable; that the common possession and use of all the natural sources and means of social production can alone guarantee the individual against a recurrence of inequality and its attendants, government and slavery. My personal conviction is that both forms of society, as well as many intermediations, would, in the absence of government, be tried in various localities, according to the instincts and material condition of the people, but that well founded objections may be offered to both. Liberty and experiment alone can determine the best forms of society. Therefore I no longer label myself otherwise than as "anarchist" simply.

I would not, however, have the world think that I am an "anarchist by trade." Outsiders have some very curious notions about us, one of them being that anarchists never work. On the contrary, anarchists are nearly always poor, and it is only the rich who live without work. Not only this, but it is our belief that every healthy human being will, by the laws of his own activity choose to work, though certainly not as now, for at present there is little opportunity for one to find his true vocation. Thus I, who in freedom would have selected otherwise, am a teacher of language. Some twelve years since, being in Philadelphia and without employment, I accepted the proposition of a small group of Russian Jewish factory workers to form an evening class in the common English branches. I know well enough that behind the desire to help me to make a living lay the wish that I might thus take part in the propaganda of our common cause. But the incidental became once more the principal, and a teacher of working men and women I have remained from that day. In those twelve years that I have lived and loved and worked with foreign Jews I have taught over a thousand, and found them as a rule, the brightest, the most persistent and sacrificing students, and in youth dreamers of social ideals. While the "intelligent American" has been cursing him as the "ignorant foreigner," while the short-sighted working man has been making life for the "sheeny" as intolerable as possible, silent and patient the despised man has worked his way against it all. I have myself seen such genuine heroism in the cause of education practised by girls and boys, and even by men and women with families, as would pass the limits of belief to the ordinary. Cold, starvation, self-isolation, all endured for years in order to obtain the means for study; and, worse than all, exhaustion of body even to emaciation—this is common. Yet in the midst of all this, so fervent is the imagination of the young that most of them find time besides to visit the various clubs and societies where radical thought is discussed, and sooner or later ally themselves either with the socialist Sections, the Liberal Leagues, the Single Tax Clubs, or the anarchist Groups. The greatest socialist daily in America is the Jewish *Vorwaerts*, and the most active and competent practical workers are Jews. So they are among the anarchists. I am no propagandist at all costs, or I would leave the story here; but the truth compels me to add that as the years pass and the gradual filtration and absorption of successful professionals, the golden mist of enthusiasm vanishes, and the old teacher must turn for comradeship to the new youth, who still press forward with burning eyes, seeing what is lost forever to those whom common success has satisfied and stupefied. It brings tears sometimes, but as Kropotkin says, "Let them go; we have had the best of them." After all, who are the really old?

Those who wear out in faith and energy, and take to easy chairs and soft living; not Kropotkin, with his sixty years upon him, who has bright eyes and the eager interest of a little child; not fiery John Most, "the old warhorse of the revolution," unbroken after his ten years of imprisonment in Europe and America; not grey-haired Louise Michel, with the aurora of the morning still shining in her keen look which peers from behind the barred memories of New Caledonia ; not Dyer D. Lum, who still smiles in his grave, I think; nor Tucker, nor Turner, nor Theresa Clairmunt, nor Jean Grave—not these. I have met them all, and felt the springing life pulsating through heart and hand, joyous, ardent, leaping into action. Not such are the old, but your young heart that goes bankrupt in social hope, dry-rotting in this stale and purposeless society. Would you always be young? Then be an anarchist, and live with the faith of hope, though you be old. I doubt if any other hope has the power to keep the fire alight as I saw it in 1897, when we met the Spanish exiles released from the fortress of Montjuich. Comparatively few persons in America ever knew the story of that torture, though we distributed fifty thousand copies of the letters smuggled from the prison and some few newspapers did reprint them. They were the letters of men incarcerated on mere suspicion for the crime of an unknown person, and subjected to tortures the bare mention of which makes one shudder. Their nails were torn out, their heads compressed in metal caps, the most sensitive portions of the body twisted between guitar strings, their flesh burned with red hot irons; they had been fed on salt codfish after days of starvation, and refused water; Juan One, a boy nineteen years old, had gone mad; another had confessed to something he had never done and knew nothing of. This is no horrible imagination. I who write have myself shaken some of those scarred hands. Indiscriminately, four hundred people of all sorts of beliefs—Republicans, trade unionists, socialists, Free Masons, as well as anarchists—had been cast into dungeons and tortured in the infamous "zero." Is it a wonder that most of them came out anarchists? There were twenty-eight in the first lot that we met at Euston Station that August afternoon, homeless wanderers in the whirlpool of London, released without trial after months of imprisonment, and ordered to leave Spain in forty-eight hours! They had left it, singing their prison songs; and still across their dark and sorrowful eyes one could see the eternal Maytime bloom. They drifted away to South America chiefly, where four or five new anarchist papers have since arisen, and several colonising experiments along anarchist lines are being tried. So tyranny defeats itself, and the exile becomes the seed-sower of the revolution.

And not only to the heretofore unaroused does he bring awakening, but the entire character of the world movement is modified by this circulation of the comrades of all nations among themselves. Originally the American movement, the native creation which arose with Josiah Warren in 1829. was purely individualist; the student of economy will easily understand the material and historical cause for such development. But within the last twenty years the communist idea has made great progress owing primarily to that concentration in capitalist production which has driven the American workingmen to grasp at the idea of solidarity, and, secondly, the expulsion of active communist propagandists from Europe. Again, another change has come within the last ten years. Till then the application of the idea was chiefly narrowed to industrial matters, and the economic schools mutually denounced each other; today a large and genial tolerance is growing. The young generation recognises the immense sweep of the idea through all the realms of art, science, literature, education, sex relations, and personal morality, as well as social economy, and welcomes the accession to the ranks of those who struggle to realise the free life, no matter in what field. For this is what anarchism finally means, the whole unchaining of life after two thousand years of Christian asceticism and hypocrisy.

Apart from the question of ideals, there is the question of method. "How do you propose to get all this?" is the question most frequently asked us. The same modification has taken place here. Formerly there were "Quakers" and "Revolutionists"; so there are still. But while they neither thought well of the other, now both have learned that each has his own use in the great play of world forces. No man is in himself a unit, and in every soul Jove still makes war on Christ. Nevertheless, the spirit of Peace grows; and while it would be idle to say that anarchists in general believe that any of the great industrial problems will be solved without the use of force it would be equally idle to suppose that they consider force itself a desirable thing, or that it furnishes a final solution to any problem, From peaceful experiment alone can come final solution, and that the advocates of force know and believe as well as the Tolstoyans. Only they think that the present tyrannies provoke resistance. The spread of Tolstoy's "War and Peace" and "The Slavery of Our Times," and the growth of numerous Tolstoy clubs having for their purpose the dissemination of the literature of non-resistance, is an evidence that many receive the idea that it is easier to conquer war with peace. I am one of these. I can see no end of retaliation unless someone ceases to retaliate. But let no one mistake this for servile submission or meek abnegation; my right shall be asserted no matter at what cost to me, and none shall trench upon it without my protest.

Good-natured satirists often remark that "the best way to cure an anarchist is to give him a fortune." Substituting "corrupt" for "cure," I would subscribe to this; and believing myself to be no better than the rest of men, I earnestly hope that as so far it has been my lot to work, and work hard, and for no fortune, so I may continue to the end; for let me keep the intensity of my soul, with all the limitations of my material conditions, rather than become the spineless and idealless creation of material needs. My reward is that I live with the young; I keep step with my comrades; I shall die in the harness with my face to the east—the East and the Light.

8

SOCIALISM, ANARCHISM AND FEMINISM

Carol Ehrlich

> You are a woman in a capitalist society. You get pissed off: about the job, about the bills, about your husband (or ex), about the kids' school, the housework, being pretty, not being pretty, being looked at, not being looked at (and either way, not listened to), etc. If you think about all these things and how they fit together and what has to be changed, and then you look around for some words to hold all these thoughts together in abbreviated form, you almost have to come up with 'socialist feminism.' [1]

From all indications a great many women have "come up" with socialist feminism as the solution to the persistent problem of sexism. "Socialism" (in its astonishing variety of forms) is popular with a lot of people these days, because it has much to offer: concern for working people, a body of revolutionary theory that people can point to (whether or not they have read it), and some living examples of industrialised countries that are structured differently from the United States and its satellites.

For many feminists, socialism is attractive because it promises to end the economic inequality of working women. Further, for those women who believe that an exclusively feminist analysis is too narrow to encompass all the existing inequalities, socialism promises to broaden it, while guarding against the dilution of its radical perspective.

For good reasons, then, women are considering whether or not "socialist feminism" makes sense as a political theory. For socialist feminists do seem to be both sensible and radical—at least, most of them evidently feel a strong antipathy to some of the reformist and solipsistic traps into which increasing numbers of women seem to be stumbling.

To many of us more unromantic types, the Amazon Nation, with its armies of strong-limbed matriarchs riding into the sunset, is unreal, but harmless. A more serious matter is the current obsession with the Great Goddess and assorted other objects of worship, witchcraft, magic, and psychic phenomena. As a feminist concerned with transforming the structure of society, I find this anything but harmless.

Item One: Over fourteen hundred women went to Boston in April, 1976 to attend a women's spirituality conference dealing in large part with the above matters. Could not the energy invested in chanting, swapping the latest pagan ideas, and attending workshops on bellydancing and menstrual rituals have been put to some better and more feminist use?

Item Two: According to reports in at least one feminist newspaper, a group of witches tried to levitate Susan Saxe out of jail. If they honestly thought this would free Saxe, then they were totally out of touch with the realities of patriarchal oppression. If it was intended to be a light-hearted joke, then why isn't anyone laughing?

Reformism is a far greater danger to women's interests than are bizarre psychic games. I know that "reformist" is an epithet that may be used in ways that are neither honest nor very useful—principally to demonstrate one's ideological purity, or to say that concrete political work of any type is not worth doing because it is potentially co-optable. In response, some feminists have argued persuasively that the right kinds of reforms can build a radical movement.[2]

Just the same, there are reformist strategies that waste the energies of women, that raise expectations of great change, and that are misleading and alienating because they cannot deliver the goods. The best (or worst) example is electoral politics. Some socialists (beguiled by the notion of gradualism) fall for that one. Anarchists know better. You cannot liberate yourself by non-liberatory means; you cannot elect a new set of politicians (no matter how sisterly) to run the same old corrupt institutions—which in turn run *you*. When the National Organisation of Women (NOW)'s Majority Caucus—the radical branch of that organisation—asks women to follow them "out of the mainstream, into the revolution" by means that include electoral politics, they will all drown in the depths of things as they are.

Electoral politics is an obvious, everyday kind of trap. Even a lot of non-radicals have learned to avoid it. A more subtle problem is capitalism in the guise of feminist economic power. Consider, for example, the Feminist Economic Network. The name might possibly fool you. Ostensibly it was a network of alternative businesses set up to erode capitalism from within by creating economic self-sufficiency for women. That is an appealing idea. Yet, FEN's first major project opened in Detroit in April, 1976. For an annual membership fee of $100, privileged women could swim in a private pool, drink in a private bar, and get discounts in a cluster of boutiques. FEN paid its female employees $2.50 per hour to work there. Its director, Laura Brown, announced this venture as "the beginning of the feminist economic revolution."[3]

When two of the same old games—electoral politics and hip capitalism—are labeled "revolution," the word has been turned inside out. It's not surprising that a socialist brand of feminism seems to be a source of revolutionary sanity to many women who don't want to be witches, primitive warriors, senators, or small capitalists, but who do want to end sexism while creating a transformed society. Anarchist feminism could provide a meaningful theoretical framework, but all too many feminists have either never heard of it, or else dismiss it as the ladies' auxiliary of male bomb-throwers.

Socialist feminism provides an assortment of political homes. On the one hand, there are the dingy, cramped quarters of Old Left sects such as the Revolutionary Communist Party (formerly the Revolutionary Union), the October League, and the International Workers Party. Very few women find these habitable. On the other hand, a fair number of women are moving into the sprawling, eclectic establishments built by newer Left groups such as the New American Movement, or by various autonomous "women's unions."

The newer socialist feminists have been running an energetic and reasonably effective campaign to recruit nonaligned women. In contrast, the more rigid Old Left groups have largely rejected the very idea that lesbians, separatists, and assorted other scruffy and unsuitable feminists could work with the noble inheritors of Marx, Trotsky (although the Trotskyists are unpredictable), Stalin, and Mao. Many reject the idea of an autonomous women's movement that cares at all about women's issues. To them, it is full of "bourgeois" (most damning of all Marxist epithets!) women bent on "doing their own thing," and it "divides the working class," which is a curious assumption that workers are dumber than everyone else. Some have a hysterical antipathy to lesbians: the most notorious groups are the October League and the Revolutionary Communist Party, but they are not alone. In this policy, as in so many others, the anti-lesbian line follows that of the communist countries. The RCP, for example, released a position paper in the early 1970s (back in its pre-party days, when it was the plain old Revolutionary Union) which announced that homosexuals are "caught in the mire and muck of bourgeois decadence," and that gay liberation is "anti-working class and counter revolutionary." All the Old Left groups are uneasy with the idea that any women outside the "proletariat" are oppressed at all. The working class, of course, is a marvelously flexible concept: in the current debates on the Left, it ranges from point-of-production workers (full stop) to an enormous group that takes in every single person who sells her or his labour for wages, or who depends on someone else who does. That's almost all of us. (So, Papa Kari, if ninety per cent of the people of the United States are the vanguard, why haven't we had the revolution yet?)

The newer socialist feminists have been trying in all manner of inventive ways to keep a core of Marxist-Leninist thought, update it, and graft it to contemporary radical feminism. The results are sometimes peculiar. In July, 1975, the women of the New American Movement and a number of autonomous groups held the first national conference on socialist feminism. It was not especially heavily advertised in advance, and everyone seemed to be surprised that so many women (over sixteen hundred, with more turned away) wanted to spend the July 4th weekend in Yellow Springs, Ohio.

On reading the speeches given at the conference, as well as extensive commentary written by other women who attended,[4] it is not at all clear what the conference organisers thought they were offering in the name of "socialist feminism." The *Principles of Unity* that were drawn up prior to the conference included two items that have always been associated with radical feminism, and that in fact are typically thought of as *antithetical* to a socialist perspective. The first principle stated: "We recognise the need for and support the existence of the autonomous women's movement throughout the revolutionary process." The second read: "We agree that all oppression, whether based on race, class, sex, or lesbianism, is interrelated and the fights for liberation from oppression must be simultaneous and cooperative." The third principle merely remarked that "socialist feminism is a strategy for revolution"; and the fourth and final principle called for holding discussions "in the spirit of struggle and unity."

This is, of course, an incredible smorgasbord of tasty principles—a menu designed to appeal to practically everyone. But when "socialist" feminists serve up the independent women's movement as the main dish, and when they say class oppression is just one of several oppressions, no more important than any other, then (as its Marxist critics say) it is no longer socialism.

However, socialist feminists do not follow out the implications of radical feminism all the way. If they did, they would accept another principle: that non-hierarchical structures are essential to feminist practice. This, of course, is too much for any socialist to take. But what it means is that radical feminism is far more compatible with one type of anarchism than it is with socialism. That type is social anarchism (also known as communist anarchism), not the individualist or anarcho-capitalist varieties.

This won't come as news to feminists who are familiar with anarchist principles—but very few feminists are. That's understandable, since anarchism has veered between a bad press and none at all. If feminists were familiar with anarchism, they would not be looking very hard at socialism as a means of fighting sexist oppression. Feminists have got to be skeptical of any social theory that comes with a built-in set of leaders and followers, no matter how "democratic" this centralised structure is supposed to be. Women of all classes, races, and life circumstances have been on the receiving end of domination too long to want to exchange one set of masters for another. We know who has power and (with a few isolated exceptions) it isn't us.

Several contemporary anarchist feminists have pointed out the connections between social anarchism and radical feminism. Lynne Farrow said "feminism practices what anarchism preaches." Peggy Kornegger believes that "feminists have been unconscious anarchists in both theory and practice for years." And Marian Leighton states that "the refining distinction from radical feminist to anarcho-feminist is largely that of making a step in self-conscious theoretical development."[5]

We build autonomy
The process of ever growing synthesis
For every living creature.
We spread
Spontaneity and creation
We learn the joys of equality
Of relationships
Without dominance
Among sisters.
We destroy domination
In all its forms.

This chant appeared in the radical feminist newspaper *It Aint Me Babe*[6] whose masthead carried the line "end all hierarchies." It was not labeled an anarchist (or anarchist feminist) newspaper, but the connections are striking. It exemplified much of what women's liberation was about in the early years of the reborn movement. And it is that spirit that will be lost if the socialist feminist hybrid takes root; if goddess worship or the lesbian nation convince women to set up new forms of dominance-submission.

Radical Feminism and Anarchist Feminism

All radical feminists and all social anarchist feminists are concerned with a set of common issues: control over one's own body; alternatives to the nuclear family and to heterosexuality; new methods of child care that will liberate parents and children; economic self-determination; ending sex stereotyping in education, in the media, and in the workplace; the abolition of repressive laws; an end to male authority, ownership, and control over women; providing women with the means to develop skills and positive self-attitudes; an end to oppressive emotional relationships; and what the Situationists have called "the reinvention of everyday life."

There are, then, many issues on which radical feminists and anarchist feminists agree. But anarchist feminists are concerned with something more. Because they are anarchists, they work to end all power relationships, all situations in which people can oppress each other. Unlike some radical feminists who are not anarchists, they do not believe that power in the hands of women could possibly lead to a non-coercive society. And unlike most socialist feminists, they do not believe that anything good can come out of a mass movement with a leadership elite. In short, neither a workers' state nor a matriarchy will end the oppression of everyone. The goal, then, is not to "seize" power, as the socialists are fond of urging, but to abolish power.

Contrary to popular belief, all social anarchists are socialists. That is, they want to take wealth out of the hands of the few and redistribute it among all members of the community. And they believe that people need to co-operate with each other as a community, instead of living as isolated individuals. For anarchists, however, the central issues are always power and social hierarchy. If a state—even a state representing the workers—continues, it will re-establish forms of domination, and some people will no longer be free. People aren't free just because they are surviving, or even economically comfortable. They are free only when they have power over their own lives. Women, even more than most men, have very little power over their own lives. Gaining such autonomy, and insisting that everyone have it, is the major goal of anarchist feminists.

> *Power to no one, and to every one: To each the power over his/her own life, and no others.*[7]

On Practice

That is the theory. What about the practice? Again, radical feminism and anarchist feminism have much more in common than either does with socialist feminism.[8] Both work to build alternative institutions, and both take the politics of the personal very seriously. Socialist feminists are less inclined to think either is particularly vital to revolutionary practice.

Developing alternative forms of organisation means building self-help clinics, instead of fighting to get one radical on a hospital's board of directors; it means women's video groups and newspapers, instead of commercial television and newspapers; living collectives, instead of isolated nuclear families; rape crisis centres; food co-ops; parent-controlled daycare centres; free schools; printing co-ops; alternative radio groups, and so on.

Yet, it does little good to build alternative institutions if their structures mimic the capitalist and hierarchical models with which we are so familiar. Many radical feminists recognised this early: That's why they worked to rearrange the way women perceive the world and themselves (through the consciousness-raising group), and why they worked to rearrange the forms of work relationships and interpersonal interactions (through the small, leaderless groups where tasks are rotated and skills and knowledge shared). They were attempting to do this in a hierarchical society that provides no models except ones of inequality. Surely, a knowledge of anarchist theory and models of organisation would have helped. Equipped with this knowledge, radical feminists might have avoided some of the mistakes they made—and might have been better able to overcome some of the difficulties they encountered in trying simultaneously to transform themselves and society.

Take, for example, the still current debate over "strong women" and the closely related issue of leadership. The radical feminist position can be summarised this way:

> 1. Women have been kept down because they are isolated from each other and are paired off with men in relationships of dominance and submission.
> 2. Men will not liberate women; women must liberate themselves. This cannot happen if each woman tries to liberate herself alone. Thus, women must work together on a model of mutual aid.
> 3. "Sisterhood is powerful," but women cannot be sisters if they recapitulate masculine patterns of dominance and submission.
> 4. New organisational forms have to be developed. The primary form is the small leaderless group; the most important behaviours are egalitarianism, mutual support, and the sharing of skills and knowledge.

If many women accepted this, even more did not. Some were opposed from the start; others saw first hand that it was difficult to put into practice, and regretfully concluded that such beautiful idealism would never work out.

Ideological support for those who rejected the principles put forth by the "unconscious anarchists" was provided in two documents that quickly circulated through women's liberation newspapers and organisations. The first was Anselma dell'Olio's speech to the second Congress to Unite Women, which was held in May, 1970 in New York City. The speech, entitled *Divisiveness and Self-Destruction in the Women's Movement: A Letter of Resignation*, gave dell'Olio's reasons for leaving the women's movement. The second document was Joreen's *Tyranny of Structurelessness*, which first appeared in 1972 in *The Second Wave*. Both raised issues of organisational and personal practice that were, and still are, tremendously important to the women's movement.

> *"I have come to announce my swan-song to the women's movement... I have been destroyed... I learned three and one-half years ago that women had always been divided against one another, were self-destructive and filled with impotent rage. I never dreamed that I would see the day when this rage, masquerading as a pseudo-egalitarian radicalism under the "pro-woman" banner, would turn into frighteningly vicious anti-intellectual fascism of the Left, and used within the movement to strike down sisters singled out with all the subtlety and justice of a kangaroo court of the Ku Klux Klan. I am referring, of course, to the personal attack, both overt and odious, to which women in the movement, who have painfully managed any degree of achievement, have been subjected... If you are... an achiever you are immediately labeled a thrill-seeking opportunist, a ruthless mercenary, out to get her fame and fortune over the dead bodies of selfless sisters who have buried their abilities and sacrificed their ambitions for the greater glory of Feminism... If you have the misfortune of being outspoken and articulate, you are accused of being power-mad, elitist, racist, and finally the worst epithet of all: a MALE IDENTIFIER."*[9]

When Anselma dell'Olio gave this angry farewell to the movement, it did two things: For some women, it raised the question of how women can end unequal power relationships among themselves without destroying each other. For others, it did quite the opposite—it provided easy justification for all the women who had been dominating other women in a most unsisterly way. Anyone who was involved in women's liberation at that time knows that the dell'Olio statement was twisted by some women in exactly that fashion: Call yourself assertive, or strong, or talented, and you can re-label a good deal of ugly, insensitive, and oppressive behaviour. Women who presented themselves as tragic heroines destroyed by their envious or misguided (and, of course, far less talented) "sisters" could count on a sympathetic response from some other women.

Just the same, women who were involved in the movement at that time know that the kinds of things dell'Olio spoke about *did* happen, and they should not have happened. A knowledge of anarchist theory is not enough, of course, to prevent indiscriminate attacks on women. But in the struggle to learn new ways of relating and working with each other, such knowledge might—just might—have prevented some of these destructive mistakes.

Ironically, these mistakes were motivated by the radical feminist aversion to conventional forms of power, and the inhuman personal relationships that result from one set of persons having power over others. When radical feminists and anarchist feminists speak of abolishing power, they mean to get rid of all institutions, all forms of socialisation, all the ways in which people coerce each other—and acquiesce to being coerced.

A major problem arose in defining the nature of coercion in the women's movement. The hostility towards the "strong" woman arose because she was someone who could at least potentially coerce women who were less articulate, less self-confident, less assertive than she. Coercion is usually far more subtle than physical force or economic sanction. One person can coerce another without taking away their job, or striking them, or throwing them in jail.

Strong women started out with a tremendous advantage. Often they knew more. Certainly they had long since overcome the crippling socialisation that stressed passive, timid, docile, conformist behaviour—behaviour that taught women to smile when they weren't amused, to whisper when they felt like shouting, to lower their eyes when someone stared aggressively at them. Strong women weren't terrified of speaking in public; they weren't afraid to take on "male" tasks, or to try something new. Or so it seemed.

Put a "strong" woman in the same small group with a "weak" one, and she becomes a problem: How does she not dominate? How does she share her hard-earned skills and confidence with her sister? From the other side—how does the "weak" woman learn to act in her own behalf? How can one even conceive of "mutual" aid in a one-way situation? Of "sisterhood" when the "weak" member does not feel equal to the "strong" one?

These are complicated questions, with no simple answers. Perhaps the closest we can come is with the anarchist slogan, "a strong people needs no leaders." Those of us who have learned to survive by dominating others, as well as those of us who have learned to survive by accepting domination, need to resocialise ourselves into being strong without playing dominance-submission games, into controlling what happens to us without controlling others. This can't be done by electing the right people to office or by following the correct party line; nor can it be done by sitting and reflecting on our sins. We rebuild ourselves and our world through activity, through partial successes, and failure, and more partial successes. And all the while we grow stronger and more self-reliant.

If Anselma dell'Olio criticised the personal practice of radical feminists, Joreen raised some hard questions about organisational structure. *The Tyranny of Structurelessness*[10] pointed out that there is no such thing as a "structureless" group, and people who claim there is are fooling themselves. All groups have a structure; the difference is whether or not the structure is explicit. If it is implicit, hidden elites are certain to exist and to control the group—and everyone, both the leaders and the led, will deny or be confused by the control that exists. This is the "tyranny" of structurelessness. To overcome it, groups need to set up open, explicit structures accountable to the membership.

Any anarchist feminist, I think, would agree with her analysis—up to this point, and no further. For what Joreen also said was that the so-called "leaderless, structureless group" was incapable of going beyond talk to action. Not only its lack of open structure, but also its small size and its emphasis upon consciousness-raising (talk) were bound to make it ineffective.

Joreen did not say that women's groups should be hierarchically structured. In fact, she called for leadership that would be "diffuse, flexible, open, and temporary"; for organisations that would build in accountability, diffusion of power among the maximum number of persons, task rotation, skill-sharing, and the spread of information and resources. All good social anarchist principles of organisation! But her denigration of consciousness-raising and her preference for large regional and national organisations were strictly part of the old way of doing things, and implicitly accepted the continuation of hierarchical structures.

Large groups are organised so that power and decision-making are delegated to a few—unless, of course, one is speaking of a horizontally coordinated network of small collectives, which she did not mention. How does a group such as NOW, with its sixty thousand members in 1975, rotate tasks, share skills, and ensure that all information and resources are available to everyone? It can't, of course. Such groups have a president, and a board of directors, and a national office, and a membership—some of whom are in local chapters, and some of whom are isolated members. Few such groups have very much direct democracy, and few teach their members new ways of working and relating to one another.

The unfortunate effect of *The Tyranny of Structurelessness* was that it linked together large organisation, formal structure, and successful direct action in a way that seemed to make sense to a lot of people. Many women felt that in order to fight societal oppression a large organisation was essential, and the larger the better. The image is strength pitted against strength: You do not kill an elephant with an air gun, and you do not bring down the patriarchal state with the small group. For women who accept the argument that greater size is linked to greater effectiveness, the organisational options seem limited to large liberal groups such as NOW or to socialist organisations which are mass organisations.

As with so many things that seem to make sense, the logic is faulty. "Societal oppression" is a reification, an over-blown, paralysing, made-up entity that is large mainly in the sense that the same oppressions happen to a lot of us. But oppressions, no matter how pervasive, how predictable, almost always are done to us by some one—even if that person is acting as an agent of the state, or as a member of the dominant race, gender, or class. The massive police assaults upon our assembled forces are few; even the police officer or the boss or the husband who is carrying out his allotted sexist or authoritarian role intersects with us at a given point in our everyday lives. Institutionalized oppression does exist, on a large scale, but it seldom needs to be attacked (indeed, seldom can be attacked) by a large group. Guerilla tactics by a small group—occasionally even by a single individual—will do very nicely in retaliation.

Another unfortunate effect of the *Tyranny of Structurelessness* mentality (if not directly of the article) was that it fed people's stereotypes of anarchists. (Of course, people don't usually swallow something unless they're hungry.) Social anarchists aren't opposed to structure: They aren't even against leadership, provided that it carries no reward or privilege, and is temporary and specific to a particular task. However, anarchists, who want to abolish a *hierarchical* structure, are almost always stereotyped as wanting no structure at all. Unfortunately, the picture of a gaggle of disorganised, chaotic anarchist women, drifting without direction, caught on. For example, in 1976 *Quest* reprinted an edited transcript of an interview which Charlott Bunch and Beverly Fisher had given the Feminist Radio Network in 1972. In one way, the most interesting thing about the interview was that the *Quest* editors felt the issues were still so timely in 1976.[11] ("We see the same trashing of leaders and glorification of structurelessness that existed five years ago." (p. 13)). But what Bunch had to say at that time was also extremely interesting: according to her, the emphasis on solving problems of structure and leadership was "a very strong anarchist desire. It was a good desire, but it was an unrealistic one" (p. 4). Anarchists, who are used to being called "unrealistic," will note that the unreality of it all apparently lay in the problems which the women's movement was having in organising itself—problems of hidden leadership, of having "leaders" imposed by the media, of difficulty in reaching out to interested but uncommitted women, of over representation of middle class women with lots of time on their hands, of the amorphousness of the movement, of the scarcity of specific task groups which women could join, of hostility towards women who tried to show leadership or initiative. A heavy indictment! Yet, these very real problems were not caused by anarchism, nor will they be cured by doses of vanguardism or reformism. And by labeling these organisational difficulties "anarchist" feminists ignore a rich anarchist tradition while at the same time proposing solutions that are—although they apparently don't know it—anarchist. Bunch and Fisher laid out a model of leadership in which everyone participates in making decisions; and leadership is specific to a particular situation and is time-limited. Fisher criticised NOW for "hierarchical leadership that is not responsible to the vast membership" (p. 9), and Bunch stated, "leadership is people taking the initiative, carrying things through, having the ideas and imagination to get something started, and exhibiting particular skills in different areas" (p. 8). How do they suggest we prevent the silencing of these women under false notions of egalitarianism? "The only way women will stop putting down women who are strong is if they are strong themselves" (p. 12). Or, as I said earlier, a strong people needs no leaders. Right on!

Situationism and Anarchist Feminism

> *To transform the world and to change the structure of life are one and the same thing.*[12]
>
> *The personal is the political.*[13]

Anarchists are used to hearing that they lack a theory that would help in building a new society. At best, their detractors say patronisingly, anarchism tells us what not to do. Don't permit bureaucracy or hierarchical authority; don't let a vanguard party make decisions; don't tread on me. Don't tread on anyone. According to this perspective, anarchism is not a theory at all. It is a set of cautionary practices, the voices of libertarian conscience—always idealistic, sometimes a bit truculent, occasionally anachronistic, but a necessary reminder.

There is more than a kernel of truth to this objection. Just the same, there are varieties of anarchist thought that can provide a theoretical framework for analysis of the world and action to change it. For radical feminists who want to take that "step in self-conscious theoretical development,"[14] perhaps the greatest potential lies in Situationism.

The value of Situationism for an anarchist feminist analysis is that it combines a socialist awareness of the primacy of capitalist oppression with an anarchist emphasis upon transforming the whole of public and private life. The point about capitalist oppression is important: all too often anarchists seem to be unaware that this economic system exploits most people. But all too often socialists—especially Marxists—are blind to the fact that people are oppressed in every aspect of life: work, what passes for leisure, culture, personal relationships—all of it. And only anarchists insist that people must transform the conditions of their lives *themselves*—it cannot be done for them. Not by the party, not by the union, not by "organisers," not by anyone else.

Two basic Situationist concepts are "commodity" and "spectacle." Capitalism has made all of social relations commodity relations: The market rules all. People are not only producers and consumers in the narrow economic sense, but the very structure of their daily lives is based on commodity relations. Society "is consumed as a *whole*—the ensemble of social relationships and structures is the central product of the commodity economy."[15] This has inevitably alienated people from their lives, not just from their labour; to consume social relationships makes one a passive spectator in one's life. The *spectacle*, then, is the culture that springs from the commodity economy—the stage is set, the action unfolds, we applaud when we think we are happy, we yawn when we think we are bored, but we cannot leave the show, because there is no world outside the theatre for us to go to.

In recent times, however, the societal stage has begun to crumble, and so the possibility exists of constructing another world outside the theatre—this time, a real world, one in which each of us directly participates as subject, not as object. The situationist phrase for this possibility is "the reinvention of everyday life."

How is daily life to be reinvented? By creating situations that disrupt what seems to be the natural order of things—situations that jolt people out of customary ways of thinking and behaving. Only then will they be able to act, to destroy the manufactured spectacle and the commodity economy—that is, capitalism in all its forms. Only then will they be able to create free and un-alienated lives.

The congruence of this activist, social anarchist theory with radical feminist theory is striking. The concepts of commodity and spectacle are especially applicable to the lives of women. In fact, many radical feminists have described these in detail, without placing them in the Situationist framework.[16] To do so broadens the analysis, by showing women's situation as an organic part of the society as a whole, but at the same time without playing socialist reductionist games. Women's oppression is part of the over-all oppression of people by a capitalist economy, but it is not less than the oppression of others. Nor—from a Situationist perspective—do you have to be a particular variety of woman to be oppressed; you do not have to be part of the proletariat, either literally, as an industrial worker, or metaphorically, as someone who is not independently wealthy. You do not have to wait breathlessly for socialist feminist manifestos to tell you that you qualify—as a housewife (reproducing the next generation of workers), as a clerical worker, as a student or a middle-level professional employed by the state (and therefore as part of the "new working class"). You do not have to be part of the Third World, or a lesbian, or elderly, or a welfare recipient. All of these women are objects in the commodity economy; all are passive viewers of the spectacle. Obviously, women in some situations are far worse off than are others. But, at the same time, none are free in every area of their lives.

Women and the Commodity Economy

Women have a dual relationship to the commodity economy—they are both consumers and consumed. As housewives, they are consumers of household goods purchased with money not their own, because not "earned" by them. This may give them a certain amount of purchasing power, but very little power over any aspect of their lives. As young, single heterosexuals, women are purchasers of goods designed to make them bring a high price on the marriage market. As anything else—lesbians, or elderly single, or self-sufficient women with "careers," women's relationship to the marketplace as consumers is not so sharply defined. They are expected to buy (and the more affluent they are, the more they are expected to buy), but for some categories of women, buying is not defined primarily to fill out some aspect of a woman's role.

So what else is new? Isn't the idea of woman-as-passive-consumer, manipulated by the media, patronised by slick Madison Avenue men, an overdone movement cliche? Well, yes—and no. A Situationist analysis ties consumption of economic goods to consumption of *ideological* goods, and then tells us to create situations (guerrilla actions on many levels) that will break that pattern of socialised acceptance of the world as it is. No guilt-tripping; no criticising women who have "bought" the consumer perspective. For they have indeed *bought* it: It has been sold to them as a way of survival from the earliest moments of life. Buy this: It will make you beautiful and lovable. Buy *this*: It will keep your family in good health. Feel depressed? Treat yourself to an afternoon at the beauty parlour or to a new dress.

Guilt leads to inaction. Only action, to *re-invent* the everyday and make it something else, will change social relations.

The Gift

Thinking she was the gift
they began to package it early.
they waxed its smile
they lowered its eyes
they tuned its ears to the telephone
they curled its hair
they straightened its teeth
they taught it to bury its wishbone
they poured honey down its throat
they made it say yes yes and yes
they sat on its thumbs
That box has my name on it,
said the man. *It's for me.*
And they were not surprised.
While they blew kisses and winked
he took it home. He put it on a table

where his friends could examine it
saying *dance* saying *faster.*
He plunged its tunnel
he burned his name deeper.
Later he put it on a platform
under the Klieg lights
saying *push* saying *harder*
saying *just what I wanted*
you've given me a son.

Carole Oles[17]

Women are not only consumers in the commodity economy; they are consumed as commodities. This is what Oles' poem is about, and it is what Tax has labeled "female schizophrenia." Tax constructs an inner monologue for the housewife-as-commodity: "I am nothing when I am by myself. In myself, I am nothing. I only know that I exist because I am needed by someone who is real, my husband, and by my children."[18]

When feminists describe socialisation into the female sex role, when they point out the traits female children are taught (emotional dependence, childishness, timidity, concern with being beautiful, docility, passivity, and so on), they are talking about the careful production of a commodity—although it isn't usually called that. When they describe the oppressiveness of sexual objectification, or of living in the nuclear family, or of being a Supermother, or of working in the kinds of low-level, underpaid jobs that most women find in the paid labour force, they are also describing woman as commodity. Women are consumed by men who treat them as sex objects; they are consumed by their children (whom they have produced!) when they buy the role of the Supermother; they are consumed by authoritarian husbands who expect them to be submissive servants; and they are consumed by bosses who bring them in and out of the labour force and who extract a maximum of labour for a minimum of pay. They are consumed by medical researchers who try out new and unsafe contraceptives on them. They are consumed by men who buy their bodies on the street. They are consumed by church and state, who expect them to produce the next generation for the glory of god and country; they are consumed by political and social organisations that expect them to "volunteer" their time and energy. The have little sense of self, because their selfhood has been sold to others.

Women and the Spectacle

It is difficult to consume people who put up a fight, who resist the cannibalising of their bodies, their minds, their daily lives. A few people manage to resist, but most don't resist effectively, because they can't. It is hard to locate our tormentor, because it is so pervasive, so familiar. We have known it all our lives. It is our culture.

Situationists characterise our culture as a *spectacle*. The spectacle treats us all as passive spectators of what we are told are our lives. And the culture-as-spectacle covers everything: We are born into it, socialised by it, go to school in it, work and relax and relate to other people in it. Even when we rebel against it, the rebellion is often defined by the spectacle. Would anyone care to estimate the number of sensitive, alienated adolescent males who a generation ago modeled their behaviour on James Dean in *Rebel Without a Cause*? I'm talking about a *movie*, whose capitalist producers and whose star made a great deal of money from this Spectacular.

Rebellious acts, then tend to be acts of *opposition* to the spectacle, but seldom are so different that they *transcend* the spectacle. Women have a set of behaviours that show dissatisfaction by being the opposite of what is expected. At the same time these acts are cliches of rebellion, and thus are almost prescribed safety valves that don't alter the theatre of our lives. What is a rebellious woman supposed to do? We can all name the behaviours—they appear in every newspaper, on prime time television, on the best-seller list, in popular magazines—and, of course, in everyday life. In a setting that values perfectionist housekeeping, she can be a slob; in a subculture that values large families, she can refuse to have children. Other predictable insurgencies? She can defy the sexual double standard for married women by having an affair (or several); she can drink; or use what is termed "locker room" language; or have a nervous breakdown; or—if she is an adolescent—she can "act out" (a revealing phrase!) by running away from home and having sex with a lot of men.

Any of these things may make an individual woman's life more tolerable (often, they make it less so); and all of them are guaranteed to make conservatives rant that society is crumbling. But these kinds of scripted insurrections haven't made it crumble yet, and, by themselves, they aren't likely to. Anything less than a direct attack upon all the conditions of our lives is not enough.

When women talk about changing destructive sex role socialisation of females, they pick one of three possible solutions: (a) girls should be socialised more or less like boys to be independent, competitive, aggressive, and so forth. In short, it is a man's world, so a woman who wants to fit in has to be "one of the boys." (b) We should glorify the female role, and realize that what we have called weakness is really strength. We should be proud that we are maternal, nurturant, sensitive, emotional, and so on. (c) The only healthy person is an androgynous person: We must eradicate the artificial division of humanity into "masculine" and "feminine," and help both sexes become a mix of the best traits of each.

Within these three models, personal solutions to problems of sexist oppression cover a wide range: stay single; live communally (with both men and women, or with women only). Don't have children; don't have male children; have any kind of children you want, but get parent and worker-controlled child care. Get a job; get a better job; push for affirmative action. Be an informed consumer; file a lawsuit; learn karate; take assertiveness training. Develop the lesbian within you. Develop your proletarian identity. All of these make sense in particular situations, for particular women. But all of them are partial solutions to much broader problems, and none of them necessarily require seeing the world in a qualitatively different way.

So, we move from the particular to more general solutions. Destroy capitalism. End patriarchy. Smash heterosexism. All are obviously essential tasks in the building of a new and truly human world. Marxists, other socialists, social anarchists, feminists—all would agree. But what the socialist, and even some feminists, leave out is this: We must smash all forms of domination. That's not just a slogan, and it is the hardest task of all. It means that we have to see through the spectacle, destroy the stage sets, know that there are other ways of doing things. It means that we have to do more than react in programmed rebellions—we must act. And our actions will be collectively taken, while each person acts autonomously. Does that seem contradictory? It isn't—but it will be very difficult to do. The individual cannot change anything very much; for that reason, we have to work together. But that work must be without leaders as we know them, and without delegating any control over what we do and what we want to build.

Can the socialists do that? Or the matriarchs? Or the spirituality-trippers? You know the answer to that. Work with them when it makes sense to do so, but give up nothing. Concede nothing to them, or to anyone else.

The past leads to us if we force it to.
Otherwise it contains us
in its asylum with no gates.
We make history or it
makes us.[19]

Notes

1. Barbara Ehrenreich, "What is Socialist Feminism?," *Win Magazine*, June 3, 1976, p.4.
2. The best of these arguments I've encountered are "Socialist Feminism; A Strategy for the Women's Movement," by the Hyde Park Chapter, Chicago Women's Liberation Union, 1972; and Charlotte Bunch, "The Reform Tool Kit," *Quest*, 1:1, Summer 1974, pp.37-51.
3. Reports by Polly Anna, Kana Trueblood, C. Corday and S. Tufts, The Fifth Estate, May, 1976, pp. 13, 16. The " revolution" failed: FEN and its club shut down.
4. People who are interested in reading reports of the conference will find them in almost every feminist or socialist newspaper that appeared in the month or so after July 4th. Speeches by Barbara Ehrenreich, Michelle Russell, and the Berkeley-Oakland Women's Union are reprinted in Socialist Revolution, No. 26, October-December 1975; and the speech by Charlotte Bunch, "Not for Lesbians Only," appears in Quest, 2:2, Fall 1975. A thirty-minute audiotape documentary is available from the Great Atlantic Radio Conspiracy, 2743 Maryland Avenue, Baltimore, Maryland 21218.
5. Farrow, "Feminism as Anarchism," Aurora, 4, 1974, p.9; Kornegger, "Anarchism: The Feminist Connection," *Second Wave*, 4: 1, Spring 1975, p.31; Leighton, "Anarcho-Feminism and Louise Michel," *Black Rose*, 1, April 1974, p. 14.
6. December, 1, 1970, p.11.
7. Lilith's Manifesto, from the Women's Majority Union of Seattle, 1969. Reprinted in Robin Morgan (ed.), *Sisterhood is Powerful*. N.Y.: Random House, 1970, p.529.
8. The best and most detailed description of the parallels between radical feminism and anarchist feminism is found in Kornegger, op cit.
9. The speech is currently available from KNOW, Inc.
10. The Second Wave, 2:1, 1972.
11. "What Future for Leadership?," *Quest*, 2:4, Spring 1976, pp.2-13.
12. Strasbourg Situationists, *Once the Universities Were Respected*, 1968, p.38.
13. Carol Hanisch, "The Personal is Political," *Notes from the Second Year*. N.Y.: Radical Feminism, 1970, pp. 76-78.
14. Leighton, op cit.
15. Point-Blank!, "The Changing of the Guard," in *Point-Blank*, October 1972, p.16.
16. For one of the most illuminating of these early analyses, see Meredith Tax, "Woman and Her Mind: The Story of Everyday Life," Boston: Bread and Roses Publication, 1970.
17. Carole Oles, "The Gift," in *13th Moon*, II: 1, 1974, p. 39.
18. Tax, op cit., p. 13.
19. Marge Piercy, excerpt from "Contribution to Our Museum," in Living in the Open. N.Y.: Knopf, 1976, pp.74-75.

9

UNTYING THE KNOT

FEMINISM, ANARCHISM AND ORGANISATION

Original Introduction by CS

(Originally published in print by Dark Star Press and Rebel Press, 1984.)

Jo Freeman's perceptive essay (*"The Tyranny of Structurelessness," Berkeley Journal of Sociology* 1970, reprinted by ORA and the Anarchist Workers Association in 1972) on the dynamics of small, unstructured groups, and Cathy Levine's reply (*"The Tyranny of Tyranny," Black Rose* no 1 / Rising Free Collective), were to have a profound influence not only on the women's movement, to which they were originally directed, but also on the anarchist movement in a new period of growth.

The question how do we organise, rather than simply why, had become of great importance. Women were aware that they had been playing an almost invisible role in the male-dominated Left. The women's movement put women in focus for the first time, and offered the chance to consider methods not just purpose, individuals not just theories.

The personal was to be political from now on.

Ironically, despite the fact that these were long-term concerns of the anarchist movement, it took feminists to show how libertarian organisation could look. "Feminism is what anarchism preaches," wrote Lynne Farrow in 1974. A little simplistic, perhaps, but it was certainly true that the feminist practice of small, leaderless groups was an anarchist ideal.

Clearly the unstructured group had an important role to play. But at times it could be dominated by informal structures and elites, and it was often prone to internal arguments and insularity. How far, then, should the leaderless principle be taken? This was where Jo Freeman was to challenge both the women's and anarchist movements. For her answer—a return to "democratic structuring" for all except consciousness-raising groups—seemed to some to spell the beginning of a new and positive era, and to others, like Cathy Levine, to spell a return to the stifling bureaucratic movement-building of the past. These articles, and the issues they confront, are as fresh today as they were when they were written in the early 1970s.

10

THE TYRANNY OF STRUCTURELESSNESS

Jo Freeman AKA Joreen

THE EARLIEST VERSION OF THIS ARTICLE WAS GIVEN AS A TALK AT a conference called by the Southern Female Rights Union, held in Beulah, Mississippi in May 1970. It was written up for Notes from the Third Year (1971), but the editors did not use it. It was then submitted to several movement publications, but only one asked permission to publish it; others did so without permission. The first official place of publication was in Vol. 2, No. 1 of The Second Wave (1972). This early version in movement publications was authored by Joreen. Different versions were published in the Berkeley Journal of Sociology, Vol. 17, 1972-73, pp. 151-16, and Ms. magazine, July 1973, pp. 76-78, 86-89, authored by Jo Freeman. This piece spread all over the world. Numerous people have edited, reprinted, cut, and translated "Tyranny" for magazines, books and web sites, usually without the permission or knowledge of the author. The version below is a blend of the three cited here.

During the years in which the women's liberation movement has been taking shape, a great emphasis has been placed on what are called leaderless, structureless groups as the main—if not sole—organisational form of the movement. The source of this idea was a natural reaction against the over-structured society in which most of us found ourselves, and the inevitable control this gave others over our lives, and the continual elitism of the Left and similar groups among those who were supposedly fighting this overstructuredness.

The idea of "structurelessness," however, has moved from a healthy counter to those tendencies to becoming a goddess in its own right. The idea is as little examined as the term is much used, but it has become an intrinsic and unquestioned part of women's liberation ideology. For the early development of the movement this did not much matter. It early defined its main goal, and its main method, as consciousness-raising, and the "structureless" rap group was an excellent means to this end. The looseness and informality of it encouraged participation in discussion, and its often supportive atmosphere elicited personal insight. If nothing more concrete than personal insight ever resulted from these groups, that did not much matter, because their purpose did not really extend beyond this.

The basic problems didn't appear until individual rap groups exhausted the virtues of consciousness-raising and decided they wanted to do something more specific. At this point they usually foundered because most groups were unwilling to change their structure when they changed their tasks. Women had thoroughly accepted the idea of "structurelessness" without realizing the limitations of its uses. People would try to use the "structureless" group and the informal conference for purposes for which they were unsuitable out of a blind belief that no other means could possibly be anything but oppressive.

If the movement is to grow beyond these elementary stages of development, it will have to disabuse itself of some of its prejudices about organisation and structure. There is nothing inherently bad about either of these. They can be and often are misused, but to reject them out of hand because they are misused is to deny ourselves the necessary tools to further development. We need to understand why "structurelessness" does not work.

Formal and Informal Structures

Contrary to what we would like to believe, there is no such thing as a structureless group. Any group of people of whatever nature that comes together for any length of time for any purpose will inevitably structure itself in some fashion. The structure may be flexible; it may vary over time; it may evenly or unevenly distribute tasks, power and resources over the members of the group. But it will be formed regardless of the abilities, personalities, or intentions of the people involved. The very fact that we are individuals, with different talents, predispositions, and backgrounds makes this inevitable. Only if we refused to relate or interact on any basis whatsoever could we approximate structurelessness—and that is not the nature of a human group.

This means that to strive for a structureless group is as useful, and as deceptive, as to aim at an "objective" news story, "value-free" social science, or a "free" economy. A "laissez faire" group is about as realistic as a "laissez faire" society; the idea becomes a smokescreen for the strong or the lucky to establish unquestioned hegemony over others. This hegemony can be so easily established because the idea of "structurelessness" does not prevent the formation of informal structures, only formal ones. Similarly "laissez faire" philosophy did not prevent the economically powerful from establishing control over wages, prices, and distribution of goods; it only prevented the government from doing so. Thus structurelessness becomes a way of masking power, and within the women's movement is usually most strongly advocated by those who are the most powerful (whether they are conscious of their power or not). As long as the structure of the group is informal, the rules of how decisions are made are known only to a few and awareness of power is limited to those who know the rules. Those who do not know the rules and are not chosen for initiation must remain in confusion, or suffer from paranoid delusions that something is happening of which they are not quite aware.

For everyone to have the opportunity to be involved in a given group and to participate in its activities the structure must be explicit, not implicit. The rules of decision-making must be open and available to everyone, and this can happen only if they are formalized. This is not to say that formalization of a structure of a group will destroy the informal structure. It usually doesn't. But it does hinder the informal structure from having predominant control and make available some means of attacking it if the people involved are not at least responsible to the needs of the group at large. "Structurelessness" is organisationally impossible. We cannot decide whether to have a structured or structureless group, only whether or not to have a formally structured one. Therefore the word will not be used any longer except to refer to the idea it represents. Unstructured will refer to those groups which have not been deliberately structured in a particular manner. Structured will refer to those which have. A Structured group always has formal structure, and may also have an informal, or covert, structure. It is this informal structure, particularly in Unstructured groups, which forms the basis for elites.

The Nature of Elitism

"Elitist" is probably the most abused word in the women's liberation movement. It is used as frequently, and for the same reasons, as "pinko" was used in the fifties. It is rarely used correctly. Within the movement it commonly refers to individuals, though the personal characteristics and activities of those to whom it is directed may differ widely: an individual, as an individual can never be an elitist, because the only proper application of the term "elite" is to groups. Any individual, regardless of how well-known that person may be, can never be an elite.

Correctly, an elite refers to a small group of people who have power over a larger group of which they are part, usually without direct responsibility to that larger group, and often without their knowledge or consent. A person becomes an elitist by being part of, or advocating the rule by, such a small group, whether or not that individual is well known or not known at all. Notoriety is not a definition of an elitist. The most insidious elites are usually run by people not known to the larger public at all. Intelligent elitists are usually smart enough not to allow themselves to become well known; when they become known, they are watched, and the mask over their power is no longer firmly lodged.

Elites are not conspiracies. Very seldom does a small group of people get together and deliberately try to take over a larger group for its own ends. Elites are nothing more, and nothing less, than groups of friends who also happen to participate in the same political activities. They would probably maintain their friendship whether or not they were involved in political activities; they would probably be involved in political activities whether or not they maintained their friendships. It is the coincidence of these two phenomena which creates elites in any group and makes them so difficult to break.

These friendship groups function as networks of communication outside any regular channels for such communication that may have been set up by a group. If no channels are set up, they function as the only networks of communication. Because people are friends, because they usually share the same values and orientations, because they talk to each other socially and consult with each other when common decisions have to be made, the people involved in these networks have more power in the group than those who don't. And it is a rare group that does not establish some informal networks of communication through the friends that are made in it.

Some groups, depending on their size, may have more than one such informal communications network. Networks may even overlap. When only one such network exists, it is the elite of an otherwise Unstructured group, whether the participants in it want to be elitists or not. If it is the only such network in a Structured group it may or may not be an elite depending on its composition and the nature of the formal Structure. If there are two or more such networks of friends, they may compete for power within the group, thus forming factions, or one may deliberately opt out of the competition, leaving the other as the elite. In a Structured group, two or more such friendship networks usually compete with each other for formal power. This is often the healthiest situation, as the other members are in a position to arbitrate between the two competitors for power and thus to make demands on those to whom they give their temporary allegiance.

The inevitably elitist and exclusive nature of informal communication networks of friends is neither a new phenomenon characteristic of the women's movement nor a phenomenon new to women. Such informal relationships have excluded women for centuries from participating in integrated groups of which they were a part. In any profession or organisation these networks have created the "locker room" mentality and the "old school" ties which have effectively prevented women as a group (as well as some men individually) from having equal access to the sources of power or social reward. Much of the energy of past women's movements has been directed to having the structures of decision-making and the selection processes formalized so that the exclusion of women could be confronted directly. As we well know, these efforts have not prevented the informal male-only networks from discriminating against women, but they have made it more difficult.

Because elites are informal does not mean they are invisible. At any small group meeting anyone with a sharp eye and an acute ear can tell who is influencing whom. The members of a friendship group will relate more to each other than to other people. They listen more attentively, and interrupt less; they repeat each other's points and give in amiably; they tend to ignore or grapple with the "outs" whose approval is not necessary for making a decision. But it is necessary for the "outs" to stay on good terms with the "ins." Of course the lines are not as sharp as I have drawn them. They are nuances of interaction, not prewritten scripts. But they are discernible, and they do have their effect. Once one knows with whom it is important to check before a decision is made, and whose approval is the stamp of acceptance, one knows who is running things.

Since movement groups have made no concrete decisions about who shall exercise power within them, many different criteria are used around the country. Most criteria are along the lines of traditional female characteristics. For instance, in the early days of the movement, marriage was usually a prerequisite for participation in the informal elite. As women have been traditionally taught, married women relate primarily to each other, and look upon single women as too threatening to have as close friends. In many cities, this criterion was further refined to include only those women married to New Left men. This standard had more than tradition behind it, however, because New Left men often had access to resources needed by the movement—such as mailing lists, printing presses, contacts, and information—and women were used to getting what they needed through men rather than independently. As the movement has changed through time, marriage has become a less universal criterion for effective participation, but all informal elites establish standards by which only women who possess certain material or personal characteristics may join. They frequently include: middle-class background (despite all the rhetoric about relating to the working class); being married; not being married but living with someone; being or pretending to be a lesbian; being between the ages of twenty and thirty; being college educated or at least having some college background; being "hip"; not being too "hip"; holding a certain political line or identification as a "radical"; having children or at least liking them; not having children; having certain "feminine" personality characteristics such as being "nice"; dressing right (whether in the traditional style or the antitraditional style); etc. There are also some characteristics which will almost always tag one as a "deviant" who should not be related to. They include: being too old; working full time, particularly if one is actively committed to a "career"; not being "nice"; and being avowedly single (i.e., neither actively heterosexual nor homosexual).

Other criteria could be included, but they all have common themes. The characteristics prerequisite for participating in the informal elites of the movement, and thus for exercising power, concern one's background, personality, or allocation of time. They do not include one's competence, dedication to feminism, talents, or potential contribution to the movement. The former are the criteria one usually uses in determining one's friends. The latter are what any movement or organisation has to use if it is going to be politically effective.

The criteria of participation may differ from group to group, but the means of becoming a member of the informal elite if one meets those criteria art pretty much the same. The only main difference depends on whether one is in a group from the beginning, or joins it after it has begun. If involved from the beginning it is important to have as many of one's personal friends as possible also join. If no one knows anyone else very well, then one must deliberately form friendships with a select number and establish the informal interaction patterns crucial to the creation of an informal structure. Once the informal patterns are formed they act to maintain themselves, and one of the most successful tactics of maintenance is to continuously recruit new people who "fit in." One joins such an elite much the same way one pledges a sorority. If perceived as a potential addition, one is "rushed" by the members of the informal structure and eventually either dropped or initiated. If the sorority is not politically aware enough to actively engage in this process itself it can be started by the outsider pretty much the same way one joins any private club. Find a sponsor, i.e., pick some member of the elite who appears to be well respected within it, and actively cultivate that person's friendship. Eventually, she will most likely bring you into the inner circle.

All of these procedures take time. So if one works full time or has a similar major commitment, it is usually impossible to join simply because there are not enough hours left to go to all the meetings and cultivate the personal relationship necessary to have a voice in the decision-making. That is why formal structures of decision making are a boon to the overworked person. Having an established process for decision-making ensures that everyone can participate in it to some extent.

Although this dissection of the process of elite formation within small groups has been critical in perspective, it is not made in the belief that these informal structures are inevitably bad—merely inevitable. All groups create informal structures as a result of interaction patterns among the members of the group. Such informal structures can do very useful things But only Unstructured groups are totally governed by them. When informal elites are combined with a myth of "structurelessness," there can be no attempt to put limits on the use of power. It becomes capricious.

This has two potentially negative consequences of which we should be aware. The first is that the informal structure of decision-making will be much like a sorority—one in which people listen to others because they like them and not because they say significant things. As long as the movement does not do significant things this does not much matter. But if its development is not to be arrested at this preliminary stage, it will have to alter this trend. The second is that informal structures have no obligation to be responsible to the group at large. Their power was not given to them; it cannot be taken away. Their influence is not based on what they do for the group; therefore they cannot be directly influenced by the group. This does not necessarily make informal structures irresponsible. Those who are concerned with maintaining their influence will usually try to be responsible. The group simply cannot compel such responsibility; it is dependent on the interests of the elite.

The "Star" System

The idea of "structurelessness" has created the "star" system. We live in a society which expects political groups to make decisions and to select people to articulate those decisions to the public at large. The press and the public do not know how to listen seriously to individual women as women; they want to know how the group feels. Only three techniques have ever been developed for establishing mass group opinion: the vote or referendum, the public opinion survey questionnaire, and the selection of group spokespeople at an appropriate meeting. The women's liberation movement has used none of these to communicate with the public. Neither the movement as a whole nor most of the multitudinous groups within it have established a means of explaining their position on various issues. But the public is conditioned to look for spokespeople.

While it has consciously not chosen spokespeople, the movement has thrown up many women who have caught the public eye for varying reasons. These women represent no particular group or established opinion; they know this and usually say so. But because there are no official spokespeople nor any decision-making body that the press can query when it wants to know the movement's position on a subject, these women are perceived as the spokespeople. Thus, whether they want to or not, whether the movement likes it or not, women of public note are put in the role of spokespeople by default.

This is one main source of the ire that is often felt toward the women who are labeled "stars." Because they were not selected by the women in the movement to represent the movement's views, they are resented when the press presumes that they speak for the movement. But as long as the movement does not select its own spokeswomen, such women will be placed in that role by the press and the public, regardless of their own desires.

This has several negative consequences for both the movement and the women labeled "stars." First, because the movement didn't put them in the role of spokesperson, the movement cannot remove them. The press put them there and only the press can choose not to listen. The press will continue to look to "stars" as spokeswomen as long as it has no official alternatives to go to for authoritative statements from the movement. The movement has no control in the selection of its representatives to the public as long as it believes that it should have no representatives at all. Second, women put in this position often find themselves viciously attacked by their sisters. This achieves nothing for the movement and is painfully destructive to the individuals involved. Such attacks only result in either the woman leaving the movement entirely-often bitterly alienated—or in her ceasing to feel responsible to her "sisters." She may maintain some loyalty to the movement, vaguely defined, but she is no longer susceptible to pressures from other women in it. One cannot feel responsible to people who have been the source of such pain without being a masochist, and these women are usually too strong to bow to that kind of personal pressure. Thus the backlash to the "star" system in effect encourages the very kind of individualistic nonresponsibility that the movement condemns. By purging a sister as a "star," the movement loses whatever control it may have had over the person who then becomes free to commit all of the individualistic sins of which she has been accused.

Political Impotence

Unstructured groups may be very effective in getting women to talk about their lives; they aren't very good for getting things done. It is when people get tired of "just talking" and want to do something more that the groups flounder, unless they change the nature of their operation. Occasionally, the developed informal structure of the group coincides with an available need that the group can fill in such a way as to give the appearance that an Unstructured group "works." That is, the group has fortuitously developed precisely the kind of structure best suited for engaging in a particular project.

While working in this kind of group is a very heady experience, it is also rare and very hard to replicate. There are almost inevitably four conditions found in such a group;

1) It is task oriented. Its function is very narrow and very specific, like putting on a conference or putting out a newspaper. It is the task that basically structures the group. The task determines what needs to be done and when it needs to be done. It provides a guide by which people can judge their actions and make plans for future activity.

2) It is relatively small and homogeneous. Homogeneity is necessary to insure that participants have a "common language" or interaction. People from widely different backgrounds may provide richness to a consciousness-raising group where each can learn from the others' experience, but too great a diversity among members of a task-oriented group means only that they continually misunderstand each other. Such diverse people interpret words and actions differently. They have different expectations about each other's behaviour and judge the results according to different criteria. If everyone knows everyone else well enough to understand the nuances, these can be accommodated. Usually, they only lead to confusion and endless hours spent straightening out conflicts no one ever thought would arise.

3) There is a high degree of communication. Information must be passed on to everyone, opinions checked, work divided up, and participation assured in the relevant decisions. This is only possible if the group is small and people practically live together for the most crucial phases of the task. Needless to say, the number of interactions necessary to involve everybody increases geometrically with the number of participants. This inevitably limits group participants to about five, or excludes some from some of the decisions. Successful groups can be as large as 10 or 15, but only when they are in fact composed of several smaller subgroups which perform specific parts of the task, and whose members overlap with each other so that knowledge of what the different subgroups are doing can be passed around easily.

4) There is a low degree of skill specialization. Not everyone has to be able to do everything, but everything must be able to be done by more

than one person. Thus no one is indispensable. To a certain extent, people become interchangeable parts.

While these conditions can occur serendipitously in small groups, this is not possible in large ones. Consequently, because the larger movement in most cities is as unstructured as individual rap groups, it is not too much more effective than the separate groups at specific tasks. The informal structure is rarely together enough or in touch enough with the people to be able to operate effectively. So the movement generates much motion and few results. Unfortunately, the consequences of all this motion are not as innocuous as the results' and their victim is the movement itself.

Some groups have formed themselves into local action projects if they do not involve many people and work on a small scale. But this form restricts movement activity to the local level; it cannot be done on the regional or national. Also, to function well the groups must usually pare themselves down to that informal group of friends who were running things in the first place. This excludes many women from participating. As long as the only way women can participate in the movement is through membership in a small group, the nongregarious are at a distinct disadvantage. As long as friendship groups are the main means of organisational activity, elitism becomes institutionalized.

For those groups which cannot find a local project to which to devote themselves, the mere act of staying together becomes the reason for their staying together. When a group has no specific task (and consciousness raising is a task), the people in it turn their energies to controlling others in the group. This is not done so much out of a malicious desire to manipulate others (though sometimes it is) as out of a lack of anything better to do with their talents. Able people with time on their hands and a need to justify their coming together put their efforts into personal control, and spend their time criticising the personalities of the other members in the group. Infighting and personal power games rule the day. When a group is involved in a task, people learn to get along with others as they are and to subsume personal dislikes for the sake of the larger goal. There are limits placed on the compulsion to remould every person in our image of what they should be.

The end of consciousness-raising leaves people with no place to go, and the lack of structure leaves them with no way of getting there. The women the movement either turn in on themselves and their sisters or seek other alternatives of action. There are few that are available. Some women just "do their own thing." This can lead to a great deal of individual creativity, much of which is useful for the movement, but it is not a viable alternative for most women and certainly does not foster a spirit of cooperative group effort. Other women drift out of the movement entirely because they don't want to develop an individual project and they have found no way of discovering, joining, or starting group projects that interest them.

Many turn to other political organisations to give them the kind of structured, effective activity that they have not been able to find in the women's movement. Those political organisations which see women's liberation as only one of many issues to which women should devote their time thus find the movement a vast recruiting ground for new members. There is no need for such organisations to "infiltrate" (though this is not precluded). The desire for meaningful political activity generated in women by their becoming part of the women's liberation movement is sufficient to make them eager to join other organisations when the movement itself provides no outlets for their new ideas and energies. Those women who join other political organisations while remaining within the women's liberation movement, or who join women's liberation while remaining in other political organisations, in turn become the framework for new informal structures. These friendship networks are based upon their common non-feminist politics rather than the characteristics discussed earlier, but operate in much the same way. Because these women share common values, ideas, and political orientations, they too become informal, unplanned, unselected, unresponsible elites—whether they intend to be so or not.

These new informal elites are often perceived as threats by the old informal elites previously developed within different movement groups. This is a correct perception. Such politically oriented networks are rarely willing to be merely "sororities" as many of the old ones were, and want to proselytize their political as well as their feminist ideas. This is only natural, but its implications for women's liberation have never been adequately discussed. The old elites are rarely willing to bring such differences of opinion out into the open because it would involve exposing the nature of the informal structure of the group.

Many of these informal elites have been hiding under the banner of "anti-elitism" and "structurelessness." To effectively counter the competition from another informal structure, they would have to become "public," and this possibility is fraught with many dangerous implications. Thus, to maintain its own power, it is easier to rationalize the exclusion of the members of the other informal structure by such means as "red-baiting," "reformist-baiting," "lesbian-baiting," or "straight-baiting." The only other alternative is to formally structure the group in such a way that the original power structure is institutionalized. This is not always possible. If the informal elites have been well structured and have exercised a fair amount of power in the past, such a task is feasible. These groups have a history of being somewhat politically effective in the past, as the tightness of the informal structure has proven an adequate substitute for a formal structure. Becoming Structured does not alter their operation much, though the institutionalization of the power structure does open it to formal challenge. It is those groups which are in greatest need of structure that are often least capable of creating it. Their informal structures have not been too well formed and adherence to the ideology of "structurelessness" makes them reluctant to change tactics. The more Unstructured a group is, the more lacking it is in informal structures, and the more it adheres to an ideology of "structurelessness,"' the more vulnerable it is to being taken over by a group of political comrades.

Since the movement at large is just as Unstructured as most of its constituent groups, it is similarly susceptible to indirect influence. But the phenomenon manifests itself differently. On a local level most groups can operate autonomously; but the only groups that can organise a national activity are nationally organised groups. Thus, it is often the Structured feminist organisations that provide national direction for feminist activities, and this direction is determined by the priorities of those organisations. Such groups as NOW, WEAL, and some leftist women's caucuses are simply the only organisations capable of mounting a national campaign. The multitude of Unstructured women's liberation groups can choose to support or not support the national campaigns, but are incapable of mounting their own. Thus their members become the troops under the leadership of the Structured organisations. The avowedly Unstructured groups have no way of drawing upon the movement's vast resources to support its priorities. It doesn't even have a way of deciding what they are.

The more unstructured a movement is, the less control it has over the directions in which it develops and the political actions in which it engages. This does not mean that its ideas do not spread. Given a certain amount of interest by the media and the appropriateness of social conditions, the ideas will still be diffused widely. But diffusion of ideas does not mean they are implemented; it only means they are talked about. Insofar as they can be applied individually they may be acted on; insofar as they require coordinated political power to be implemented, they will not be.

As long as the women's liberation movement stays dedicated to a form of organisation which stresses small, inactive discussion groups among friends, the worst problems of Unstructuredness will not be felt. But this style of organisation has its limits; it is politically inefficacious, exclusive, and discriminatory against those women who are not or cannot be tied into the friendship networks. Those who do not fit into what already exists because of class, race, occupation, education, parental or marital status, personality, etc., will inevitably be discouraged from trying to participate. Those who do fit in will develop vested interests in maintaining things as they are.

The informal groups' vested interests will be sustained by the informal structures which exist, and the movement will have no way of determining who shall exercise power within it. If the movement continues deliberately to not select who shall exercise power, it does not thereby abolish power. All it does is abdicate the right to demand that those who do exercise power and influence be responsible for it. If the movement continues to keep power as diffuse as possible because it knows it cannot demand responsibility from those who have it, it does prevent any group or person from totally dominating. But it simultaneously ensures that the movement is as ineffective as possible. Some middle ground between domination and ineffectiveness can and must be found.

These problems are coming to a head at this time because the nature of the movement is necessarily changing. Consciousness-raising as the main function of the women's liberation movement is becoming obsolete. Due to the intense press publicity of the last two years and the numerous overground books and articles now being circulated, women's liberation has become a household word. Its issues are discussed and informal rap groups are formed by people who have no explicit connection with any movement group. The movement must go on to other tasks. It now needs to establish its priorities, articulate its goals, and pursue its objectives in a coordinated fashion. To do this it must get organised—locally, regionally, and nationally.

Principles of Democratic Structuring

Once the movement no longer clings tenaciously to the ideology of "structurelessness," it is free to develop those forms of organisation best suited to its healthy functioning. This does not mean that we should go to the other extreme and blindly imitate the traditional forms of organisation. But neither should we blindly reject them all. Some of the traditional techniques will prove useful, albeit not perfect; some will give us insights into what we should and should not do to obtain certain ends with minimal costs to the individuals in the movement. Mostly, we will have to experiment with different kinds of structuring and develop a variety of techniques to use for different situations. The Lot System is one such idea which has emerged from the movement. It is not applicable to all situations, but is useful in some. Other ideas for structuring are needed. But before we can proceed to experiment intelligently, we must accept the idea that there is nothing inherently bad about structure itself—only its excess use.

While engaging in this trial-and-error process, there are some principles we can keep in mind that are essential to democratic structuring and are also politically effective:

1) Delegation of specific authority to specific individuals for specific tasks by democratic procedures. Letting people assume jobs or tasks only by default means they are not dependably done. If people are selected to do a task, preferably after expressing an interest or willingness to do it, they have made a commitment which cannot so easily be ignored.

2) Requiring all those to whom authority has been delegated to be responsible to those who selected them. This is how the group has control over people in positions of authority. Individuals may exercise power, but it is the group that has ultimate say over how the power is exercised.

3) Distribution of authority among as many people as is reasonably possible. This prevents monopoly of power and requires those in positions of authority to consult with many others in the process of exercising it. It also gives many people the opportunity to have responsibility for specific tasks and thereby to learn different skills.

4) Rotation of tasks among individuals. Responsibilities which are held too long by one person, formally or informally, come to be seen as that person's "property" and are not easily relinquished or controlled by the group. Conversely, if tasks are rotated too frequently the individual does not have time to learn her job well and acquire the sense of satisfaction of doing a good job.

5) Allocation of tasks along rational criteria. Selecting someone for a position because they are liked by the group or giving them hard work because they are disliked serves neither the group nor the person in the long run. Ability, interest, and responsibility have got to be the major concerns in such selection. People should be given an opportunity to learn skills they do not have, but this is best done through some sort of "apprenticeship" programme rather than the "sink or swim" method. Having a responsibility one can't handle well is demoralizing. Conversely, being blacklisted from doing what one can do well does not encourage one to develop one's skills. Women have been punished for being competent throughout most of human history; the movement does not need to repeat this process.

6) Diffusion of information to everyone as frequently as possible. Information is power. Access to information enhances one's power. When an informal network spreads new ideas and information among themselves outside the group, they are already engaged in the process of forming an opinion—without the group participating. The more one knows about how things work and what is happening, the more politically effective one can be.

7) Equal access to resources needed by the group. This is not always perfectly possible, but should be striven for. A member who maintains a monopoly over a needed resource (like a printing press owned by a husband, or a darkroom) can unduly influence the use of that resource. Skills and information are also resources. Members' skills can be equitably available only when members are willing to teach what they know to others.

When these principles are applied, they ensure that whatever structures are developed by different movement groups will be controlled by and responsible to the group. The group of people in positions of authority will be diffuse, flexible, open, and temporary. They will not be in such an easy position to institutionalize their power because ultimate decisions will be made by the group at large. The group will have the power to determine who shall exercise authority within it.

11

THE TYRANNY OF TYRANNY

Cathy Levine

AN ARTICLE ENTITLED "THE TYRANNY OF STRUCTURELESSNESS" which has received wide attention around the women's movement, (in *MS, Second Wave,* etc.) assails the trend towards "leaderless," "structureless" groups, as the main—if not sole—organisational form of the movement, as a dead-end. While written and received in good faith, as an aid to the movement, the article is destructive in its distortion and maligning of a valid, conscious strategy for building a revolutionary movement. It is high time that we recognise the direction these tendencies are pointing in, as a real political alternative to hierarchical organisation, rather than trying to nip it in the bud.

There are (at least) two different models for building a movement, only one of which does Joreen acknowledge: a mass organisation with strong, centralised control, such as a Party. The other model, which consolidates mass support only as a coup de grace necessity, is based on small groups in voluntary association.

A large group functions as an aggregate of its parts—each member functions as a unit, a cog in the wheel of the large organisation. The individual is alienated by the size, and relegated, to struggling against the obstacle created by the size of the group—as example, expending energy to get a point of view recognised.

Small groups, on the other hand, multiply the strength of each member. By working collectively in small numbers, the small group utilizes the various contributions of each person to their fullest, nurturing and developing individual input, instead of dissipating it in the competitive survival-of-the-fittest/smartest/wittiest spirit of the large organisation.

Joreen associates the ascendency of the small groups with the consciousness-raising phase of the women's movement, but concludes that, with the focus shifting beyond the changing of individual consciousness towards building a mass revolutionary movement, women should begin working towards building a large organisation. It is certainly true and has been for some time that many women who have been in consciousness-raising groups for a while feel the need to expand their political activities beyond the scope of the group and are at a loss as to how to proceed. But it is equally true that other branches of the Left are at a similar loss, as to how to defeat capitalist, imperialist, quasi-fascist Amerika.

But Joreen fails to define what she means by the women's movement, which is an essential prerequisite to a discussion of strategy or direction.

The feminist movement in its fullest sense, that is, as a movement to defeat Patriarchy, is a revolutionary movement and a socialist movement, Placing it under the umbrella of the Left. A central problem of women determining strategy for the women's movement is how to relate to the male Left; we do not want to take their Modus Operandi as ours, because we have seen them as a perpetuation of patriarchal, and latterly, capitalist values.

Despite our best efforts to disavow and dissassociate ourselves from the male Left, we have, nonetheless, had our energy. Men tend to organise the way they fuck—one big rush and then that "wham, slam, thank you maam," as it were. Women should be building our movement the way we make love—gradually, with sustained involvement, limitless endurance—and of course, multiple orgasms. Instead of getting discouraged and isolated now, we should be in our small groups—discussing, Planning, creating and making trouble. We should always be making trouble for patriarchy and always supporting women—we should always be actively engaging in and creating feminist activity, because we ail thrive on it; in the absence of feminist activity, women take to tranquilizers, go insane and commit suicide.

The other extreme from inactivity, which seems to plague politically active people, is over-involvement, which led, in the late '60s, to a generation of burnt-out radicals. A feminist friend once commented that, to her, "being in the women's movement" meant spending approximately 25% of her time engaging in group activities and 75% of her time developing herself. This is a real, important time allocation for "movement" women to think about. The male movement taught us that "movement" people are supposed to devote 24 hours a day to the Cause, which is consistent with female socialisation towards self-sacrifice. Whatever the source of our selflessness, however, we tend to plunge ourselves head-first into organisational activities, neglecting personal development, until one day we find we do not know what we are doing and for whose benefit, and we hate ourselves as much as before the movement. (Male over-involvement, on the other hand, obviously unrelated to any sex-linked trait of self-sacrifice, does however smell strongly of the Protestant/Jewish, work/achievement ethic, and even more flagrantly, of the rational, cool, unemotional facade with which Machismo suppresses male feelings.)

These perennial pitfalls of movement people, which amount to a bottomless pit for the movement, are explained by Joreen as part of the "Tyranny of Structurelessness," which is a joke from the standpoint that sees a nation of quasi-automatons, struggling to maintain a semblance of individuality against a post-technological, military/industrial bulldozer.

What we definitely don't need is more structures and rules, providing us with easy answers, pre-fab alternatives and no room in which to create our own way of life. What is threatening the female Left and the other branches even more, is the "tyranny of tyranny," which has prevented us from relating to individuals, or from creating organisations in ways that do not obliterate individuality with prescribed roles, or from liberating us from capitalist structure.

Contrary to Joreen's assumption, then, the consciousness-raising phase of the movement is not over. Consciousness-raising is a vital process which must go on, among those engaged in social change, to and through the revolutionary liberation. Raising our consciousness—meaning, helping each other extricate ourselves from ancient shackles—is the main way in which women are going to turn their personal anger into constructive energy, and join the struggle. Consciousness-raising, however, is a loose term—a vacuous nothingism, at this point—and needs to be qualified. An offensive television commercial can raise a woman's consciousness as she irons her husbands shirts alone in her house; it can remind her of what she already knows, i.e. that she is trapped, her life is meaningless, boring, etc.—but it will probably not encourage her to leave the laundry and organise a houseworkers' strike. Consciousness-raising, as a strategy for revolution, just involves helping women translate their personal dissatisfaction into class-consciousness and making organised women accessible to all women.

In suggesting that the next step after consciousness-raising groups is building a movement, Joreen not only implies a false dichotomy between one and the other, but also overlooks an important process of the feminist movement, that of building a women's culture. While, ultimately, a massive force of women (and some men) will be necessary to smash the power of the state, a mass movement itself does not a revolution make. If we hope to create a society free of male supremacy, when we overthrow capitalism and build international socialism, we had better start working on it right away, because some of our very best anti-capitalist friends are going to give us the hardest time. We must be developing a visible women's culture, within which women can define and express themselves apart from patriarchal standards, and which will meet the needs of women where patriarchy has failed.

Culture is an essential part of a revolutionary movement—and it is also one of the greatest tools of counter-revolution. We must be very careful to specify that the culture we are discussing is revolutionary, and struggle constantly to make sure it remains inveterately opposed to the father culture.

The culture of an oppressed or colonized class or caste is not necessarily revolutionary. America contains—both in the sense of "having" and in preventing the spread of—many "subcultures" which, though defining themselves as different from the father culture, do not threaten the status quo. In fact, they are part of the "pluralistic" American one-big-happy-family society/ethnic cultures, the "counter-culture." They are acknowledged, validated, adopted and ripped off by the big culture. Cooptation.

The women's culture faces that very danger right now, from a revolutionary new liberating girdle to *MS magazine*, to *The Diary of a Mad Housewife*. The New Woman, i.e. middle-class, college-educated, male-associated, can have her share of the American Pie. Sounds scrumptious—but what about revolution? We must constantly re-evaluate our position to make sure we are not being absorbed into Uncle Sam's ever-open arms.

The question of women's culture, while denigrated by the arrogant and blind male Left, is not necessarily a revisionist issue. The polarization between masculine and feminine roles as defined and controlled by male society, has not only subjugated women, but has made all men, regardless of class or race, feel superior to women—this feeling of superiority, countering anti-capitalist sentiment, is the lifeblood of the system. The aim of feminist revolution is for women to achieve our total humanity, which means destroying the masculine and feminine roles which make both men and women only half human. Creating a woman's culture is the means through which we shall restore our lost humanity.

The question of our lost humanity brings up the subject that vulgar Marxists of every predilection have neglected in their analysis for over half a century—the psycho-sexual elements in the character structure of each individual, which acts as a personal policeman within every member of society. Wilhelm Reich began to describe, in narrow, heterosexual, male-biased form, the character armor in each person, which makes people good fascists or, in our society, just good citizens. Women experience this phenomenon every day, as the repressed feelings, especially obvious among our male friends, who find it so difficult to express or even 'expose' their feelings honestly. The psychic crippling which capitalist psychology coerces us into believing is the problems of the individuals, is a massive social condition which helps advanced capitalist society to hold together.

Psychic crippling of its citizens makes its citizens report to work, fight in wars, suppress its women, non-whites, and all nonconformists vulnerable to suppression. In our post-technological society, every member of which recognises this as being the most advanced culture, the psychic crippling is also the most advanced—there is more shit for the psyche to cut through, what with Jonathan Livingston Seagull and the politics of "You're okay, I'm okay," not to mention post-neo-Freudians and the psycho-surgeons. For the umpteenth time, let it be said that, unless we examine inner psychic shackles, at the time we study outer, political structures and the relationship between the two, we will not succeed in creating a force to challenge our enemy; in fact, we will not even know the enemy. The Left has spent hours and tomes trying to define the ruling class; the ruling class has representative pigs inside the head of every member of society—thus, the logic behind so-called paranoia. The tyranny of tyranny is a deeply-entrenched foe.

Where psychological struggle intersects political involvement is the small group. This is why the question of strategy and tactics and methods of organisation are so crucial at this moment. The Left has been trying for decades to rally people into the streets, always before a number sufficient to make a dent exist. As Stone pointed out, you can't make a revolution when four-fifths of the people are happy. Nor should we wait until everyone is ready to become radical. While on the one hand, we should constantly suggest alternatives to capitalism, through food co-ops, anti-corporate actions and acts of personal rebellion, we should also be fighting against capitalist psychic structures and the values and living patterns which derive from them. Structures, chairmen, leaders, rhetoric—when a meeting of a Leftist group becomes indistinguishable in style from a session of a US Senate, we should not laugh about it, but re-evaluate the structure behind the style, and recognise a representative of the enemy.

The origin of the small group preference in the women's movement—and by small group I refer to political collectives—was, as Joreen explains, a reaction against the over-structured, hierarchical organisation of society in general, and male Left groups in particular. But what people fail to realize is that we are reacting against bureaucracy because it deprives us of control, like the rest of this society; and instead of recognising the folly of our ways by returning to the structured fold, we who are rebelling against bureaucracy should be creating an alternative to bureaucratic organisation. The reason for building a movement on a foundation of collectives is that we want to create a revolutionary culture consistent with our view of the new society; it is more than a reaction; the small group is a solution.

Because the women's movement is tending towards small groups and because the women's movement lacks direction at this time, some people conclude that small groups are to blame for the lack of direction. They wave the shibboleth of "structure" as a solution to the strategic stalemate, as if structure would give us theoretical insight or relief from personal anxieties. It might give us a structure into which to "organise," or fit more women, but in the absence of political strategy we may create a Kafkaesque irony, where the trial is replaced by a meeting.

The lack of political energy that has been stalking us for the last few years, less in the women's movement than in the male Left, probably relates directly to feelings of personal shittiness that tyrannize each and every one of us. Unless we confront those feelings directly and treat them with the same seriousness as we treat the bombing of Hanoi, paralysis by the former will prevent us from retaliating effectively against the latter.

Rather than calling for the replacement of small groups with structured, larger groups, we need to encourage each other to get settled into small, unstructured groups which recognise and extol the value of the individual. Friendships, more than therapy of any kind, instantly relieve the feelings of personal shittiness—the revolution should be built on the model of friendships.

The omnipresent problem which Joreen confronts, that of elites, does not find solution in the formation of structures. Contrary to the belief that lack of up-front structures lead to insidious, invisible structures based on elites, the absence of structures in small, mutual trust groups fights elitism on the basic level—the level of personal dynamics, at which the individual who counters insecurity with aggressive behaviour rules over the person whose insecurity maintains silence. The small personally involved group learns, first to recognise those stylistic differences, and then to appreciate and work with them; rather than trying to either ignore or annihilate differences in personal style, the small group learns to appreciate and utilize them, thus strengthening the personal power of each individual. Given that each of us has been socialised in a society in which individual competition with every other individual is the way of existence, we are not going to obliterate personal-styles-as-power, except by constant recognition of these differences, and by learning to let differences of personal style exist together. Insofar as we are not the enemy, but the victims, we need to nurture and not destroy each other. The destructive elements will recede gradually as we grow stronger. But in the meantime we should guard against situations which reward personal style with power.

Meetings award prizes to the more aggressive, rhetorical, charismatic, articulate (almost always male). Considering how much the various derivatives of the term 'anarchism' are bandied about, very few people in the Left have studied anarchism with any seriousness. For people priding themselves on cynicism about social taboos, we sure are sucked in by this taboo against anarchism.

Like masturbation, anarchism is something we have been brought up to fear, irrationally and unquestioningly, because not to fear it might lead us to probe it, learn it and like it. For anyone who has ever considered the possibility that masturbation might provide more benefits than madness, a study of anarchism is highly recommended—all the way back to the time of Marx, when Bakunin was his most radical socialist adversary... most radical, because he was a dialectical giant step beyond Marx, trusting the qualities of individuals to save humanity.

Why has the Left all but ignored anarchism? It might be because the anarchists have never sustained a revolutionary victory. Marxism has triumphed, but so has capitalism. What does that prove, or what does it suggest but that maybe the loser, up to this point is on our side? The Russian anarchists fiercely opposed the very revisionist tyranny among the Bolsheviks that the new Left would come to deride with sophomoric callousness, before their old Left parents in the '60s. Sure, the old generation of American Leftists were narrow-minded not to see capitalism regenerating in Russia; but the tunnel vision with which we have charted a path of Marxist-Leninist dogma is not something to be proud of either.

Women, of course, have made it out of the tunnel way before most men, because we found ourselves in the dark, being led by the blind men of the new Left, and split. Housewife for the revolution or prostitute for the proletariats; amazing how quickly our revision restored itself. All across the country independent groups of women began functioning without the structure, leaders and other factotems of the male Left, creating independently and simultaneously, organisations similar to those of anarchists of many decades and locales. No accident either.

The style, the audacity of Emma Goldman, has been touted by women who do not regard themselves as anarchists... because Emma was so right-on. Few women have gotten so many men scared for so long as Emma Goldman. It seems logical that we should study Emma, not to embrace her every thought, but to find the source of her strength and love of life. It is no accident, either, that the anarchist Red Terror named Emma was also an advocate and practitioner of free-love; she was an affront to more capitalist shackles than any of her Marxist contemporaries.

12

SOCIAL DEMOCRACY AND ANARCHISM

Charlotte Wilson

IT HAS NOT YET BEEN RECOGNISED IN ENGLAND THAT THE socialism which is being put forward throughout the civilised world as a remedy for the acknowledged evils of modem society—wears two distinct faces. When it is said that a man is a socialist, it is implied that he regards the monopoly of private property in the means of production as the cause of the existing unequal distribution of wealth and its attendant ills; but the philosophical grounds of his belief, and his practical deductions from them remain indefinite as ever. Putting aside those so-called socialists, who only aim at reforming our present social arrangements so as to relieve, for the moment, the misery, without an attempt to fathom either its ultimate cause, or its ultimate issue; socialists are divided into the centralising and decentralising parties, the party of the State and the party of the federatic commune, and this political difference is the outward sign of a grave difference of principle.

It is needless to dwell here at great length upon the beliefs of the socialists of the State, the Social Democrats: their views are already familiar to the English Public through the publications of the Social Democratic Federation.

Roughly speaking they may be summed up as follows: Man, is the creature of his conditions. His moral, social, and political state at any given time is exactly what his economic circumstances have made it. Human progress means increasing ability to derive from Nature the largest amount of subsistence with the smallest expenditure of energy, and the discovery of the best social arrangements for the distribution of what is so obtained. The problem now before us, is, how to modify the external conditions of human existence so as to secure to all men the most complete enjoyment. The means for working it out, lie ready to our hands. Misery has resulted from individual monopoly of the means of production, let us therefore, transfer land and capital to the State. The State, as it is now, is the engine of class rule; it can only reflect the economic phase through which we are passing. True Democracy—the government of the people by themselves—can only advance hand in hand with socialism. The advance of the people to political power will serve us as a lever to bring about their economic salvation. We can make use of the organised force of the State as it is to transform the machinery of Government into that, and the State as it ought to be. The main business of society, organised for self-government, should be the regulation of the business of production and exchange in such a manner that each citizen shall be obliged to perform his fair share of social labour and receive in return a corresponding share of social produce.

Thus men are to be freed from wrong and oppression by the alteration of their external conditions, and their external conditions must be altered by organised force: i.e., by seizing upon the State as it is. To obtain a hold on the State we must enter in political arena and use political methods: political methods in a democracy mean the art of obtaining command over the strength of numbers, and these numbers must be won by an appeal that the masses can understand. The lofty ideal of the socialised State appeals to the moral sense of the thoughtful few: but to the ignorant masses in their bitter need, must be preached the gospel of hate and spoliation. The people supply both the dynamic force and the raw material essential to eager social reconstructors, and so each one scrambles for a place in the popular favour that he may have opportunities to work out his scheme in his own way. As in other political conflicts—other things being equal—the man who wins is he with the loudest voice, the readiest flow of words, the quickest wit and the most self-assertive personality. Immediately it becomes the business of the minor personalities to drag him down, and the old struggle for place and power repeats itself within the very socialistic societies themselves. There is authority on one side and revolt on the other, and the very forms which are supposed to be the safeguards of liberty are made engines of personal enmities.

Social democracy in every land is thus setting out for the new Jerusalem, along the same old muddy political tracks, of which some of us are so weary, and the Holy City to which it aspires, is to be built up of the old bricks and mortar of property and authority: but the bricks are to be set the other way up and refaced so as to look smart from the outside. In economics, in the renunciation of the individual monopoly of capital, social democracy belongs to the future; but in politics, in its conception of the community organised administratively, it belongs to the past.

The history of men living in a social state is one long record of a never-ending contest between certain opposing natural impulses developed by the life in common. The slow development, the contest between these opposing instincts, within each man, has repeated itself within each society. As the one set of impulses or the other have triumphed in the individual man or woman, he or she has sided with one party or other in the community. But in the vast majority of cases no definite triumph has been won: the man or woman has been swayed hither and thither between social and anti-social desires, without conscious realisation of their nature. Looked at for short periods the life of society seems to bear the same impress of fluctuation and uncertainty, but regarded as a whole, it becomes distinctly apparent that the slow course of evolution is tending to eliminate the one sort of impulse and to develop the other into increasing activity.

The struggle of which we are beginning to be dimly conscious within our own nature and in the world of men around us, is that between the antisocial desire to monopolise and dominate, and the social desires which find their highest expression in fraternity—the equal brotherhood of men. This distinction is not equivalent to that often drawn between altruism and egoism, between the self-regarding impulses and those which regulate our relations with our fellows—neither is it another mode of expressing the difference in human relations commonly expressed in the words selfish and unselfish. A selfish man may find it more for his own ease and interest not to attempt to dominate or monopolise, and an unselfish man may be honestly convinced that it is his painful duty to rule his neighbours for their own good.

The desire to dominate is the desire to make oneself superior to one's fellows, to be distinguished from them or placed above them by some acknowledgement of superiority. It is the desire to take and keep whatever may conduce to one's own superiority or importance. The social impulses and desires summed up in "fraternity" are the reverse of all this. They prompt the wish to be on terms of equal companionship with our fellowmen, to share with them all gifts of nature or circumstances, to exchange ideas or opinions on their own merits, and to decide on common action by mutual agreement and sufferance.

The increasing consciousness of self which marks our age, is revealing to us more clearly these opposing currents of desire, both in ourselves and others. We are often keenly aware within ourselves of a desire to rule some fellow-creature, who tempts us by his servility or his feeble defiance: of a sense of equal social relationship towards another who meets us on a ground of equality and equal self-respect; or of an instinct of self-defence called out by the aggressive personality of a third. It is this personal experience which is leading us to a clearer conception of the true meaning of the strife we see around us.

The battle is for freedom, for the deliverance of the spirit of each one of us, and of humanity as a whole, from the government of man by man; whether such coercion justify itself on the plea of superior strength or superior wisdom, of divine light or necessity, of utility or expedience; whether it take the form of force or fraud, of exacted conformity to an arbitrary moral code, or an arbitrary social system, of the open robbery of the means of subsistence, or the legal appropriation of the universal birthright of land, and the fruit of social labour.

This freedom is the necessary preliminary to any true and equal human association, and until this is recognised in theory as the basis of human relationship, state social union is impossible.

Anarchism is the conscious recognition of this naked truth. It stands face to face with the spirit of greed and domination, and declares a moral compromise out of the question. In the light of past victories, won upon many a changing and ill-defined battle-ground, it confronts the enemy of to-day in the latest of his protean shapes, and demands the destruction of the monopoly of property, and of its guardian—the law. Slavery and serfdom are past, political despotism is shrinking away towards the East, and constitutional monarchy is withering before our eyes. Wage slavery and class supremacy is doomed, and our Bourgeois Parliaments are on the high road to talk themselves out of existence, but property and law are still hedged about by that divinity which has ceased to smile on kings.

Property is the *domination* of an individual, or a coalition of individuals, over things; it is not the claim of any person or persons to the use of things—this is, usufruct, a very different matter. Property means the monopoly of wealth, the right to prevent others using it, whether the owner needs it or not. Usufruct implies the claim to the use of such wealth as supplies the user's needs. If any individual shuts off a portion of it (which he is not using, and does not need for his own use) from his fellows, he is defrauding the whole community.* The only claims which any member of a community can fairly put forward to a share of the social wealth are: first, that he requires it to develop and maintain in efficiency all his faculties and powers. Secondly that he has contributed towards the production of that wealth to the best of his ability. Thirdly that (as regards any particular article) he has put so much of his personal labour into it as to have a prior claim to its first use. The first claim is a part of that larger claim that each individual has upon the social feeling of the community of which he is a member; the claim that he shall—as far as the means of the community will admit—have space and opportunity for the fullest development of which his nature is capable. What is required for such development only the individual himself can judge, it varies in every particular instance. But not only is such opportunity pleaded for by the social feelings of such of us as believe the highest development to lead to the highest happiness, but it is urged by the self-interest of the community; for the best developed members of a community are certainly the most useful to it as a whole. It is the highly developed who feel most strongly that healthy desire for the exercise of their faculties which leads to the doing of the best and most earnest work, and this is the most effectual stimulant to exertion. That stimulant which is afforded by the desire to appropriate as much wealth as possible from the general produce—is not only inferior to intensity but it leads a man to choose—not that work which is most useful or for which he has most natural appetite, but rather such work as pays best: a choice which naturally results in "scamping" and inferior workmanship. The utilitarian arguments for the monopoly of property would not suffice to uphold it against the sense of justice which has grown up in humanity, were it not for the guardianship of law. Law encircles private property with some of its own sanctity—a sanctity arising from the fact that it is supposed to represent—in some mysterious manner—that which is in the abstract eternally right. "Thou shalt not steal" as embodied in the statute book is supposed to afford a special sanction to monopolists in possession, however their wealth may have been come by, or is used.

"This reverence has a foundation, in fact, there is a certain small kernel of written law that does represent the social code of habits, customary and desirable in daily life, habits the utility of which has commended itself to the common moral sense of mankind, as a rough generalisation from experience, But men have forgotten that the conditions to which that experience applies vary slightly in each individual case, and in each succeeding generation. To have this social morality—written and fixed is an obstacle to social progress, to enforce it upon the individual by price is an insult to humanity. It is to suppose men suddenly deprived of those higher self-regarding and social instincts, from the free play of which all such morality has sprung, and to deprive them of that sense of responsibility for their own conduct, which is at once the safeguard of life in common, and the earnest of its future development."

But even this inner kernel of law, as it now exists, has been so fatally vitiated by admixtures introduced by the desire to dominate that it is more often opposed to than in accordance with the social sentiments it professes to represent. Take one instance in which the advance of knowledge has come to the aid of struggling social feeling and enlarged our moral sense. I mean the case of so-called criminals. We are now perfectly aware that individuals who commit an outrage upon their fellows are, in the majority of cases, the victims of a defective organisation, or of social arrangements which are a disgrace to our humanity. Yet some of them we brutally murder in cold blood because, in a moment of homicidal mania, they have destroyed human life; others, to whom we have troubled ourselves to give no opportunities of mental or physical development, and who have consequently felt the force of no social obligations, we consign to the tender mercies of a system described by Michael Davitt—after his personal experience of it—as follows:[1]

Penal servitude has become so elaborated that it is now a huge punishing machine, destitute through centralised control and responsibility, of discrimination, feeling, or sensitiveness, and its non-success as a deterrent from crime, its complete failure in reformative effect upon criminal character, are owing to its essential tendency to deal with erring human beings—who are still men despite their crimes—in a manner which mechanically reduces them to a uniform level of disciplined brutes.

And all this we acquiesce in, stifling our natural sensations of horror and pity, because it is the work of the law. We confound the fact that the individual who is ignorant enough to run counter to any natural law, whether it be an observed series of sequences in an inanimate nature, or in the social relationships of men must necessarily suffer for his want of understanding; with a sort of crude instinct of retaliation for the infliction of personal inconvenience which still unhappily survives amongst us, and is exactly that which leads a cat to scratch the person who treads upon her tail. Thus we talk with approval of society avenging itself upon the criminal, or rewarding him according to his misdeeds, when the one just attitude of his brother-men towards him, would be that sense of sorrowing sympathy which would lead them to feel themselves in part responsible for the injury done to himself and others, and for its reparation.

This instance is enough to show what I mean by the vitiation of that small portion of existing law which represents the social sentiments. In truth it has fallen into the hands of the dominators of mankind. It has been formulated by priests, and administered by fighting-men with all the narrowness and cruelty of their crafts until it has practically ceased to represent the moral sense of the people, and become the possession of the privileged classes, who claim the exclusive right of expounding it and carrying it into effect. Moreover they have taken advantage of the respect it commanded to overlay it with a vast mass of regulations in their own interests, for which they have claimed equal reverence, and which exist purely (1st.) to support, define, and defend the monopoly of property (2nd.), to regulate the machinery which upholds it, i.e., Government.

This then is the position of anarchism at the present moment. It finds itself confronted by the spirit of domination in the concrete form of Property, guarded by law, upheld by the organised force of Government, and backed by the yet undestroyed desire to dominate in certain individuals, ignorance of the issues involved in others, (the majority), and the cowardice, folly, idleness, and selfishness, of mankind in general. In this position what are the practical measures to be taken? What are we anarchists to do?

To answer this question fully would be to out-step the limits of the present article, for it would be necessary to trace out the relation of the conviction I have been describing to the economic and social tendencies at present existing in society. Now I can only summarise as briefly as possible—necessarily omitting many important considerations.

As a preliminary, we endeavour to discard the principle of domination from our own lives. In the next place, we associate ourselves with others in working for that social revolution, which for us means the destruction of all monopoly and all government, and the direct seizure by the workers of the means of production. It is our aim to give conscious expression to the voiceless cry of the oppressed, believing that as the knowledge of the real causes of their distress slowly dawns upon the victims of despair, with fuller consciousness will come the energy of hope. It is only the incomprehensible which is paralysing. As to the means to be employed—besides the free association of those who share one hope and one belief—they rest with each man's conscience and his opportunities. The employment of force to coerce others is unjustifiable: but as a means of escaping from coercion, if it is available when other means have failed, it is not only excusable, it is a moral obligation. Each man owes it to himself and to society to be free.

Society can relieve itself of monopoly by force; but social re-formation is the work of silent growth, not of conscious, sudden effort, and it may fairly be predicted, that the old will not be thrown off until the new is sufficiently developed to take its place. Already, for the careful and unbiased observer of present tendencies, it is possible to form some conception of the free community of the future. Federated, self-organised, and self-directed trade and distributing societies, voluntary associations of workers, utilising a common capital, and sharing amongst themselves and with one another the produce of their labour, are no startling innovations. But delivered from the yoke of property, which exacts interest, creates monopoly value and competition in consumption, and makes its possessor arbiter of the destiny of his fellows, such associations will obviously exist in a new atmosphere. When each person directs his own life, then, and then only, he throws his whole soul into the work he has chosen, and makes it the expression of his intensest purpose and desire, then, and then only, labour becomes pleasure, and its produce a work of art.

With the cessation of the luxury and misery, which are the exciting causes of crime and vice, and the substitution of a free scope for human energy, it will become possible to treat the decreasing number of criminals, as science and humanity dictate, i.e., as patients suffering from mental or physical aberration, needing the voluntary attention of skilful physicians and nurses. As for the expression of the collective life of the community, and the raising of such members of it as have lagged behind the social standard of conduct, it is enough to note the marvelous growth of public opinion since the emancipation of speech and the press, to become aware that social expressions of opinion and social codes of morality, unsupported by law or Government, are able to exercise a pressure so strong as to be overwhelming, and to take action with a rapidity unrivalled by any police officer. Indeed, they constitute a serious danger to individual freedom, which, as it is a natural result of life in common, can only be met by a higher moral culture.

It follows from what has been said that anarchism is not a system, but a theory of human development; not a Utopian dream of the future, but a faith for the present; not a nostrum for the cure of all human ills, by the alteration of the material conditions of society, but a protest against certain definite evils, pointed out by reason and experience, as entrenched behind the prejudices of our moral blindness. This protest, this theory, this faith, it carries into every department of life as it is, confident that men will one day see the beauty of life as it might be.

[The Practical Socialist, Volume 1, Number 1, January 1886]

* Property—in the sense understood by the Proudhon School—may perhaps be defined as wealth controlled by one who does not use it except to make an engine of extortion against someone who does use it. In this sense a field let by a landlord is his property, but a similar field cultivated by the owner is his possession—EDITOR.

1 *Contemporary Review*, August 1883

What Socialism Is

INTRODUCTION

The last three centuries of English history have been characterised by a political, agricultural and industrial revolution.

At the Reformation, the increasingly important trading class in the cities formed the main strength of the Crown as against the Church and the Baronage. The Civil Wars and the Revolution of 1688–9 placed direct political influence within the reach of this growing middle class; and, from the early part of this century, its wealth has made it the supreme power in the State, through the medium of representative govemment. Meanwhile, the destruction of the feudal system, consummated by the decimation of the English Baronage in the Wars of the Roses, had tended to place a large portion of the land of the country at the immediate disposal of the King; and the Reformation added the bulk of the territorial possessions of the Church to the estates with which the Tudors were enabled to reward their favourites and supporters. In accordance with the new ideas of property introduced into Northern Europe during that period by the revived influence of Roman law, these estates were granted in private ownership, subject only to the dues to the Crown, abolished in 1645, and replaced in 1660 by a royal revenue raised by general taxation. In these arrangements the claims of the peasantry settled upon the soil from time immemorial were completely ignored. In consequence, these peasants were driven from the land to become hired labourers, vagabonds and paupers. The destruction of the legal rights of the majority of Englishmen in their native soil was completed by the enclosure of common lands, and the removal of small yeomen-farmers to clear the way for large estates farmed by tenants, which took place during the eighteenth and at the beginning of the present century. Thus the English peasantry were transformed into proletarian wage-workers: an instrument ready to the hand of capitalist production.

The discoveries of North and South America and of the passage to India round the Cape of Good Hope, and the era of colonisation which followed opened out new fields for English enterprise. The invention of the steam-engine and of machinery in the eighteenth century completely changed our industrial as well as our agricultural system. The small industries, in which the producer utilised his own capital, were superseded by production on a large scale, with its infinitesimal division of labour, its divorce of capital and the workman, its complete separation of the toil of head and hand, and its competition of capital for profit and of labour for the right to employment. The Napoleonic Wars, checking industry on the Continent, whilst, by raising the price of provisions, increasing agricultural profits at home, enabled England to retain the advantage in commercial development which her inventions had procured her; and, when peace was declared, she was in a position so to utilise the new machinery and facilities of transport and communication as to make herself mistress of the markets of the world. Free trade income has enabled her, until lately, to maintain this position; but signs are not wanting that her pre-eminence—and with it high rates of profit for capital, and average sufficiency of employment for wage-labour—is upon the wane.

From this political and economic revolution have sprung alike the enormous increase in our national wealth, and the unsatisfactory nature of its social distribution.

The foundation upon which our modem economic system rests is the monopoly of land and capital (the means of production) by individuals. This monopoly, i.e., *ownership* as distinct from *usufruct,* originated in the ages of violence and open robbery, and is now protected by the legal and political system gradually fabricated for their own security by the monopolist class. The possessors of property in the means of production have thus been enabled to take advantage of the necessities of the propertyless, and to induce them to work on condition of receiving such a share of the produce of their labour as suffices to keep them alive. The man who has nothing but his labour-force, sells that to the owner of land or machinery or raw material, at a price which is always tending to be forced to a lower level by the competition of increasing population. It is true that, on the other hand, this price may be, and sometimes is, raised by the insistence of the workers upon an increased standard of subsistence; but as machinery tends to oust personal skill in labour the mass of unskilled workmen forced to undersell one another for starvation wages continually augments. The existence of this surplus labour in the market is a necessity of capitalist production, since it is only in consequence of competition amongst labourers for work that the capitalist is able to force his workmen to leave him the lion's share of the produce. The difference between the value produced by the workers and the wages they receive is appropriated by the landlord and capitalist class; and each individual landlord or capitalist keeps as much for his personal share as the competition of other owners of land and employers of labour will admit. This competition appears to return a certain amount of surplus value (difference between the produce of labour and its remuneration, absorbed by the non-producing classes as profits, interest, rent, &c.) to the workers as consumers; but increased cheapness of living in one direction, e.g., bread and groceries, tends to be counterbalanced by increased dearness in others, e.g., rent and meat, so that, for the majority of the workers, real wages remain practically at the level of subsistence. Labour combinations, such as Trades Unions and the like, and the higher standard of comfort, upon which so much stress has recently been laid, have only operated by enabling a certain proportion of the more skilful and prudent workers to exact a fluctuating and uncertain advance of wages in particular trades, where personal ability has not yet been superseded by machinery. But the rapid increase of mechanical agency, the alarming development of commercial gambling in its various forms of speculation, manipulation of the money-market, political wire-pulling, over-production, &c., and the recurring periods of alternate inflation and depression which are the necessary result of production for profit, not for use, combine to render the worker's position every day more insecure. In all such cases, he is the helpless and irresponsible victim of the action of others; he has been forced to sell himself for a mess of pottage, and is consequently deprived of the guidance of his own life and the direction of his own labour. For the so-called freedom of contract between wage-payer and wage-receiver is the bargain of Jacob and Esau, in which one party possesses those necessaries of existence that the other must obtain or starve.

But this evolution of economic conditions, fatal to national prosperity, and degrading alike to the idle and to the working population, has brought with it tendencies which are an earnest of remedy. The Great Industry, massing the workers in large cities, and rendering all the branches of production mutually interdependent, has socialised labour and paved the way for co-operation.

The conscious growth of social feeling thus stimulated, and the inevitable development of the representative system towards Democracy, have resulted in State interference on behalf of the exploited class. Education and political power have been the means of suggesting to the oppressed the possibility of changing their social condition by legal methods, and in this direction such English socialism as exists has hitherto mainly moved.

In other parts of the civilised world the economic problem has been longer and more scientifically discussed, and socialist opinion has taken shape in two distinct schools, Collectivist and anarchist. English socialism is not yet anarchist or Collectivist, nor yet definite enough in point of policy to be classified. There is a mass of socialistic feeling not yet conscious of itself as socialism. But when the unconscious socialists of England discover their position, they also will probably fall into two parties: a Collectivist party supporting a strong central administration, and a counterbalancing anarchist party defending individual initiative against that administration. In some such fashion progress and stability will probably be secured under socialism by the conflict of the ineradicable Tory and Whig instincts in human nature. In view of this probability, the theories and ideals of both parties, as at present formulated, are set forth below; though it must be carefully borne in mind that the majority of English socialists are not committed to either, but only tend more or less unconsciously in one or other direction.

COLLECTIVISM

Summarised from Bebel's *Woman in the Past, Present and Future*

The monopoly of the means of production being proved by an examination of the history of past and present economic and social development to be the underlying cause of the existing confusion in production and inequality in distribution, Collectivists propose to transfer the control of land and capital to the State; or rather to the community organised administratively; for the State as we know it—an organisation for the maintenance of monopoly—will abolish itself by the act of expropriating the expropriators. "The government of persons will be replaced by the administration of things."

The machinery of the Collectivist State will consist of executive committees in each local commune or district, representing each branch of industry, elected by universal suffrage for brief periods of office, and paid at the rate of ordinary workmen; and of a central executive committee, consisting of delegates chosen in like manner, or else directly appointed by the local communal councils. These to be supplemented, where necessary, by intermediate provincial committees.

The business of this executive agency will be to calculate the resources of the community and its needs, and, by comparison of the statistics collected, to regulate production according to consumption. Just as such statistics furnish material for the Budget and for the trading enterprises of large firms today, they will furnish the standard for social labour in the society of the future. They will determine the daily social labour required from each; and as the amount of this at any given period will depend upon the relation between the development of the needs of society and the advance in the arts of production, and as it will be for the interest of each and all to shorten as much as possible the hours of necessary toil, invention and ingenuity will be thereby as much stimulated as now they are discouraged by the lack of interest of the workers in the introduction of labour-saving appliances and more powerful motors.

Production will be carried on only for the purpose of consumption and not for profit, therefore there will be no buying and selling of commodities. The social value of articles will be measured by the average length of the working time required to produce them under average conditions. The calculated average value of ten minutes of social work in one trade will be exchangeable for ten minutes of social work in another. The labour of each worker will be rewarded according to this estimated average standard, by labour notes or certificates of time; and each may work as long as he finds necessary to supply his individual needs, after which he will be free to employ his time and earnings as he likes. As regards the real equality of this system of remuneration, each is free to choose the productive occupation he prefers; and in conditions which afford to all equal physical and mental advantages, the differences of capacity, where choice of function is allowed, are very slight. In cases, however, in which the supply of labour does not equal the demand, the executive must interfere and re-arrange matters, e.g., in the relative numbers of labourers required in town and country at different seasons of the year. But when regard for human welfare has replaced regard for profit, it will be the interest of all to render every kind of labour both pleasant and safe; and mining, sea-faring, factory-work, &c, will be carried on under scientific, sanitary, and artistic conditions now undreamt of; for their introduction would not repay the individual capitalist. Labour will be directed by foremen elected by the workers, and paid at the same rate; and, as society improves, this office will probably be filled by all in turn.

The exchange of articles of consumption will be effected by communal and district depots under the control of the executive; and thus useless middlemen will be set free for productive labour. This change will also simplify the transport service by preventing the unnecessary passing hither and thither of goods of doubtful utility, and thus the executive will be able to extend the means of transit in such a manner as to facilitate the decentralisation of the population.

The collective possession of land will allow of agriculture being treated as a physical problem on a wider basis than has been possible under the regime of private proprietorship. The highest fertility of the soil does not depend so much on the skill or care expended upon small portions of land as upon topographic conditions only capable of national and international treatment: e.g., elevation, forests, water supply. We are unable to estimate the increase in productiveness obtainable by wholesale improvements in irrigation, drainage, levelling, tree-felling and planting, the alteration of the chemical constituents of soil by the scientific use of sewage and other manures, and so forth, or the freedom from toil such improvements will bring in their train.

Finally, the organisation of society must provide for the needs of the old and sick, and the nurture and education of children from the moment they are weaned until they are of age, education for boys and girls alike being compulsory, physical, intellectual and technical.

As to the immediate methods by which the new social and economic condition is to be introduced, Collectivists are divided into Revolutionists, who disdain all political action, and wait till evolution brings the moment for radical change; and Opportunists, who by political action aim at using the organised force of the State as it is, to transform it into the State as it ought to be.

ANARCHISM

Drawn up by C.M. Wilson, on behalf of the London Anarchists

Anarchism is a theory of human development which lays no less stress than Collectivism upon the economic or materialistic aspect of social relations; but, whilst granting that the immediate cause of existing evils is economic, anarchists believe that the solution of the social problem can only be wrought out from the equal consideration of the whole of the experience at our command, individual as well as social, internal as well as external. Life in common has developed social instinct in two conflicting directions, and the history of our experience in thought and action is the record of this strife within each individual, and its reflection within each society. One tendency is towards domination; in other words, towards the assertion of the lesser, sensuous self as against the similar self in others, without seeing that, by this attitude, true individuality impoverishes, empties and reduces itself to nonentity. The other tendency is towards equal brotherhood, or to the self-affirmation of fulfilment of the greater and only true and human self, which includes all nature, and thus dissolves the illusion of mere atomic individualism.

Anarchism is the conscious recognition that the first of these tendencies is, and has always been, fatal to real social union, whether the coercion it implies be justified on the plea of superior strength or superior wisdom, of divine right or necessity, of utility or expedience; whether it takes the form of force or fraud, of exacted conformity to an arbitrary legal system or an arbitrary ethical standard, of open robbery or legal appropriation of the universal birthright of land and the fruits of social labour. To compromise with this tendency is to prefer the narrower to the wider expediency, and to delay the possibility of that moral development which alone can make the individual at one in feeling with his fellow, and organic society, as we are beginning to conceive of it, a realisable ideal.

The leading manifestations of this obstructive tendency at the present moment are Property, or the domination over things, the denial of the claim of others to their use; and Authority, the government of man by man, embodied in majority rule; that theory of representation which, whilst admitting the claim of the individual to self-guidance, renders him the slave of the simulacrum that now stands for society.

Therefore, the first aim of anarchism is to assert and make good the dignity of the individual human being, by his deliverance from every description of arbitrary restraint—economic, political and social; and, by so doing, to make apparent in their true force the real social bonds which already knit men together, and, unrecognised, are the actual basis of such common life as we possess. The means of doing this rest with each man's conscience and his opportunities. Until it is done any definite proposals for the reorganisation of society are absurd. It is only possible to draw out a very general theory as to the probable course of social reconstruction from the observation of growing tendencies.

Anarchists believe the existing organisation of the State only necessary in the interest of monopoly, and they aim at the simultaneous overthrow of both monopoly and State. They hold the centralised "administration of productive processes" a mere reflection of the present middle-class government by representation upon the vague conception of the future. They look rather for voluntary productive and distributive associations utilising a common capital, loosely federated trade and district communities practising eventually complete free communism in production and consumption. They believe that in an industrial community in which wealth is necessarily a social not an individual product, the only claims which any individual can fairly put forward to a share in such wealth are: firstly, that he needs it: secondly, that he has contributed towards it to the best of his ability: thirdly (as regards any special article), that he has thrown so much of his own personality into its creation that he can best utilise it. When this conception of the relation between wealth and the individual has been allowed to supersede the idea now upheld by force, that the inherent advantage of possessing wealth is to prevent others from using it, each worker will be entirely free to do as nature prompts, i.e., throw his whole soul into the labour he has chosen, and make it the spontaneous expression of his intensest purpose and desire. Under such conditions only labour becomes pleasure and its produce a work of art. But all coercive organisation working with machine-like regularity is fatal to the realisation of this idea. It has never proved possible to perfectly free human beings to co-operate spontaneously with the precision of machines. Spontaneity, or artificial order and symmetry must be sacrificed. And as spontaneity is life, and the order and symmetry of any given epoch only the forms in which life temporarily clothes itself, anarchists have no fears that in discarding the Collectivist dream of the scientific regulation of industry, and inventing no formulas for social conditions as yet unrealised, they are neglecting the essential for the visionary.

The like reasoning is applicable to the moral aspect of social relations. Crime as we know it is a symptom of the strain upon human fellowship involved in the false and artificial social arrangements which are enforced by authority, and its main cause and sanction will disappear with the destruction of monopoly and the State. Crime resulting from defective mental and physical development can surely be dealt with both more scientifically and more humanely, by fraternal medical treatment and improved education, than by brute force, however elabourated and disguised.

As for the expression of the common life of the community, and the practical persuasion and assistance desirable to raise those who have lagged behind the average of moral development, it is enough to note the marvelous growth of public opinion since the emancipation of platform and press to become aware that no artificial machinery is needful to enforce social verdicts and social codes of conduct without the aid of written laws administered by organised violence. Indeed, when arbitrary restraints are removed, this form of the rule of universal mediocrity is, and has always been, a serious danger to individual freedom; but as it is a natural, not an artificial result of life in common, it can only be counteracted by broader moral culture.

Anarchism is not a Utopia, but a faith based upon the scientific observation of social phenomena, In it the individualist revolt against authority, handed down to us through Radicalism and the philosophy of Herbert Spencer, and the socialist revolt against private ownership of the means of production, which is the foundation of Collectivism, find their common issue. It is a moral and intellectual protest against the unreality of a society which, as Emerson says, "is everywhere in conspiracy against the manhood of every one of its members." Its one purpose is by direct personal action to bring about a revolution in every department of human existence, social, political and economic. Every man owes it to himself and to his fellows to be free.

[*What Socialism Is,* Fabian Society, Tract Number 4, June 1886]

The Principles and Aims of Anarchists

The key-note of the anarchist contention is, that the vitiation of social life is produced by the domination of man by man. The spirit of domination is the disintegrating element, which, constantly tending to break up society, is the fundamental cause of confusion and disorder.

This impulse in men to dominate their fellows, i.e., impose their will upon them and assert their own superiority, would seem to be an ignorant misdirection of the healthy impulse to assert human dignity, the unity of man, as distinct but not separate from the unity of nature, and the dignity and spontaneity of the individual human being as distinct but not separate from associated humanity. The misdirection of this impulse has been encouraged by the absence of knowledge as to the nature and method of natural processes, which has resulted in superstitious awe of all uncomprehended manifestations of force in external nature and in man. This awe has been utilised by the stronger and more cunning of the human race to sanction their domination.

As knowledge has penetrated the governed masses, their submission to the oppression of the dominators, whether priests, lawyers, or warriors, has decreased; and the people have revolted against the form of authority then felt most intolerable. This spirit of revolt in the individual and in the masses, is the natural and necessary fruit of the spirit of domination; the vindication of human dignity, and the saviour of social life.

Anarchism is recognition and acknowledgement of this truth, that social peace and the possibility of full social developments depend on the accordance of the equal social claim of each sane adult to the responsibility of guiding his own thoughts, speech and action by the law of his own conscience, and not by the will of any other individual or collection of individuals.

Considering the spirit of domination as the great cause of human misery, and the present disorganisation of social life, anarchists declare war against its present principal forms of expression—property, and law manufactured and administered by majority rule.

Property is the monopoly of social wealth; the claim to an individual right not only to use such wealth, but to prevent others from using it. Wealth being the product of the collective labour of society past and present, of associated mankind, can only belong to society. When it is monopolised by the force or cunning of individuals, other individuals who have been prevented by larger and more generous social feeling, want of strength, of ability or opportunity, from monopolising also, must necessarily become subordinate to the monopolists; since they must work to obtain wherewithal to exist, and cannot work without the monopolised instruments of production. Hence the monopoly of social wealth is the main agent of domination.

Its justification on the ground of its social necessity as an inducement to labour, unless forced labour be substituted, is contradicted by the experience of the possibility of voluntary labour for a common object, whether sustenance or social improvements in the common labour of all primitive peoples, of such historical associations as the guilds of the Middle Ages, of the innumerable spontaneous societies and associations for every variety of social effort of the present day. It is also contradicted by scientific observations as to the pleasure experienced by all healthy animals in the exercise of function, and the obvious preference of healthy and free human beings for such occupations as produce a tangible result, satisfy the whole nature morally and physically, and win the approbation of their fellows. Work which is the result of free choice is best done. But the desire to obtain the largest possible share of wealth by labour, injures workmanship and leads to the choice of the most profitable rather than the fittest sort of work.

The monopoly of wealth would have no chance against the sense of social justice and the needs of mankind, unless sanctioned and protected by law.

The kernel of law, which commends it to the respect of the moral sense of men, is the crystallised social custom—result of common experience, social feeling spontaneously called forth by life in common—which our written law contains. But this reasonable respect has been twice converted into superstitious awe by the dominators of men, who have pretended for law the origin of a direct divine revelation, and who have used the reverence thus inspired to cover the whole of the enactments they have made for their own advantage, and the maintenance of their supremacy.

The manufacture and administration of law by the delegates of a majority, changes nothing of its oppressive character; its only purpose remains to impose the will of certain individuals upon the rest, and to maintain certain privileges and distinctions. With the resignation of claim and monopoly of every sort, its occupation is gone.

Apart from this, law is essentially the attempt on the part of certain persons to draw a hard and fast line for the conduct of others; and as the circumstances, motives and personal inspiration of no two individuals is the same, it is a perennial source of injustice and wrong. The pressure and the inspiration which is the natural and inevitable action of the surrounding social atmosphere upon the social sensibilities of the individual, are in all normal cases more than sufficient to secure the possibility of agreement and corporate action. With the removal of arbitrary bonds and hard and fast restraints their strength is more fully recognised, and the aroused sense of responsibility which follows the absence of coercion, tends to make opposition to social claims a matter of conscience rather than of caprice. In abnormal cases, the want of social feeling can be most humanely and more effectually met by an active display of brotherly care and attention; the spirit of resistance to all aggression in the name of human dignity, not of personal self-assertion, and the generous attempt to relieve the physical deformity or disease, or the moral blindness which has led to the aggression.

Anarchism is a protest against the government of man by man in every shape and form as the disturber of social life, an assertion that the free play of the social nature of free and equal human beings is the only solid basis of society.

This is an abstract of paper read before the London Dialectical Society on the 2nd of June [1886]

The Present Day, Number 38 (Old Series), Number 2 (New Series), July 1886.

A WOMAN WITHOUT A COUNTRY

Emma Goldman

THE TITLE IS PERHAPS MISLEADING BECAUSE, IN A TECHNICAL sense, I am not without a country. Legally I am a "subject of His Britannic Majesty." But in a deeper, spiritual sense, I am indeed a woman without a country, as I shall try to make plain in the course of this article.

To have a country implies, first of all, the possession of a certain guarantee of security, the assurance of having some spot you can call your own and that no one can alienate from you. That is the essential significance of the idea of country, of citizenship. Divested of that, it becomes sheer mockery.

Up to the World War citizenship actually did stand for such a guarantee. Save for an occasional exception in the more backward European countries, the native or naturalized citizen had the certainty that somewhere on this globe he was at home, in his own country, and that no reversals of personal fortune could deprive him of his inherent right to have his being there. Moreover, he was at liberty to visit other lands and wherever he might be he knew that he enjoyed the protection of his citizenship.

But the War has entirely changed the situation. Together with countless lives it also destroyed the fundamental right to be, to exist in a given place with any degree of security. This peculiar and disquieting condition of affairs has been brought about by a usurpation of authority that is quite incredible, nothing short of divine. Every government now arrogates to itself the power to determine what person may or may not continue to live within its boundaries, with the result that thousands, even hundreds of thousands, are literally expatriated. Compelled to leave the country in which they happen to live at the time, they are set adrift in the world, their fate at the mercy of some bureaucrat vested with authority to decide whether they may enter "his" land. Vast numbers of men and women, even of children, have been forced by the War into this terrible predicament. Hunted from place to place, driven hither and thither in their search for a spot where they might be permitted to breathe, they are never certain whether they may not be ordered at any moment to leave for other parts—where the same fate is awaiting them. Veritable Wandering Jews, these unfortunates, victims of a strange perversion of human reason that dares question any person's right to exist.

From every "civilised" country men and women may now be expelled any time it suits the police or the government. It is not only foreigners who are thus virtually driven off the face of the earth. Since the World War citizens are also subject to the same treatment. Citizenship has become bankrupt. It has lost its essential meaning, its one-time guarantee. Today the native is no more safe in "his own" country than the citizen by adoption. Deprivation of citizenship, exile and deportation are practiced by every government; they have become established and accepted methods. So common are these proceedings that no one is any more shocked by them or made sufficiently indignant to voice an effective protest. Yet, for all their "legality," denaturalization and expatriation are of the most primitive and cruel inhumanity.

The War has exacted a terrific price in the stupendous number of human lives lost, men maimed and crippled, countless hearts broken and homes destroyed. But even more fearful is the effect of that holocaust upon the living. It has dehumanized and brutalized mankind, has injected the poison of hatred into our hearts, has roused man's worst instincts, made life cheap, and human safety and liberty of the smallest consideration. Intolerance and reaction are rampant, and their destructive spirit is nowhere so evident as in the growing despotism of official authority and in its autocratic attitude toward all criticism and opposition. A wave of political dictatorship is sweeping Europe, with its inevitable evils of irresponsible arbitrariness and oppression. Fundamental rights are being abolished, vital ethical conceptions scorned and flouted. Our most precious possession, the cultural values which it has taken centuries to create and develop, are being destroyed. Brute force has become the sole arbiter, and its verdict is accepted with the servile assent of silence, often even with approval.

Till 1917 the United States had fortunately not become affected by the internecine madness which was devastating the Old World. The idea of war was very unpopular, and American sentiment was virtually unanimous against mixing up in the European imbroglio. Then, suddenly, the entire situation changed: a peace-insisting nation was transformed, almost over night, into a martial maniac run amuck. A study of that strange phenomenon would no doubt be an interesting contribution to our understanding of collective psychology, but the subject is outside the present discussion. Here it must suffice to recollect that, after having elected Woodrow Wilson president because he "had kept them out of war," the American people were somehow persuaded to join the European war. The President's decision, very unwillingly concurred in by a no-war Congress, had the effect of changing the entire psychology of the United States. The tranquil country became a land of flaming jingoism, and a deluge of intolerance and persecuting bigotry overwhelmed the people. The vials of mutual suspicion, of hatred and compulsion were poured out from North to South and from East to West, setting man against man, and brother against brother. In the halls of legislation the spirit of the new militarism manifested itself in draconic laws passed against every critic and protestant.

The sanguine European struggle for territory and markets was proclaimed a holy crusade in behalf of freedom and democracy, and forcible conscription was hailed as "the best expression of a free citizenry." The war orgy evidenced a psychosis on a nationwide scale never before witnessed in the United States. Compared with it the temporary American aberration that followed the violent death of President McKinley, in 1901, was a mere flurry. On that occasion, as will be remembered, the Federal Government rushed through special legislation outlawing everything that indicated the least symptom of non-conformism or dissent. I am referring to the notorious anti-anarchist law, which for the first time in the history of the United States introduced the principle of government by deportation. Persons suspected of anarchist tendencies, disbelievers in organised government, were not to be allowed entry to the United States, the land of the free; or, if already there could be sent out of the country within a period of three years. According to that law men like Tolstoy and Kropotkin would have been refused permission to visit the United States, or deported if found within its boundaries.

That law, however, product of a short-lived panic, virtually remained a dead letter. But the war-time psychosis revived the forgotten anti-anarchist statutes and broadened them to include everyone who was persona non grata to the powers that be, without the benefit of time limitation. There began a national hunt for "undesirables." Men and women were gathered in by the hundred, arrested on the street or taken from their work-benches, to be administratively deported, without hearing or trial, frequently because of their foreign appearance or on account of wearing a red shawl or necktie.

The war cyclone, having swept Europe, gained increased momentum in America. The movement to make the world safe for democracy and liberty, solidly supported by the "liberal" intelligentsia of press and pulpit, made the United States the most dangerous place for democrat and libertarian. An official reign of terror ruled the country, and thousands of young men were literally driven into the army and navy for fear of their neighbors and of the stigma of "slacker" cast upon everyone in civilian dress—cast mostly by idle ladies of fashion who paraded the streets to aid the cause of "humanity." Everyone who dared raise his voice to stem the tide of the war-mania was shouted down and maltreated as an enemy, an anarchist and public menace. Jails and prisons were filled with men and women ordered deported. Most of them were persons that had lived many years in their adopted country, peacefully following their vocations; some of the others had spent almost their entire lives in America. But length of sojourn and useful occupation made no difference. The great Government of the United States stooped even to the subterfuge of secretly depriving naturalized citizens of their citizenship, so as to be able to deport them as "undesirable foreigners."

Future historians will wonder at the peculiar phenomenon of American war psychology: while Europe experienced its worst reaction as a result of the war, the United States—in keeping with its spirit of "get there first"—reached its greatest reactionary zenith before entering the war. Without warning, as it were, it forswore all its revolutionary traditions and customs, openly and without shame, and introduced the worst practices of the Old World. With no more hesitation than necessary it transplanted to America methods of autocracy which had required centuries to develop in Europe, and it initiated expatriation, exile and deportation on a whole scale, irrespective of any considerations of equity and humanity.

To be sure, the pacifist intellectuals who prepared America for war solemnly insisted that the summary abrogation of constitutional rights and liberties was a temporary measure necessitated by the exigencies of the situation, and that all war-legislation was to be abolished as soon as the world would be made safe for democracy. But more than a decade has passed since, and in vain I have been scanning American newspapers, journals and magazines for the least indication of the promised return to normalcy. It is easier to make laws than abolish them, and oppressive laws are particularly notorious for their longevity.

With its habitual recklessness it has outdone the effete Old World in its preparedness. The former great democracy of Thomas Jefferson, the land of Paine and Emerson, the one-time rebel against State and Church, has turned persecutor of every social protestant. The historic champion of the revolutionary principle, "No taxation without representation," compelled its people to fight in a war waged without their consent! The refuge of the Garibaldis, the Kossuths and Schurzes practises deportation of heretics. America, whose official functions always begin with a prayer to the Nazarene who had commanded "Thou shalt not kill" has imprisoned and tortured men who scrupled to take human life, and has hounded those who proclaimed "peace and good will on earth." Once a haven for the persecuted and oppressed of other lands, the United States has since shut its doors in the face of those seeking refuge from the tyrant. A new twentieth-century Golgotha for its "foreign" Saccos and Vanzettis, it silences its native "undesirables," its Mooneys and Billingses, by burying them alive in prison. It glorifies its flying Lindberghs, but damns their thinking fathers. It crucifies manhood and expatriates opinion.

The practice of deportation places America, in a cultural sense, far below the European level. Indeed, there is less freedom of thought in the United States than in the Old World. Few countries are as unsafe for the man or woman of independence and idealism. No offence more heinous there than an unconventional attitude; every crime may be forgiven but that of unapproved opinion. The heretic is anathema, the iconoclast the worst culprit. For such there is no room in the great United States. In a singular manner that country combines industrial initiative and economic self-help with an almost absolute taboo against ethical freedom and cultural expression. Morals and behaviour are prescribed by draconic censorship, and woe to him who dares step out of the beaten path. By substituting rule by deportation for its fundamental law, America has recorded itself thoroughly reactionary. It has erected formidable barriers against its cultural development and progress. In the last analysis such policies are a means of depriving the people of the finer values and higher aspirations. The great body of labour is, of course, the most direct victim of this menace. It is designed to stifle industrial discontent, to eliminate the spokesmen of popular unrest, and subjugate the inarticulate masses to the will of the masters of life.

Unfortunately it is the workers themselves who are the main bulwark of reaction. No body of any toilers in any country is as mentally undeveloped and as lacking in economic consciousness as the American Federation of Labour. The horizon of their leaders is sadly limited, their social short-sightedness positively infantile. Their role in the World War days was most pitiful and subservient in their vieing to outdo each other as trade drummers for the Moloch of slaughter. They championed the most reactionary measures, too fatuous to understand that the same will remain a post-war weapon in the hands of the employers of labour. They learned nothing from past experience and have forgotten the lesson of the Sherman Law, passed by the efforts of the workers to check the industrial trusts but since applied by the American courts to weaken and emasculate the organisations of labour. As was to be foreseen, the "temporary" war legislation, sponsored by the American Federation of Labour, is now being used in the industrial struggles against the toilers.

It was Fridjof Nansen, the famous explorer, who was one of the first to realize the far-reaching effects of the war psychosis in relation to these expatriated. He introduced the special passport that bears his name and which is designed to insure at least a modicum of safety to the increasing number of refugees. Because of Nansen's great services in organising the millions of homeless and parentless children during the war, the League of Nations was induced to approve his project and established the so-called Nansen passport. Few countries, however, recognise its validity, and that half-heartedly, and in no case does it guarantee its holder against exile and deportation. But the very fact of its existence goes to prove the havoc wrought by post-war developments in the matter of citizenship and the utterly wretched situation of the thousands of expatriated and countryless.

It should not be assumed that the latter consists mostly of political refugees. In that huge army of exile there are great numbers of entirely apolitical people, of men and women whom territorial rapacity and the Versailles "peace" have deprived of their country. Most of them do not even get the benefit of the Nansen passport, since the latter is intended only for the political refugees of certain nationalities. Thus thousands find themselves without legal papers of any kind, and in consequence may not be permitted to stay anywhere. A young woman of my acquaintance, for instance, a person who has never been interested in any social or political activities, is at this very moment adrift in this Christian world of ours, without the right of making any country her home, without fatherland or abode, and constantly at the mercy of the passport police. Though a native of Germany, she is refused citizenship in that country because her father (now dead) was an Austrian. Austria, on the other hand, does not recognise her a citizen because her father's birthplace, formerly belonging to Austria, has by the terms of the Versailles treaty become part of Rumania. Rumania, finally, declines to consider the young woman as a citizen on the ground that she is not a native, and never lived in the country, does not speak its language and has no relatives there. The unfortunate woman is literally without a country, with no legal right to live anywhere on earth, save by the temporary toleration of some passport officials.

Still more hazardous is the existence of the vast army of political refugees and expatriated. They live in ever present fear of being deported, and such a doom is equivalent to a sentence of death when these men are returned, as is only too often the case, to countries ruled by dictatorships. Quite recently a man I know was arrested in the place of his sojourn and ordered deported to his native land, which happened to be Italy. Had the order been carried out, it would have meant torture and execution. I am familiar with a number of cases of political refugees not permitted to remain in the countries where they had sought refuge and deported to Spain, Hungary, Rumania or Bulgaria, where their lives are in jeopardy. For the arm of reaction is long. Thus Poland has on several occasions lately decreed the deportation of Russian political refugees to their native country, where the Tcheka executioner was ready to receive them. It was only through the timely intercession of influential friends abroad that the men and their families were saved from certain death. European despotism reaches even across the seas, to the United States and South America; repeatedly politicals of Spanish and Italian descent have been deported to their native lands as an act of "Courtesy" to a friendly power.

These are not exceptional instances. Large numbers of refugees are in a similar position. Not to speak of the thousands of non-political, denaturalized and expatriated and despoiled of abode. In Turkey and France, to mention two countries only, there are at present over half a million of them, victims of the World War, of Fascism, of Bolshevism, of Post-war territorial changes and of the mania for exiling and deporting. Most of them are being merely tolerated, for the time being, and are always subject to an order to "move on"—somewhere else. Lesser but still very considerable numbers are scattered throughout the world, particularly in Belgium, Holland, Germany and in the various countries of Southern Europe.

There is nothing more tragic than the fate of those men and women thrown upon the mercy of our Christian world. I know from personal experience what it means to be torn out of the environment of a lifetime, dug out by the very roots from the soil you have had your being in, compelled to leave the work to which all your energies have been devoted, and to part from those nearest and dearest to you. Most disastrous are the effects of such expatriation particularly on persons of mature age, as were the greater number of those deported by America. Youth may adapt itself more readily to a new environment and acclimatize itself in a strange world. But for those of more advanced age such transplantation is a veritable crucifixion. It requires years of application to master the language, custom and habits of a new land, and a very long time to take root, to form new ties and secure one's material existence,—not to speak of the mental anguish and agony a sensitive person suffers in the face of wrong and inhumanity.

As for myself, in the deeper significance of spiritual values, I feel the United States "my country." Not to be sure, the United States of the Ku Kluxers, of moral censors in and out of office, of the suppressionists and reactionaries of every type. Not the America of Tammany or of Congress, of respectable inanity, of the highest skyscrapers and fattest moneybags. Not the United States of petty provincialism, narrow nationalism, vain materialism and naive exaggeration. There is, fortunately, another United States—the land of Walt Whitmans, the Lloyd Garrisons, the Thoreaus, the Wendell Phillipses. The country of Young America of life and thought, or of art and letters; the America of the new generation knocking at the door, of men and women with ideals, with aspirations for a better day; the America of social rebellion and spiritual promise, of the glorious “undesirables” against whom all the exile, expatriation and deportation laws are aimed.

It is to THAT America that I am proud to belong.

THE TRAGEDY OF WOMAN'S EMANCIPATION

Emma Goldman

From the 1917 edition of Anarchism and Other Essays

I BEGIN WITH AN ADMISSION: REGARDLESS OF ALL POLITICAL and economic theories, treating of the fundamental differences between various groups within the human race, regardless of class and race distinctions, regardless of all artificial boundary lines between woman's rights and man's rights, I hold that there is a point where these differentiations may meet and grow into one perfect whole.

With this I do not mean to propose a peace treaty. The general social antagonism which has taken hold of our entire public life today, brought about through the force of opposing and contradictory interests, will crumble to pieces when the reorganisation of our social life, based upon the principles of economic justice, shall have become a reality.

Peace or harmony between the sexes and individuals does not necessarily depend on a superficial equalization of human beings; nor does it call for the elimination of individual traits and peculiarities. The problem that confronts us today, and which the nearest future is to solve, is how to be one's self and yet in oneness with others, to feel deeply with all human beings and still retain one's own characteristic qualities. This seems to me to be the basis upon which the mass and the individual, the true democrat and the true individuality, man and woman, can meet without antagonism and opposition. The motto should not be: Forgive one another; rather, Understand one another. The oft-quoted sentence of Madame de Stael: "To understand everything means to forgive everything," has never particularly appealed to me; it has the odor of the confessional; to forgive one's fellow-being conveys the idea of pharisaical superiority. To understand one's fellow-being suffices. The admission partly represents the fundamental aspect of my views on the emancipation of woman and its effect upon the entire sex.

Emancipation should make it possible for woman to be human in the truest sense. Everything within her that craves assertion and activity should reach its fullest expression; all artificial barriers should be broken, and the road towards greater freedom cleared of every trace of centuries of submission and slavery.

This was the original aim of the movement for woman's emancipation. But the results so far achieved have isolated woman and have robbed her of the fountain springs of that happiness which is so essential to her. Merely external emancipation has made of the modern woman an artificial being, who reminds one of the products of French arboriculture with its arabesque trees and shrubs, pyramids, wheels, and wreaths; anything, except the forms which would be reached by the expression of her own inner qualities. Such artificially grown plants of the female sex are to be found in large numbers, especially in the so-called intellectual sphere of our life.

Liberty and equality for woman! What hopes and aspirations these words awakened when they were first uttered by some of the noblest and bravest souls of those days. The sun in all his light and glory was to rise upon a new world; in this world woman was to be free to direct her own destiny—an aim certainly worthy of the great enthusiasm, courage, perseverance, and ceaseless effort of the tremendous host of pioneer men and women, who staked everything against a world of prejudice and ignorance.

My hopes also move towards that goal, but I hold that the emancipation of woman, as interpreted and practically applied today, has failed to reach that great end. Now, woman is confronted with the necessity of emancipating herself from emancipation, if she really desires to be free. This may sound paradoxical, but is, nevertheless, only too true.

What has she achieved through her emancipation? Equal suffrage in a few States. Has that purified our political life, as many well-meaning advocates predicted? Certainly not. Incidentally, it is really time that persons with plain, sound judgment should cease to talk about corruption in politics in a boarding-school tone. Corruption of politics has nothing to do with the morals, or the laxity of morals, of various political personalities. Its cause is altogether a material one. Politics is the reflex of the business and industrial world, the mottos of which are: "To take is more blessed than to give"; "buy cheap and sell dear"; "one soiled hand washes the other." There is no hope even that woman, with her right to vote, will ever purify politics.

Emancipation has brought woman economic equality with man; that is, she can choose her own profession and trade; but as her past and present physical training has not equipped her with the necessary strength to compete with man, she is often compelled to exhaust all her energy, use up her vitality, and strain every nerve in order to reach the market value. Very few ever succeed, for it is a fact that women teachers, doctors, lawyers, architects, and engineers are neither met with the same confidence as their male colleagues, nor receive equal remuneration. And those that do reach that enticing equality, generally do so at the expense of their physical and psychical well-being. As to the great mass of working girls and women, how much independence is gained if the narrowness and lack of freedom of the home is exchanged for the narrowness and lack of freedom of the factory, sweat-shop, department store, or office? In addition is the burden which is laid on many women of looking after a "home, sweet home"—cold, dreary, disorderly, uninviting—after a day's hard work. Glorious independence! No wonder that hundreds of girls are willing to accept the first offer of marriage, sick and tired of their "independence" behind the counter, at the sewing or typewriting machine. They are just as ready to marry as girls of the middle class, who long to throw off the yoke of parental supremacy. A so-called independence which leads only to earning the merest subsistence is not so enticing, not so ideal, that one could expect woman to sacrifice everything for it. Our highly praised independence is, after all, but a slow process of dulling and stifling woman's nature, her love instinct, and her mother instinct.

Nevertheless, the position of the working girl is far more natural and human than that of her seemingly more fortunate sister in the more cultured professional walks of life—teachers, physicians, lawyers, engineers, etc., who have to make a dignified, proper appearance, while the inner life is growing empty and dead.

The narrowness of the existing conception of woman's independence and emancipation; the dread of love for a man who is not her social equal; the fear that love will rob her of her freedom and independence; the horror that love or the joy of motherhood will only hinder her in the full exercise of her profession—all these together make of the emancipated modern woman a compulsory vestal, before whom life, with its great clarifying sorrows and its deep, entrancing joys, rolls on without touching or gripping her soul.

Emancipation, as understood by the majority of its adherents and exponents, is of too narrow a scope to permit the boundless love and ecstasy contained in the deep emotion of the true woman, sweetheart, mother, in freedom.

The tragedy of the self-supporting or economically free woman does not lie in too many but in too few experiences. True, she surpasses her sister of past generations in knowledge of the world and human nature; it is just because of this that she feels deeply the lack of life's essence, which alone can enrich the human soul, and without which the majority of women have become mere professional automatons.

That such a state of affairs was bound to come was foreseen by those who realized that, in the domain of ethics, there still remained many decaying ruins of the time of the undisputed superiority of man; ruins that are still considered useful. And, what is more important, a goodly number of the emancipated are unable to get along without them. Every movement that aims at the destruction of existing institutions and the replacement thereof with something more advanced, more perfect, has followers who in theory stand for the most radical ideas, but who, nevertheless, in their every-day practice, are like the average Philistine, feigning respectability and clamoring for the good opinion of their opponents. There are, for example, socialists, and even anarchists, who stand for the idea that property is robbery, yet who will grow indignant if anyone owe them the value of a half-dozen pins.

The same Philistine can be found in the movement for woman's emancipation. Yellow journalists and milk-and-water litterateurs have painted pictures of the emancipated woman that make the hair of the good citizen and his dull companion stand up on end. Every member of the woman's rights movement was pictured as a George Sand in her absolute disregard of morality. Nothing was sacred to her. She had no respect for the ideal relation between man and woman. In short, emancipation stood only for a reckless life of lust and sin; regardless of society, religion, and morality. The exponents of woman's rights were highly indignant at such representation, and, lacking humor, they exerted all their energy to prove that they were not at all as bad as they were painted, but the very reverse. Of course, as long as woman was the slave of man, she could not be good and pure, but now that she was free and independent she would prove how good she could be and that her influence would have a purifying effect on all institutions in society. True, the movement for woman's rights has broken many old fetters, but it has also forged new ones. The great movement of TRUE emancipation has not met with a great race of women who could look liberty in the face. Their narrow, Puritanical vision banished man, as a disturber and doubtful character, out of their emotional life. Man was not to be tolerated at any price, except perhaps as the father of a child, since a child could not very well come to life without a father. Fortunately, the most rigid Puritans never will be strong enough to kill the innate craving for motherhood. But woman's freedom is closely allied with man's freedom, and many of my so-called emancipated sisters seem to overlook the fact that a child born in freedom needs the love and devotion of each human being about him, man as well as woman. Unfortunately, it is this narrow conception of human relations that has brought about a great tragedy in the lives of the modern man and woman.

About fifteen years ago appeared a work from the pen of the brilliant Norwegian, Laura Marholm, called *Woman, A Character Study*. She was one of the first to call attention to the emptiness and narrowness of the existing conception of woman's emancipation, and its tragic effect upon the inner life of woman. In her work Laura Marholm speaks of the fate of several gifted women of international fame: the genius, Eleonora Duse; the great mathematician and writer, Sonya Kovalevskaia; the artist and poet-nature, Marie Bashkirtzeff, who died so young. Through each description of the lives of these women of such extraordinary mentality runs a marked trail of unsatisfied craving for a full, rounded, complete, and beautiful life, and the unrest and loneliness resulting from the lack of it. Through these masterly psychological sketches, one cannot help but see that the higher the mental development of woman, the less possible it is for her to meet a congenial mate who will see in her, not only sex, but also the human being, the friend, the comrade and strong individuality, who cannot and ought not lose a single trait of her character.

The average man with his self-sufficiency, his ridiculously superior airs of patronage towards the female sex, is an impossibility for woman as depicted in the *Character Study* by Laura Marholm. Equally impossible for her is the man who can see in her nothing more than her mentality and her genius, and who fails to awaken her woman nature.

A rich intellect and a fine soul are usually considered necessary attributes of a deep and beautiful personality. In the case of the modern woman, these attributes serve as a hindrance to the complete assertion of her being. For over a hundred years the old form of marriage, based on the Bible, "till death doth part," has been denounced as an institution that stands for the sovereignty of the man over the woman, of her complete submission to his whims and commands, and absolute dependence on his name and support. Time and again it has been conclusively proved that the old matrimonial relation restricted woman to the function of a man's servant and the bearer of his children. And yet we find many emancipated women who prefer marriage, with all its deficiencies, to the narrowness of an unmarried life; narrow and unendurable because of the chains of moral and social prejudice that cramp and bind her nature.

The explanation of such inconsistency on the part of many advanced women is to be found in the fact that they never truly understood the meaning of emancipation. They thought that all that was needed was independence from external tyrannies; the internal tyrants, far more harmful to life and growth—ethical and social conventions—were left to take care of themselves; and they have taken care of themselves. They seem to get along as beautifully in the heads and hearts of the most active exponents of woman's emancipation, as in the heads and hearts of our grandmothers.

These internal tyrants, whether they be in the form of public opinion or what will mother say, or brother, father, aunt, or relative of any sort; what will Mrs. Grundy, Mr. Comstock, the employer, the Board of Education say? All these busybodies, moral detectives, jailers of the human spirit, what will they say? Until woman has learned to defy them all, to stand firmly on her own ground and to insist upon her own unrestricted freedom, to listen to the voice of her nature, whether it call for life's greatest treasure, love for a man, or her most glorious privilege, the right to give birth to a child, she cannot call herself emancipated. How many emancipated women are brave enough to acknowledge that the voice of love is calling, wildly beating against their breasts, demanding to be heard, to be satisfied.

The French writer, Jean Reibrach, in one of his novels, *New Beauty*, attempts to picture the ideal, beautiful, emancipated woman. This ideal is embodied in a young girl, a physician. She talks very cleverly and wisely of how to feed infants; she is kind, and administers medicines free to poor mothers. She converses with a young man of her acquaintance about the sanitary conditions of the future, and how various bacilli and germs shall be exterminated by the use of stone walls and floors, and by the doing away with rugs and hangings. She is, of course, very plainly and practically dressed, mostly in black. The young man, who, at their first meeting, was overawed by the wisdom of his emancipated friend, gradually learns to understand her, and recognises one fine day that he loves her. They are young, and she is kind and beautiful, and though always in rigid attire, her appearance is softened by a spotlessly clean white collar and cuffs. One would expect that he would tell her of his love, but he is not one to commit romantic absurdities. Poetry and the enthusiasm of love cover their blushing faces before the pure beauty of the lady. He silences the voice of his nature, and remains correct. She, too, is always exact, always rational, always well behaved. I fear if they had formed a union, the young man would have risked freezing to death. I must confess that I can see nothing beautiful in this new beauty, who is as cold as the stone walls and floors she dreams of. Rather would I have the love songs of romantic ages, rather Don Juan and Madame Venus, rather an elopement by ladder and rope on a moonlight night, followed by the father's curse, mother's moans, and the moral comments of neighbors, than correctness and propriety measured by yardsticks. If love does not know how to give and take without restrictions, it is not love, but a transaction that never fails to lay stress on a plus and a minus.

The greatest shortcoming of the emancipation of the present day lies in its artificial stiffness and its narrow respectabilities, which produce an emptiness in woman's soul that will not let her drink from the fountain of life. I once remarked that there seemed to be a deeper relationship between the old-fashioned mother and hostess, ever on the alert for the happiness of her little ones and the comfort of those she loved, and the truly new woman, than between the latter and her average emancipated sister. The disciples of emancipation pure and simple declared me a heathen, fit only for the stake. Their blind zeal did not let them see that my comparison between the old and the new was merely to prove that a goodly number of our grandmothers had more blood in their veins, far more humor and wit, and certainly a greater amount of naturalness, kind-heartedness, and simplicity, than the majority of our emancipated professional women who fill the colleges, halls of learning, and various offices. This does not mean a wish to return to the past, nor does it condemn woman to her old sphere, the kitchen and the nursery.

Salvation lies in an energetic march onward towards a brighter and clearer future. We are in need of unhampered growth out of old traditions and habits. The movement for woman's emancipation has so far made but the first step in that direction. It is to be hoped that it will gather strength to make another. The right to vote, or equal civil rights, may be good demands, but true emancipation begins neither at the polls nor in courts. It begins in woman's soul. History tells us that every oppressed class gained true liberation from its masters through its own efforts. It is necessary that woman learn that lesson, that she realize that her freedom will reach as far as her power to achieve her freedom reaches. It is, therefore, far more important for her to begin with her inner regeneration, to cut loose from the weight of prejudices, traditions, and customs. The demand for equal rights in every vocation of life is just and fair; but, after all, the most vital right is the right to love and be loved. Indeed, if partial emancipation is to become a complete and true emancipation of woman, it will have to do away with the ridiculous notion that to be loved, to be sweetheart and mother, is synonymous with being slave or subordinate. It will have to do away with the absurd notion of the dualism of the sexes, or that man and woman represent two antagonistic worlds.

Pettiness separates; breadth unites. Let us be broad and big. Let us not overlook vital things because of the bulk of trifles confronting us. A true conception of the relation of the sexes will not admit of conqueror and conquered; it knows of but one great thing: to give of one's self boundlessly, in order to find one's self richer, deeper, better. That alone can fill the emptiness, and transform the tragedy of woman's emancipation into joy, limitless joy.

15

MAKE YOUR OWN TEA
WOMEN'S REALM AND OTHER RECIPES AND PATTERNS

Alice Nutter

This essay originally appeared in the Class War *final issue, Summer 1997*

THIS PIECE IS WRITTEN FOR *ALL* REVOLUTIONARIES. THIS IS NOT the token 'women's bit' that's stuck in for the sake of appearances. This is an attempt to look at how and why the Left, and Class War in particular, has not just failed to attract women, but alienated, patronised and looked upon them as a minority group. How can half the working class be treated as a minority? We're not claiming that we have solutions for the gender imbalance but we are saying that it's time to stop ignoring the problem. Any revolutionary movement which doesn't address why there are so few women in its ranks isn't a true revolutionary movement, just a complacent reflection of the status quo.

Dazed and Confused

In the early years of Class War, the attitude was that feminist demands did not go far enough. We said why call for equal pay? Equal rights under capitalism was putting out a begging bowl for equal gender exploitation and was spectacularly unambitious. Class War were calling not for equal pay packets but for the abolition of money. The feminist fixation with voting rights was another half measure. Why choose between two evils when there's so much more to be had? Class War tried to support the principle of gender equality while disagreeing with the reformist tendencies of established feminism.

In the mid-1980s the Left was in its victim stage. 'All men are bad, all women are good' arguments were being waged by feminists who wanted the moral advantage and brownie points. Class War wasn't about pushing the politics of middle class guilt. By showing images of women who were taking control of their lives and fighting back, Class War thought it was supporting working class women. Whether it was or not is up for discussion, but the paper's intentions were honourable. The approach was simplistic, but at least it wasn't as confused as other sections of the Left—who were dancing round Goddess-based 'alternative' religions and calling them politics.

Class War's early issues show that there was a commitment to talking to *all* the working class as opposed to just young white males. Cervical cancer information sat on the same page as 'Battered Bobby.' Articles about sexism (admittedly basic and often moralistic as opposed to libertarian) made regular appearances. The politics were often misguided, with one article offering instructions to working class men to support women's struggles by offering physical protection. This paternalistic attitude reflected society's but it didn't make it right.

But to put Class War in context, other lefty groups and papers had even worse attitudes. Militant and the SWP's politics were so entrenched in old-fashioned rhetoric that women only featured in their papers when they slotted in to the traditional 'worker' slot. Grunwick was their finest hour: workers who were women and Asian to boot. Women Against Pit Closures and 'miners' wives' were the only other photos of a woman they'd use. Those pictures from 1977 and 1984 had to see them through almost 20 years of papers.

In 1987 a Brixton woman wrote to Class War questioning our coverage of the Brixton riots. She said that living in a police no-go area had ended not in Utopia, but in women suffering intimidation, physical and sexual violence. To Class War's credit, the paper responded with an article about the dangers of romanticising violence, and started up a debate about communities providing their own policing.

However, a lot of women who agree with Class War's aims and principles, think the organisation is too Boy's Own to become involved with. Class War's attitude to violence is alienating for women—no amount of wishful thinking will alter the fact that working class men and women have very different attitudes to violence. Class War's hard image, its music and boots are meant to attract young, white males. It's questionable whether concentrating on attracting one area of the working class (and alienating other sections of it) is worth the price, but even on its own terms this tactic fails.

What Did You Do in the War, Mum?

Looking at Class War in isolation won't tell us much about why the Left has put gender politics on the back-burner. Class War came in to being at a time when the women's movement was in crisis. Without sketching a rough run-down of some of the events that preceded that crisis, it's impossible to challenge the cliché that feminism is merely the plaything of the middle classes.

In lefty circles all you have to do to discredit a movement or an idea is call it middle class. It's become a non-specific term of abuse. The feminist movement *did* have a lot of middle class women in it, but that doesn't mean that all of them opposed the interests of working class women. Nor does it mean that feminist ideas aren't useful to working class women.

In the early seventies feminist ideas began to permeate through society. The media (as always) looked for leaders and personalities. Rather than talk about the anger, the ideas and the needs that were propelling feminism forward, the emphasis was on individuals. Germaine Greer and Co. fitted the media bill.

But this didn't stop women seizing the idea of liberation. Suddenly there were theories which explained why life was so miserable for the majority of women. The middle classes were the first to catch them because they had more access to education, but many working class women weren't all that far behind. The only solution to women's troubles was to change society, which was the last thing that the right wanted.

Women got down to the serious job of showing we'd no longer tolerate male domination and violence. In 1972 the first refuge for battered women opened. In 1976 the first Rape Crisis Centre opened, run on feminist lines. It mushroomed and by the mid-1980s there were centres in almost every city.

The *Reclaim the Night* marches started in Soho in protest against the exploitation of the sex industry. The women's movement was making it up as it went along—and at that point it hadn't had to take account of the views of women actually working in the industry. In Leeds and York the Reclaim the Night marches took on a different significance. Peter Sutcliffe, the so-called 'Yorkshire Ripper,' was still on the loose in Northern industrial towns. We were sick of living in a climate of fear, of being told that the only way to stay safe was to stay in doors or under male protection. Last but not least we'd had enough of the state and media distinction between 'good' and 'bad' girls; between the prostitute women who the media implied deserved to be murdered and the good, asexual, family-type women who didn't. Feminism provided the framework for women to realise that we had a right to be sexual and safe. We were angrily rejecting the hypocritical morality of the times as well as celebrating our presence on the streets.

Women: They all Look the Same to me

The women's liberation movement had its own internal problems. the rhetoric of 'sisterhood' above all else meant that class and race, other great defining aspects of our lives, were in danger of being buried under the 'all girls together' mentality. Working-class and non-white women fought the fallacy that class and race were less important than gender. They said that middle class women were fighting for their independence from patriarchy, while keeping the perks of their class. Working class women weren't trying to destroy sisterhood; they were insisting that it be made more substantial. Some working class women said that sisterhood had to start with income sharing.

Black women refused to let the reality of having to live in a racist society be obscured by an umbrella of sisterhood. The women's liberation movement was predominantly white and middle class, but to say that the white middle class women constantly held sway is to under-value black and working class women's contributions. They forced the women's liberation movement to take account of them—whether it wanted to or not. In 1978 *The Working Class Women's Liberation Newsletter* was launched. To go along with the myth that working class women played no part in changing society, is to repeat the lie that we were too thick to read the writing on the wall, and add our own quotes.

Separatism helped create more schisms and split feminism into non-complementary strands. The main bugbear was whether women working or having relationships with men were letting the side down by fraternising with 'the enemy.' In retrospect separatism looks like just more Stalinist power-play. Arguments about desire and free choice were put down to women trying to hang on to their 'heterosexual privilege.' Capitalism's privileges weren't given much attention. No wonder the women's movement split.

Despite internal sex wars, the women's movement continued to have a positive influence on society. The one good thing about radical feminism was that it taught women to recognise the full extent of male domination. Women who chose not to live or work apart from men finally picked up on the way that trade unions/political groups/partners made few concessions to women. The revolutionary movement was found wanting.

The Enemy Within

The women's movement would have survived and still politically progressed if the right hadn't intervened. The American Weyrich was the first of many new right leaders to declare feminist women a threat to state power: *"There are people who want a different political order. Symbolised by the women's liberation movement, they believe the future for their political power lies in the restructuring of the traditional family, and in downgrading the male or the father role in the traditional family."*

Thatcher and her followers had their own think-tanks which drew the same conclusions. By the mid-1980s equality seemed like a sensible proposition to most women, so the media responded by declaring that feminism was outdated, a 1970s thing like flares. 'Post-feminism' was the new thing. It came complete with a younger generation who hated the women's movement. 'Post-feminist' was anti-feminist and it was set off not by women achieving their demands but by the fact that they looked in danger of getting too stroppy, too much of a threat.

The old feminist 'leadership' were now part of the media establishment Greer and Co. happily went back on their past calls for equality and independence. The new, revisionist line was that feminism had robbed us of our right to be mothers and home bodies. Greer declared that the model woman was the old-fashioned peasant wife up to her neck in onions and kids. One after another the old guard trundled out to tell us that women were at their most fulfilled when their influence was restricted to the home-front. Unsurprisingly, the media loved this U-turn and printed every word of it. It was the worst sort of careerism, but the right has always diffused subversive ideas by rewarding changes of opinion. Post-feminist theory smelled a lot like old-fashioned servitude.

You"ll Always Find me in the Kitchen at Parties

Class War was formed at the height of this period of post-feminism. The entire Left was confused by the infighting and the right's full-scale assault. Class War didn't stand back and look at what was happening, but neither did anybody else. It was a time when one after another all the women's papers collapsed under the weight of the onslaught. Feminism was too old hat to be bought, so most of the radical women's papers folded. The only voices we were hearing were the new right and its lackeys telling us to get back into the kitchen.

It's an elaborate confidence trick. The new right wants us in the traditional wifey mode, but it also wants our wage labour. The post-feminist line is that the modern women can have freedom through work, and still have the 'fulfillment' of running a home.

Capitalism needs women to work. The far right's shift to economic 'rationalism' and the expansion of the low-paid service industries mean that cheap labour is always in demand. And as far as capital is concerned, nothing comes cheaper than women. Capitalism's motto is: if you want to shell out less money and make more profits, employ women—they're worth less.

Nine out of ten single parents are women, and even in two parent households many women are the main bread-winner; yet capitalism still pretends that women's wages are 'pin money.' Women don't need a living wage, because we don't actually have to live off it. Despite a wealth of evidence to the contrary, men are still seen as the main 'providers.' Our wages pay for the little extras: food, shelter and warmth. And as we get older, in a society which judges women on appearance, we become worthless.

Single mothers on benefit are the group who have borne the worst of the post-feminism backlash. Capitalism has outlawed all non-monetary relations. In a capitalist society to have no money is to have no identity. We're not what we eat, but where we work and what we earn. Single mothers have been targeted because their existence threatens the right's social, political and economic aims. Hence the constant media attacks and housing and benefit cuts. 'Back to Basics' blamed everything from loose morals to the rising crime rate on single mothers.

Work and wages—no matter how menial and low—are often cited as proof that we've achieved our objectives and no longer need feminism. Try telling the woman who gets up at six to clean offices, that if she worked harder she too could have two homes and inter-continental air travel. The role models post-feminism holds up as 'successful' women (scum like Anita Roddick) get to the top by promoting ruthless capitalism. Gender plays no part in their story—other than their having to prove that their killer instincts are twice as sharp as men's.

One of capitalism's strategies for reducing wages is to take what has traditionally been 'men's work'—manufacturing etc.—automate the plant and then bring in 'unskilled' women at a lower rate of pay. Then it is women, rather than capitalism's sharp practice, who are blamed for men being chucked out of the workforce.

Post-feminism also makes a big fuss out of women's nurturing natures—we're supposed to like being dogsbodies. In 81 per cent of (two adult) homes where a woman works full-time, she is still responsible for the washing and ironing and the bulk of the domestic jobs. Maybe 'we've made it' means the beds. We're still acting as unpaid domestic servants; the only real change is that men think they do more. There's a million excuses for why not, but men rarely take an equal share of cooking and household chores.

Revolutionary groups seldom address the day-to-day inequalities in their own kitchens. Issues around housework are seen as trivial. Twenty years ago the expression for it was 'women's work.' Lefty 'man' may claim to be fighting for the freedom of mankind, but that doesn't mean her wants his girlfriend to stop doing his washing.

Part of the problem is that housework has been tagged 'personal politics.' 'Personal' like 'middle class' is just another way of saying irrelevant to the overall struggle. Class War has always understood that 'politics' is about improving the day-to-day realities of our lives. Unfortunately, that understanding doesn't seem to extend to women. Too often issues are prioritised on the grounds of whether or not they make men feel heroic. Rioting does; shopping doesn't. Washing up just doesn't get the adrenaline going: ask any woman.

Get Your Tits Out for the Lasses

Post-feminism has a cute chorus-line of girls flashing their knickers as a sign of liberation. We've got the Girlie Show, The Pyjama Party, and the Spice Girls sticking their tits out on prime-time TV. All three were put together by blokes. We're supposed to see them as symbols of the new 'sassy' woman, but all are a bloke's idea of the perfect feminist. They make a lot of noise but never say anything which actually threatens the status quo. They're Stepford Wives with better thighs, and a carefully programmed attitude. They're go-go dancing for equality.

At the same time there's a constant media crusade to show us what a dangerous place the world is for women. Less than eight per cent of all violent crimes are sexual attacks on women (the highest mortality rate is among young working class men), but the media loves to highlight our rapes and murders by deranged strangers. The message is that we need the security of male protection. The sub-text is: 'your relationship might be crap and abusive but look how much worse off you'd be without him.' The irony is that at least a third of all women killed in Britain are murdered by their husbands or boyfriends—the majority just after they declare their independence by breaking off the relationship.

Will this Movement Move me?

We don't live in an equal world. We need a feminist analysis as much as we ever did. All around us the gains of the last thirty years are under attack. The Left bowed out of women's struggles years ago, and since there isn't really a women's movement to speak of, individual women are left to slug it out alone. The whole point in joining a revolutionary movement is to fight alongside people who share the same dreams and ideals. There's not much incentive for women to join revolutionary groups when the general ethos is: you can fight our battles but we're not interested in yours.

Women join revolutionary organisations because they want to change the whole of society not just the sexist bit. But to survive within them we end up having to 'put up and shut up.' Just because we've prioritised class and capitalism as major oppressions doesn't mean that we don't give a shit about gender.

The old chestnut about 'single issues' distracting the focus of the struggle has been dragged out too many times when women's struggles come up. The anti-JSA campaign or prisoner support are 'single issues'; race, class and gender aren't. We can't pick up and put down our class, our skin colour or our sex. Whatever comes after Class War needs to take a less one-dimensional approach. We don't know what will make a unified movement, but we do know what won't: ignorance.

No one is 'just' working class, 'just' a woman, 'just' black. Our politics are a mesh of different experiences, and half the time there's no cosy alliance between our different oppressions. A woman's experiences under patriarchy help shape her perceptions of class. We've been guilty of pretending that working class men and women would all live happily ever after once we've banished capitalism. Not if we still have one half serving the other half. Life isn't simple. Those who are our comrades in one area may well turn out to be against us in another. When conflict comes up we're forced to say what matters most; sometimes it's our class and sometimes it isn't. We have to acknowledge difficulties before we can start to deal with them. We don't know if we can resolve these dilemmas but we're certainly willing to try.

Anonymous
was
a
Woman

16

ROTE ZORA

THE REVOLUTIONARY CELLS (RZ) FIRST APPEARED ON November 16, 1973 with an attack against ITT in West Berlin to point out the participation of this multinational corporation in Pinochet's military putsch in Chile. In 1974, the first high-explosive attack was undertaken by the wimmin of the RZ against the *Bundesverfassungsgericht* (Federal Constitutional Court) in Karlsruhe, the day after it supported the abortion law, Par. 218; a paragraph against free choice on abortion, allowing abortion only in certain cases. The wimmin naturally demanded the total right for every womyn to have an abortion, as a right to self-determination over their own bodies. In the first issue of *Revolutionärer Zorn (Revolutionary Rage)* the RZ subdivided their actions into three main categories: 1) anti-imperialist actions, 2) actions against the branches, establishments, and accomplices of Zionism in the FRG, and 3) actions supporting the struggles of workers, wimmin and youth, and attacking and punishing their enemies. This thematic spectrum was used in the following years.

One Revolutionary Cell became several Revolutionary Cells. Later on, in the late 70's, the militant actions by the RZ became also a part of the anti-nuclear movement (at that time people marched in thousands against nuclear power and reprocessing plants in Kalkar, Wyhl, Gorleban, and Brokdorf) and the Anti-Runway 18 West movement (Anti-Startbahn 18 West-Bewegung) in the Rhein-Main area. In this context, only one attack with deadly consequence was carried out: the Minister of Economy and Transportation, Herbert Karry, was assassinated on May 11, 1981 by the RZ.

From 1977 onwards, the militant feminist anti-patriarchal wimmin's urban guerrilla group Rote Zora (Red Zora) acted autonomously and independently, though some wimmin still participated in the Revolutionary Cells.

> "Wimmin were always a part of the armed groups. Their portion was mostly held back. But the times are changing ... subversive wimmin's groups like Red Zora do exist, indeed still too few, but even that will be changing."
> *Red Zora*

Red Zora attacks predominantly patriarchal institutes, companies, and persons representing and building up a male sexist society, which is oppressing and exploiting wimmin worldwide. They are conducting campaigns against porntraders, sex shops, international traders of wimmin (those who profit from importing Asian wimmin as "brides" for West German men), doctors who are carrying out forced sterilizations, the Doctor's Guild ("We see the Federal Doctor's Guild as exponents of rape in white trench-coats"), drug companies (notably Schering who produced the birth defect causing drug Duogynon), as well as computer companies such as Nixdorf and the multinational Siemens. Very popular as well was the illegal reprinting of bus and streetcar fares. In individual cases, Red Zora and the Revolutionary Cells have worked together such as in the writing of a critique of the peace movement in 1984. In this paper they criticised the peace movement as a bourgeois movement with an apocalyptic vision. The RZ and Red Zora said that the major mistake of the peace movement was to concentrate their political goal only on the preservation of peace in the metropoles instead of discussing the imperialist, context between armament and crisis; Third World misery and social cutbacks; sexism and racism.

Anti-Imperialism Today

In the last three years the RZ have concentrated their actions on the issue of West German foreigner and refugee policies. "We want to contribute to the recovery of a concrete anti-imperialism in the FPG ... Anti-imperialism doesn't mean only attacks on the military industrial complex and it is more than just solidarity with liberation movements worldwide." (Quote from *Revolutionary Rage*. October 1986).

Attacks such as the one on the Centre for the Central Register of Foreigners in Cologne on the one hand, or the Kneecapping of Hollenburg (Chief of Immigration Police in West Berlin) show the wide field of these militant politics. While those who are attacked are responsible for the racist refugee policies in the FRG and West Berlin, the intention of the attacks on institutions, whose documents, files, and data are being destroyed, is to procure a space which isn't controlled and regulated by the state. "But our actions will fizzle out ineffectually, if they don't contribute to a development of a new beginning of anti-imperialism within the radical left" (Quote by the RZ).

Since the early 70's, the RZ and Red Zora have launched over 200 attacks. Red Zora's most comprehensive and successful attack campaign so far has been the deposit of incendiary bombs in ten branches of the Adler Corporation, one of West Germany's largest clothing manufacturers selling discount clothing in the FRG, produced by low paid wimmin in South Korean and Sri Lankan factories. "The wimmin at Adler in South Korea struggle against the exploitation of their capacity for work and are putting up a fight against the daily sexism. They call for support from the FRG for their struggle. As a result, the shitty living and working conditions of wimmin in the vacuous production centres of the three continents and especially those of Adler in South Korea and Sri Lanka are becoming more widely known here through leaflets, events, and actions in front of Adler's retail centres. In these actions, anti-imperialism can be practical." (Quote from Red Zora, in their Adler statement.)

In a later released statement from Red Zora, the consideration was again concretized that the attacks were the correct strategy: "Consciousness had already been raised through leaflet actions organised by human rights groups (Terre des Femmes) and independent church groups. So preparatory work had been done. The wimmin in South Korea have taken control of and defended their own situation." They went on strike to protest low minimum wages, lay offs, deplorable work conditions, and rampant sexism from West German foremen. "So it was possible that the struggle there (by the wimmin in South Korea) and the struggle here (by Red Zora) are compatible. We aren't fighting for the wimmin in the Third World," they said, "we're fighting alongside them." This defines Red Zora's struggle against imperialism.

In 1987. when Red Zora and their sister group in West Berlin, the Amazonen, fire bombed ten Adler outlets throughout West Germany, they caused millions of dollars in damages. Because of this, Adler was forced to meet the demands of the textile workers. Red Zora and the Amazonen clearly proved that militant resistance can be very effective.

Both the Revolutionary Cells and Red Zora have anti-authoritarian structures and a decentralised decision-making process for choosing targets. As well, they point out that militant direct actions are just one part of the revolutionary movement. Although they participate in extensive and far-reaching legal work campaigns and social movements through their militant actions, these actions aren't of any more importance than handing out flyers or leaflets, going to demonstrations, having sit-ins, publishing newspapers, educating people, squatting houses, or organising strikes at work. "We don't have a hierarchical system for choosing actions. Thinking in hierarchical divisions puts actions in a perspective of privilege and is prone to a patriarchal way of thinking." (Quote by members of the RZ in an interview that appeared in *Autonomie,* 1980.)

Besides the RZ and Red Zora, there exist several other militant autonomous groups who are all integral components of the revolutionary movement in West Germany and West Berlin. Most of these groups originate from the mass social movements of the 80's. They all work independently of each other and issue political statements of their actions, much like the RZ and Red Zora. But unlike them, many of these groups haven't been around very long.

In 1986, at the peak of resistance against the nuclear power plant in Brokdorf and the nuclear reprocessing plant in

Wackersdorf, thousands of people participated in demonstrations as a part of the anti-nuclear movement. During this time, several hundred attacks were made by militant autonomous cells against certain companies and corporations to protest their involvement in the nuclear industry. The most popular activity at this time was sawing down electric power lines that were directly connected to the nuclear power plants. Around 2–300 attacks were made. Some of the militant autonomous groups from this period have survived into the present. Others have disbanded and have gone on to influence and form other groups. Following is a list of a few of these groups. It would be impossible to name all of them.

•*Revolutionäre Handwerker:* involved in direct actions against nuclear plants by sawing down electric power lines. No longer active.
•*Amazonen:* sister group of Red Zora, but independent of them. Two people are currently in jail for being members of the Amazonen.
•*Zornige Viren:* on January 2, 1989, attacked the Gen-Institut (Gene Institute) at the University of Darmstadt causing DM2,000,000 in damages.
•*Autonome Zellen Alois Sonnenleitner (AS):* autonomous anti-nuclear cell. Destroyed excavators, trucks, and building site of Hofmeister AG (an NPP company) by setting fire to them. Alois Sonnenleitner was an elderly man who was killed in Wackersdorf by the cops in 1986. Still active.
•*Revolutionäre Viren:* fighting gene technology, human genetics, and biotechnology.
•*Anti-rassistische Zellen:* carrying out actions against Shell.
•*Kämpfende Einheiten:* "Fighting Units." Anti-imperialist cells attacking military industrial complexes. One cell, Kämpfende Einheit Crespo Cepa Galende, named itself after an ETA (Basque guerrilla organisation) fighter who was killed by the Spanish authorities. Made an attack on a border police security building.

The militant direct action groups in West Germany and West Berlin have received widespread support from the larger movements there, including from some of the more liberal organisations. This is partially because the underground cells are dependent on the larger movements and, as well, are active in them. Their actions address issues that many people are already educated on and sympathetic to. For example, Red Zora has gained wide popular support because their actions appeal to the massive feminist movement already existing in West Germany, where the leftist and radical media has been doing much work for some time now to educate the public on issues involving sexism, wimmin's oppression and exploitation, and wimmin's rights to the control of their own bodies. While the RZ doesn't claim as much support as Red Zora, in 1987, supporters of the Revolutionary Cells published the book *Der Weg zum Erfolg (The Way to Success)*, explaining their strategies, politics, and actions. Less than a week after the book hit the shelves of radical bookstores, the entire, printing (around 3000) was sold out.

The high degree of effectiveness of many RZ and Red Zora actions wouldn't be possible without popular support. By themselves, their actions would only serve to alienate them from the struggle. Moreover, with the support of the mass movements, members of the RZ and Red Zora are able to work among the numbers of people active in the struggle without exposing their underground identities. In their herstory, only one womyn has been arrested for membership in Red Zora. But due to a lack of evidence against her, the charges were dropped. The RZ, however, has had a few convictions over the past 16 years. Ingrid Strobl most recently was sentenced to five years in prison on the 9th of June 1989 for being a member of the RZ. Her sentence is the longest issued to any of the convicted RZ members. While prisoner support is an important task that consumes a great amount of time, most of the work is done by the larger movement, and the RZ and Red Zora can continue organising actions against oppressive, imperialist companies and corporations.

Other revolutionaries sentenced to prison:

•*Erik Prauss and Andrea Sievering:* accused of membership in the "terrorist" organisation, Red Army Faction (RAF), and a bombing of Dornier, a war corporation, which caused 1.3 million DM in damages. Each was sentenced to 9 years in prison on January 18, 1989.
•*Norbert Hofmeier, Barbara Perau, Thomas Thoene, and Thomas Richter:* accused of membership in the RAF and a bombing. Sentenced all together to 32 years on January 20, 1989. Sentencing judge (Arend) also sentenced Ingrid

Strobl. Hofmeier: 10 years., Perau: 9, Thoene: 9.
Richter: 4.

In both of the trials involving the mentioned people. The BAW (Federal State Prosecutors) and the judges were alleging that the accused people were members of the RAF. But this was the false claim of the court to get these people stiffer sentences. Both attacks (the one at Dornier, and the other at the border police security building) were claimed by Kämpfende Einheiten. This group works independently from the RAF. But since the RAF is defined as a "terrorist" organisation by the state, conviction as a member can carry a longer sentence. Kämpfende Einheiten isn't defined as such and would not be subject to as heavy a sentence. So the BAW and the judges set up the construct of the Whole-RAF (Gesamt-RAF) and claimed that Kämpfende Einheiten is a part of the RAF.

At the trial of Erik and Andrea, Eva-Haule Frimpong, an imprisoned member of the RAF, stated on the witness stand that "in 4 years, no one but myself has been caught from the RAF. The twelve comrades of the resistance who were supposedly arrested since then (the six from Kiefernstrasse nor the people from Stuttgart) were not organised in the RAF." (Quote by Eva on November 29, 1988).

Fritz Storim: sentenced to one year in prison. A teacher, accused of supporting the RAF. Supposedly a member of the autonomous newsjournal SABOT which published articles in solidarity with the RAF.

17

INTERVIEW WITH ROTE ZORA

THE FOLLOWING INTERVIEW WAS SENT TO THE GERMAN women's magazine *Emma*, and although it wasn't an interview by *Emma,* it was published in June '84. In 1974 'women of the RZs' bombed the Supreme Court which had decided one day earlier to withdraw the reform of the abortion law. In '77 women of 'Rote Zora' bombed the Federal Doctor's Guild in Cologne stating: "We see the Federal Doctor's Guild as exponents of rape in white trenchcoats." This was followed by the attacks on pornography stores, women traders, and the Schering company which was put on trial for producing the birth defect-inducing Duogynon pill. In August 1983 they blew up the bus of Gunther Menger in front of his villa. He is a trader (buys and sells) of 'Thai-girls'. These women traders serve Germen men exotic women under 'terms of delivery' with a list of 'types' and possible 'testing'. Provision: $500(Can), but costs "will soon be compensated because girls from the Far East don't smoke and drink." The courts and police cannot see a legal way to stop these modern slave traders. *Die Spieqel* wrote at that time "These women traders only have to fear the 'Red Zora'." This interview, originally entitled *Resistance Is Possible*, is the first one where they explain why they struggle autonomously inside the RZs and the nature of their relationship to the women's movement.

Let's start with who you are.

Zora 1: If this is a personal question then we are women between the ages of 20 and 51. Some of us sell our labour. Some of us take what we need. and others are 'parasites' on the welfare state. Some have children, some don't. Some women are lesbians, others love men. We buy in disgusting supermarkets, we live in ugly houses, we like going for walks or to the cinema, the theatre, or the disco. We have parties and cultivate idleness. And of course we live with the contradiction that many things we want to do can't be done spontaneously. But after successful actions we have great fun.

What does your name mean?

Zora 2: 'The Red Zora and her Gang' (a children's book)—that is the wild street kid who steals from the rich to give to the poor. Until today it seems to be a male privilege to build gangs or to act outside the law. Yet particularly because girls and women are strangled by thousands of personal and political chains this should make us masses of 'bandits' fighting for our freedom, our dignity, and our humanity. Law and order are fundamentally against us, even if we have hardly achieved any rights and have to fight for them daily. Radical women's struggles and loyalty to the law—there is no way they go together!

Yet it is no coincidence that your name has the same first letters as the Revolutionary Cells (RZ).

Zora 1: No; of course not. Rote Zora expresses the fact that we have the same principles as the RZs, the same concept of building illegal structures and a network which is not controlled by the state apparatus. This is so we can carry our subversive direct actions—in connection with the open legal struggles of various movements. "We strike back"—this slogan of the women of May 1968 is no longer as controversial today regarding individual violence against women. But it is still very controversial, and most of the time taboo as an answer to the power conditions that steadily produce this violence.

What actions have you carried out and what was the background?

Zora 2: The women of RZ started in 1974 with the bombing of the Supreme Court in Kariaruhe because we all wanted the total abolishment of §218 (the abortion law). In the Walpurgisnight (last day of April, 'Women Take Back the Night') 1977 we bombed the Federal Doctor's Guild because they undermined even this reduced abortion reform. Then followed the bombing against Schering during its Duogynon trial, and constant attacks against sex-shops. Actually one of these porno stores should burn or be devastated every day! Therefore we think it absolutely necessary to tear the oppression of women as sexual objects and producers of children out of the 'private domain' and to show our anger and hate with fire and flames.

Zora 1: We don't limit ourselves to direct or obvious women's oppression. As women we are also concerned about social power conditions, whether it be urban or environmental destruction, or capitalist ways of production; the same conditions men are confronted with. We don't like the left 'division of labour' under the motto: the women for the women's question, the men for the general political themes. Nobody can take away from us the responsibility for changing our everyday life. Therefore, for example, we have set fire to the fancy cars of the lawyers of 'slumlord' Kanssen, who were responsible for a series of brutal evictions. Together with the RZs we printed pirate public transportation tickets and distributed them in the Rulo area to introduce a little bit of zero-tarrif.

Zora 2: Our latest bombings were directed against Siemens and the computer company Nixdorf. They promote the development of new domination technology for more sophisticated possibilities of war production and counter-revolution. They also have the function of remodeling labour, especially on the backs of women world-wide. Women here will be exploited with the technology of these companies by working isolated from each other in part-time jobs, without social security. The women of the so-called Third World will be worn out by producing these technologies. At the age of 25 they are totally ruined.

How important is the connection to the Third World, the exploitation of women there, for you?

Zora 1: In all our attacks we've declared this context, also when we attacked the women traders and the Philippine Embassy last year. We don't struggle for women in the Third World—we instead struggle with them—for example against the exploitation of women as a commodity. This modern slave trade has its equivalent in the conjugal possession condition here. The forms of oppression are different but they all have the same roots. Nobody can play cards with us any longer. The separation between men and women has its equivalent internationally in the separation between people of the First and Third World. We ourselves profit from the international division of labour. We want to break with our involvement with this system and understand our common interests with women from other countries.

You explained how you understand your practice, but you didn't explain why you organise yourself in the context of the RZs.

Zora 2: First of all the main reason is that these politics were developed by the RZs and we still think they are correct. During our development we determined our own content—therefore we organised autonomously as women—but we fall back on the experiences of the RZs. We also think that the cooperation of radical groups can strengthen the militant resistance. There were productive forms of cooperation such as the actions against the Reagan visit or the discussion paper about the peace movement.

But there are also stressful discussions. Sometimes men who otherwise transform their radical breaking with this system into a consequent practice are alarmingly far away from realizing what anti-sexist struggle means and what meaning it has for social-revolutionary perspective. Between its women it is also controversial where the limits are, when a cooperation strengthens or paralyses our women's struggle. But we think our feminist identity unites us with some women of the RZs.

Does that mean you define yourself as feminists?

Zora 1: Yes, of course, we think the personal is political. Therefore, we believe that all things social, economic and political which structure and reinforce the so-called personal are an invitation for struggle, especially for us women. These are the chains we want to tear apart. But it is incomplete to make the oppression of women here in West Germany the only turning point of politics and not to see other oppressive conditions such as class oppression, racism, or the annihilation of whole peoples through imperialism. This attitude never understands the base of misery: that the oppression of women and sexual division of labour are presuppositions which are fundamental for oppression of any kind—against other races, minorities, the old and the sick, and especially against those who revolt.

Zora 2: For us difficulties start when feminist demands are used to demand 'equal rights' and recognition in this society. We don't want women in men's positions and reject women who make their career inside the patriarchal structure under the guise of women's struggles. Such careers remain an individual act from which only some privileged women can profit. Women are only allowed to design and manage power in this society if they advocate the interests of men.

The women's movement was quite strong in the '70s. It achieved some things in a legal way. For example: the struggle against the abortion law, publicity about violence against women in the family, and rape as an act of power and violence, the building of autonomous counter structures. Why do you then maintain the necessity of armed struggle?

Zora 1: Of course, the women's movement achieved a lot and for me the most important is the development of a broad consciousness about women's oppression in this society. Also women no longer experience their oppression as an individual case or think they themselves are responsible for it, instead women come together and experience their common strength. The things that were organised by the women's movement like women's bookstores, women's centres, women's newspapers, and meetings or congresses—this has been part of the political reality for some time and is a strong part of the development of the struggle.

Zora 2: Some successes were rather an expression of the situation in a society which can allow women some leeway. Of course when they wanted women in the factories and offices they created more places in kindergartens, but this didn't lead to a basic change in the lifestyle of a woman. It requires a continuous movement whose aims cannot be integrated, whose uncompromising section cannot be forced into legal forms, whose anger and dedication to non-parliamentary struggles and anti-institutional forms is expressed without limit.

Zora 1: The legal route is not sufficient because the usual repression and structures of violence are legal. It is legal if husbands beat and rape their wives. It is legal if women traders buy our Third World sisters; and sell them to German men. It is legal when women ruin their health and do the monotonous work for subsistence wages. These are all violent conditions which we are no longer willing to accept and tolerate and which can't be changed solely by criticism. It was an important step to create a public consciousness about violence against women, but it didn't lead to its prevention. It is a phenomenon that the screaming unfairness which women suffer is met with an incredible proportion of ignorance. It is a tolerance which exposes male parasitism. This 'typical situation' is connected to the fact that there is not much resistance. Oppression is only recognised through resistance. Therefore we sabotage, boycott, damage, and take revenge for experienced violence and humiliation by attacking those who are responsible.

What do you think about the contemporary women's movement?

Zora 2: We think it wrong to talk about the women's movement. On the one hand the women's movement is understood as a result of long existing structures, of projects, encounter centres and of mysticism. There are many currents which do not reinforce each other very fruitfully, but instead partly exclude or fight each other. On the other hand new political impulses stem from different contexts where women are becoming aware of their oppression and are radically questioning patriarchal structures and developing politics in the interests of women—for example women in Latin American solidarity groups, in anti-imperialist groups, in the squatter movement. Therefore the saying "The women's movement is dead, long live the women's movement" is accurate. The women's movement is not a one issue like the anti-nuke or squatter movements, which will not survive if no more nuclear power plants are built, or no more property is available for speculation. The women's movement relates to the totality of patriarchal structures, their technology, their organisation of labour, their relationship to nature, and it is therefore a phenomenon which won't disappear with the removal of some cancerous growths, but instead in the long process of social revolution.

Zora 1: The women's movement has never really analysed its defeat around the abortion law and around the state financing of projects like shelters for battered women. It lacks a rejection of state politics. Also, it anticipated the turning point in family politics through the wave of the new motherhood in the women's movement. Also, the class question never existed; social differences were denied by the universalization of sexist oppression. This makes it difficult to find an answer to the worsening of labour conditions, increasing oppression, and reactionary family politics in the present crisis. The lack of a perspective for action in order to react appropriately to the attack leads to the dilemma of either going offensively against reactionary politics or solely preserving the unfolding of leeway for women. We can't solve this problem in theory, but we don't think the building of women's committees (in the Green Party) is an appropriate solution. The experience is that women do not come to power by ways which exist directly to exclude women and to stabilize and conserve patriarchal domination. Therefore we consider women's committees which want to organise greater influence in parties and institutions the wrong way.

Zora 2: But in the meantime other important discussions and analyses by women which consider the future development of society have begun to develop. The increasing oppression, with the help of new technologies, is investigated from the point of view of the lowest echelons of our society, new wages and work structures for women are analysed, the indirect structures of women are understood. Many women understand and reject the everyday war against women—the wave of hard core porn and propaganda contemptuous of women—and the call of the society for increased motherhood and more femininity. They also understand that the setbacks in women's and family politics are presuppositions for the crisis and the new strategies of capital. The policy of population control, for example the change of the abortion law, is the attempt to have a qualitative influence on the development of the population. Among other things its aim is to multiply the 'healthy' German middle class together with state sponsored genetic technology, which is a development we have to prevent. Today we need more urgently than ever before, a radical women's movement which has the power to prevent and break open the social and political encirclement, not only of women, but also of foreigners and minorities: a women's liberation movement which does not reduce the hope for revolution to a nice dream.

Do you understand yourself as being part of the women's movement, or of the guerilla movement, or both and how do you see the context?

Zora 1: We are part of the women's movement. We struggle for women's liberation. Beside theoretical commonalities there also exists another unity between our practice and the legal women's movement, that is the personal radicalization which can encourage other women to resist and take themselves and the struggle seriously. It is the feeling of strength if you see that you can do things which before you were afraid of, and if you see that it brings about something. We would like to share this experience. We don't think it has to happen in the forms we choose. For example, take the women who disrupted a peep show by drawing women's symbols and dropping stink bombs—these actions encourage us, strengthen us, and we hope women feel the same way about our actions. Our dream is that everywhere small bands of women will exist, that in every city a rapist, a women trader, a battering husband, a misogynist publisher, a porn trader, a pig gynecologist should have to feel that a band of women will find them to attack them and make them look silly in public. For example, that it will be written on his house who he is and what he did, on his car, at his job—women's power everywhere!

How can you take responsibility for possibly endangering the lives of innocent people with your actions?

Zora 2: Why is it that people always assume that those who deal with explosives don't care about what is self-evident for yourselves, for the women's movement or the Left. It's the opposite! Because of the possibility of endangering life we are forced to be especially responsible. You know as well as we do that we could give up if you were right with your question. It would be a paradox to struggle against a system for which life is only worthwhile as long as it is utilizable and at the same time to become as cynical and brutal as that system. There were many actions we rejected because we couldn't eliminate the danger to innocent people. Some firms know this full well which is why they prefer to move into residential buildings. They speculate with our morals if they move into residential dwellings to protect their property.

What do you say against the argument: armed actions harm the movement. They are part of the reason for increasing surveillance of the women's movement to denounce it as terrorist, that it's split and isolated from the majority of women in the women's movement.

Zora 1: To harm the movement—you talk about the installation of repression. The actions don't harm the movement! It's the opposite, they should and can support the movement directly. Our attack on the women traders, for example, helped to expose their businesses to public light, to threaten them, and they now know they have to anticipate the resistance of women if they go on with their business. These 'gentlemen' know they have to anticipate resistance. We call this a strengthening of our movement.

Zora 2: For a long time the strategy of counter-revolution has begun to split the radical wing from the rest of the movement by any means and isolate them to weaken the whole movement. In the '70s we had the experience of what it means when sectors of the left adopt the propaganda of the state, when they start to present those who struggle uncompromisingly as responsible for state persecution, destruction, and repression. They not only confuse cause with effect, but also justify implicit state terror. Therefore, they weaken their own position. They narrow the frame of their protest and their resistance.

Zora 1: Our experience: To stay uncontrolled and to protect ourselves against state attacks a strong unity is necessary. We can no longer afford to have every group repeat the same mistakes. There must be structures in which we share knowledge and experiences which are useful for the movement.

How can non-autonomous, non-radical women understand what you want? Armed actions do have a 'scare away' effect.

Zora 2: Why doesn't it have a 'scare away' effect if a guy sells women, but it does if his car burns? Behind it is the fact that traditional social violence is accepted, whereas similar reprisals 'scare away'. Maybe it is scary if everyday reality is questioned. Women who get it pounded into their heads from the time they are little girls that they are victims get insecure if they are confronted with the fact that women are neither victims nor peaceful. This is a provocation. Those women who experience their powerlessness with rage can identify with our actions. As every act of violence against one woman creates an atmosphere of threat against all women—our actions contribute—even if they aim only against the individual responsible—to the development of an atmosphere of 'Resistance is possible!'

18

MUJERES CREANDO

Bolivian Anarcha-Feminist Street Activists

MAKING WAVES

Mujeres Creando interviewed by Katherine Ainger

OVERNIGHT, IN BEAUTIFUL HANDWRITING, WORDS APPEAR ON the walls of La Paz, the high-altitude capital of Bolivia. They speak truths Bolivian women won't say out loud. Deconstructing machismo, anti-gay prejudice and neoliberalism, Bolivian anarcha-feminist group Mujeres Creando takes art back to the streets. Theirs is a politics of creativity, of interventions in everyday life. Tired of the traditional Left where, they say, 'everything was organised from the top down'.

The women only served the tea or their role was a purely sexual one, or they were nothing more than secretaries; three friends—Maria Galindo, Julieta Paredes and Monica Mendoza—started Mujeres Creando (Women Creating) in 1992. Two are the only openly lesbian activists in Bolivia. At the time, they explain, there was little talk of feminism—a militant, radical feminism, a feminism of the streets, of everyday life.

'We decided on autonomy from political parties, NGOs, the state, hegemonic groups who wish to represent us. We don't want bosses, figureheads or exalted leaders. Nobody represents anybody else—each woman represents herself.'

'We believe that how we relate to people in the street is the most important thing. We have a newspaper which we edit and sell ourselves, and creative street actions. We paint graffiti—las pintadas—this is one of the communicative forms that really gets through to people. It began as a criticism of what the Left is—and the Right. It was our response to their painting in the streets saying "vote for so-and-so." They were affirmative or negative phrases, "no to the vote," "yes to this," "no to that." What we do instead is we appeal to poetry and creativity, to suggest ideas which aren't just "yes" or "no," "Left" or "Right."'

Examples of their graffiti include 'Making your supper and your bed takes away my desire to make love to you', 'If Goni [former President Gonzalo Sanchez de Lozada] had a womb, he'd legalise abortion and privatise it', and 'Neither God, nor master, nor husband, nor party'.

They have targeted all kinds of oppression from a feminist perspective—racism, the dictatorship and debt.

Our aims aren't always centred on women's themes like abortion, reproductive rights, motherhood. The Government says: "You can dedicate yourselves to those issues, full stop." And we may say "no." Or we may say "yes, that interests us." We have positions on abortion, birth control, but don't categorize us! We are involved in everything: we are part of society. And for this reason we paint graffiti about different things. There is graffiti which provokes men, graffiti provoking the Government, graffiti which is only directed at women, graffiti about the political situation.

'For us, the street is a space like a common patio, where we can all be, including children. In Europe, everything is controlled: whether or not you can march, whether or not you can protest, whether or not you can sell things. In Bolivia, the streets belong to the people: people doing things, people selling things—the streets are ours.

'It is very important that what we do in the street interacts with people, talks to them so that they can see the graffiti, that it should provoke something in them, provoke laughter, provoke annoyance, provoke anger, provoke many things.

'People want to dispossess us of something that is ours. To turn creativity into something elitist. But creativity is human—it belongs to all women and men. It is fundamental to everything we do, in the books we make, in the street actions, in the graffiti. There are people who say to us:

"You're artists." But we are not artists, we are street activists.'

This year a group called Deudora ('debtor'), made up largely of poor women from the barrios, came to La Paz to protest at the crippling rates of interest on their microcredit loans.

'We spoke to them about pacifism, we carried out some creative actions against interest, against the banks, against money... painting murals in the streets. 'Mujeres Creando brought paint, and the Deudora group took off their shoes and dipped their feet into the pots, then lifted each other up to leave their footprints on the wall. This was a symbol of their long journey to the capital. On another street action the Mujeres threw themselves on the floor to shield the debtors' protest from attack by police.

'After three-and-a-half months, we managed to sit down with the large banking and financial associations and the Deudora group and achieved an agreement. Now people whose houses were being auctioned off have had their debts excused.

'Once an agreement was signed that benefited the debtors, we organised a kind of festival with flowers and bread. The children began to share out the bread with everyone, a symbol of the olla (collective cooking pot) of the poor—the poor who share what they have.'

Article from New Internationalist, *July 2002*

With Dynamite and Molotovs, Anarchists Occupy Government Buildings

Juventudes Libertarias (Anarchist Youth), Bolivia, July 2, 2001

Small debtors have been calling for a solution to their credit problems for 95 days. At ten o'clock this morning some of them took over government buildings. Among them were members of the anarchist-feminist group Mujeres Creando (Women's Initiative), whom the government named as responsible for the action.

About a hundred activists occupied the office of the Defensoria del Pueblo (People's Defence). Several dozen also occupied the office of the Catholic archbishop. But the most striking event occurred at the banking supervisory agency, where a thousand debtors occupied offices and detained 94 of the institution's functionaries.

One group of activists passed unnoticed by security guards, went into the banking authority building and took some of its employees as hostages. Groups were also able to enter the bishop's office and the Defensorìa before they were noticed.

Once inside the banking agency, activists sprayed the entrance hall with gasoline near the door of the superintendent's office. From the top floor of the building they threw sticks of dynamite into the Isabel la Catulica Plaza in order to prevent the police from entering. Groups of plainclothes cops attempted to retake the building.

Top-level functionaries of the banking authority were tied up in their offices and bundles of dynamite were tied to their bodies to prevent any kind of police intervention. The activists wore dozens of dynamite sticks around their bodies and some carried old military firearms.

At least a dozen activists positioned themselves on the balconies of the fifth floor of the banking authority's building and gave speeches using bullhorns.

"We are here because nobody is listening to us. These people are showing the typical hard-heartedness of bankers. We are here because we cannot pay our debts." Their words echoed loudly from their fifth floor position, accompanied by insults and songs directed against the bankers.

Carrying a bullhorn, molotov cocktails and sticks of dynamite, the small debtors walked around the building's balconies, setting off more than an explosion in the Plaza Isabel la Catulica in order to make their demands heard.

One woman protester used a bullhorn to communicate her complaint to the police surrounding the place: "For the poor there is no relief, no justice. They have taken everything from us, leaving us sticks of dynamite to eat. Because only the deal-makers have rights, we have been here, living in the street, in the cold of night, with scarcely one meal a day, for more than 90 days. And nobody will listen to us."

Representing the debtors at a press conference, another woman declared, "We cannot leave while there is no dialogue to solve our problem, and if no solution is found, we are determined to commit suicide right in front of them—because we cannot put up with this situation any longer."

This protest movement includes 12,000 workers and unemployed people who have borrowed small sums of money and have been abused by the private banks' usurious practices. Today they are demanding total cancellation of their debts, an end to the suits against them and an end to the impounding of their meager goods. For three months thousands of debtors have been coming to La Paz from all parts of Bolivia to stage daily protests. These had pacifist beginnings but later became more radical, going as far as attempting to burn banks. During the conflict, because of the misery and desperation surrounding them, more than six debtors have committed suicide. Many have been forced to give up all their belongings and live in the street. Meanwhile, the government favors the rich by pardoning their debts and granting them immense sums of money.

In the middle of the night, attempts were begun to free the 94 functionaries still held in the banking authority building. This involved a six-person committee for assuring their safety, including the anarchist Julieta P., as well as some low types such as the rightwing legislator F. Kieffer, a former paramilitary operative. While the negotiations continued the building remained closed. Included in the talks were debtors (headed by the anarchist Marìa Galindo Mujeres Creando group) and representatives of the private banks, senior Catholic clergymen, the Defensora del Pueblo (People's Defense), and members of Derechos Humanos (human Rights).

There has been a ban on cameras and bringing in food or drink. The building is constantly surrounded by a cordon of police. According to unofficial reports, sharpshooters have been positioned in the area and specially trained commando units have been brought in.

The Bolivian government is openly fascist. The genocidal President-General Banzer has had many social fighters murdered during the four years of his regime. We denounce the human rights clowns, the reactionary Catholic Church and the Bank vultures as makers of a smoke screen to divert attention to the negotiating table while the government prepares its dogs to execute a bloodbath.

The activity of the small debtors is by nature anticapitalist, because it delegitimizes private property and directly attacks profits. It utilizes direct action and self-organisation.

The Bolivian state has been called the most corrupt in the Americas. Inequality verges on the sordid. Hunger, massacres and unemployment rule. The intensity of the class struggle is making the exploited more radical in their struggles. Twelve days ago Aymara farmers blocked highways in the Altiplano region to demand an end to neoliberalism. The state responded by murdering two of them. The answer was dynamite attacks on powerline towers.

We call on the anarchist movement in particular and anticapitalists in general to protest at Bolivian embassies, to spread word of our struggles in order to stop a genocide in the making.

Violence is justifiable, insurrection is indispensable.

ONWARD TO THE SOCIAL REVOLUTION...

DIRECT ACTION AGAINST CAPITAL AND THE STATE!

19

AN INTERVIEW WITH MUJERES CREANDO

Translated by Pat Southorn March 2002

INTERVIEW WITH JULIETA PAREDES OF MUJERES CREANDO, AN anarcha-feminist group in La Paz, Bolivia.

How did Mujeres Creando (Women Creating) come about? What is its goal?

JP: Mujeres Creando is a "craziness" started by three women (Julieta Paredes, Maria Galindo and Monica Mendoza) from the arrogant, homophobic and totalitarian Left of Bolivia during the '80s, where heterosexuality was still the model and feminism was understood to be divisive. It's not really a new design in a society such as ours. So we had already been developing this kind of criticism. The other part of our criticism of the Left is toward what has been a constructed social practice; that is, it was unethical, dishonest and it had a double morality.

Revolutionary in the streets, revolutionary in their words, revolutionary in their talking, yet, at home, they were the dictators of their own families, with their own loved ones.

We have started to realize the original proposal of Mujeres Creando, and so we have been picking over all our experiences with the Left, as well as learning through our first time taking part in the San Bernard Conference in Argentina, which was an experience of all Latin American feminists.

From the viewpoint of Mujeres Creando, one way to move toward our goal is the concept of diversity (the other is creativity). Diversity is fundamental for us, because if you look at how other groups are made up, they're usually of the same kind of people (barrio [neighborhood], young people, workers, lesbians, etc.). Diversity is a way to criticise these "enclosed cubicles" in society. Mujeres Creando is made up of lesbians and heterosexuals, whites and indigenous women, young and old women, divorced and married women, women from the country and from the city, etc. The system tries to keep us in the "enclosed cubicles" and to divide us so that it can control us more effectively.

What's important is that we, through our connection with other women, are starting to observe the diversity in which Latin American feminism developed; that is, there were farmers, students, soldiers, lesbians, etc. It was beautiful and it captivated us.

Afterwards we realized that it wasn't enough just to be a woman... there were deep political differences. We keep on with the feminist movement and become feminists, and immediately we see something that seems to us like empty space: it's all good and diverse, but what was our position as to (government) power?

The difference between us and those who talk about the overthrow of capitalism is that all their proposals for a new society come from the patriarchy of the left. As feminists in Mujeres Creando we want revolution, a real change of the system; we do not want just to change capitalism, nor just to change attitudes toward women, but also a change in attitude toward young people and the environment. We want to change patriarchy, in a historical and long-lasting transformation that is being created by the feminism we dream of.

In the process of constructing organisation—no bosses, no hierarchy—I speak for myself and don't represent anybody... I've said it and I'll say it again that we're not anarchists by Bakunin or the CNT, but rather by our grandmothers, and that's a beautiful school of anarchism.

What is it to be a feminist in Latin America?

JP: To be a feminist in our society means to fight against neoliberalism and its ideology; for us, being a feminist means denouncing racism, machismo/sexism (in the Left and within anarchism, as well as feminine sexism), homophobia, domestic violence, etc. It means denouncing the sexist, bureaucratized, technocratic women of this generation (for us, those women that have fallen into neoliberalism and are administrators of the murderous politics of the World Bank, IMF, etc.) Here's the difference between us and them: they use power and are within the system, and therefore they always control the forces (military, economic, social, political) against those who oppose what they say.

So, we're not interested in power, women's offices, or ministries. We are interested in the daily construction of practice and theory in the streets and in nurturing our creativity.

Our generation denounces the unjust relationship between men and women, just as the class concept has denounced the unjust relationship between the bourgeois and the proletariat. Therefore, it should have led to a revolution, but it's changed into a concept grabbed up by the system, because the only thing that works is the description of being a man or woman today, not the denunciation of the relationship's injustice... so, the generation becomes a descriptive concept. Feminism looks for ways to recover this category, which has a descriptive aspect, but more importantly its denouncing character. We bring this character forward in our fight for the construction of our anti-patriarchal theory.

What do you think of the "lack of women" in social movements? Is it a myth or an historical reality?

JP: It seems to me like a blindfold when people ask, "where are the women?" We have been around since the beginning of revolutionary moments, always.

On the other hand, in today's era, social movements (Sem-Terra, de los Deudores, Madres y Abuelas de Plaza de Mayo) are all women-led fights resisting and confronting dictatorships. What we see is a division between public and private affairs, a blindfold, an invisibility in the struggles.

How do men and women, indoctrinated into a patriarchal society, react to the goals of Mujeres Creando?

JP: Women have sympathy as well as fear. The sexist women are much more stubborn and violent than macho men. These men are careful about having sex with us; they're afraid, it's some kind of complex... but in the end they have a certain kind of respect toward us because we have been fighting for ten or eleven years. At first, most women have sympathy, and later they're afraid because it's a demanding and radical proposal, but that's the only way to build a place where everything is not superficial and diluted. And the men that sympathize with us follow us if they're interested in everything, but they keep wanting us to be like mothers, feeding them; they're a little lazy because they don't want to accept the challenge of making their own group.

What is your vision of social change as relates to the books you [Mujeres Creando] write and the videos and graffiti you make?

JP: You can want a microphone or camera like you'd want a rifle, neither with bullets nor with audio or pictures. No, I'll say what I want to say to others.

We have given communication a high place, on the same level as creativity—that is, creativity in communication. So we have preferred to take from our roots and, by leaving them, we begin a creative communication process. In '92 we started to do graffiti. We did it in Cochabamba, Santa Cruz, and other places. And so, out of all our work that we do, the graffitis (signed Mujeres Creando) are not anonymous—we put what we want, and everybody knows that MC is in this area, and if someone wants to put us in jail, he or she comes here and does it. Whenever we've gone out to do graffiti, we have been afraid, and we're always afraid. But we've thought about our right to do it... Coca-Cola pays and paints, Repsol pays and paints, so why can't we paint without paying? The problem isn't that the walls are painted, the problem is that it's not paid for. If we must pay for public space, then it's a big contradiction in democracy. What's public and what's private?

Streets are public space, the whole city's courtyard, not a jail hallway, where you go from the jail of your house to the jail of your office job... if it's public, then everybody can use it. But if you pay for public space it becomes private. Public space doesn't exist. Let's start this discussion.

What's dirty? What's clean? "You're making my walls dirty!" Oh, so when Coca-Cola contracts a painter, it doesn't make the wall dirty? That's an aesthetic concept. It seems to me that it has made the wall dirty in a disgusting way. And what we have done, our graffiti, that's beautiful.

What are some of the next projects for Mujeres Creando? Is it possible that you will participate in IMC Bolivia?

J.P.: If we want Mujeres Creando to go on, it needs to question itself, and not embody a myth like "a cute group of feminists" because you have to have roots in society. For this, I propose to build a space (Creando Feminismo Autonomo [Creating Autonomous Feminism]) for other women and other social groups where we'd build feminism in terms of Mujeres Creando... and I think it's important to let people know about these experiences through Indymedia.

My privileged space is for women; I want to start with them. I want to start from there, to feed others and myself through the Indymedia space. I don't consider this women's space to be apart from others—I think that we can get into deeper discussion if we start with women. But I don't want it to start in Indymedia and finish with the women. It's a social proposal by women and for both women AND men.

20

THE CREATIVE FORCE OF BOLIVIAN DEBTORS

MARÍA GALINDO IS A MEMBER OF WOMEN CREATING, AN ANARchist-feminist collective in La Paz, the Bolivian capital. The group runs a small cultural centre, publishes a biweekly paper and publishes books, but is known mostly for its clever graffiti and creative direct actions. In recent months, the group has helped lead almost daily protests by about 10,000 Bolivians, mostly women, who are demanding cancellation of bank debts. In this essay, translated from Spanish by Bruce Campbell, Galindo describes another recent direct action.

All social change is born as creative action capable of breaking, of moving, of calling together. In May, I infiltrated the Bolivian Chamber of Commerce's annual Luxury Luncheon at the Radisson Hotel in downtown La Paz. My goal was to publicise a debt-cancellation demand of thousands of women ready to converge at the hotel.

The women are among half a million Bolivians with microcredit loans, the financing promoted by banks and nongovernmental organisations as a response to unemployment and hunger in the neoliberal age. The loans have gone mostly to women, whom lenders recognise as assuming the greatest responsibility for their family's survival and meeting repayment schedules most reliably. Supposedly self-employed, many of the women and often their children have ended up working 14–16 hours a day while running up debts as high as $5,000 with annual interest rates of up to 120 percent. Bolivia's economic crisis has sunk most of the businesses. Repaying the debt is unthinkable.

No such worries faced the luncheon guests. It was one of the most select gatherings since neoliberalism took root 15 years ago. The chosen, the winners, the intelligent ones and the occasional society lady—all white or whitened—had discovered how to turn a profit without wrinkling their suits and how to guarantee the loot with tear gas. They included the microcredit lenders, the invisible bosses of the street vendors, artisans, underground entrepreneurs and tradespersons. These gentlemen celebrated themselves as finance geniuses for launching businesses with capital diverted from anti-poverty programmes. Disguised as honest men, they sat down, ready to enjoy a delectable lunch.

I sat among them and stirred my soup, waiting for my moment. My table companions enjoyed the paste—slurp, smack, slurp, smack—and we discussed the stock market and the keynote speech by Banks Superintendent Fernando Calvo. They mistook me for one of their own! At 2 p.m., as the sun revealed the fat belly of boredom, dessert arrived. It was time to break in.

Just then, like Pachamama (who, I'm certain, is on our side), two television cameras arrived. As they began taping, I darted to the podium and placed our sheet of denunciations over the superintendent's notes. "We must interrupt because we are fed up with the insensitivity and the rhetoric," I announced.

From table to table, I distributed our leaflet, scolding, shouting and pestering them. I described the terror of children when lawyers brought eviction orders. I said it was impossible to extract another cent from the debtors. I called the bankers inhumane bloodsuckers.

What's the point of such direct action? It's fun. Insolence and mockery are indispensable for our movement. Without us, the luncheon would have been a warm reception for the superintendent. With us inside, the event became scandalous, shameful and profoundly unpleasant.

After saying everything that struck my fancy, I looked at my watch and calculated that my people had arrived at the hotel door. I headed outside and, according to plan, there they were. The unemployed women, formerly deluded into believing that a microcredit loan would ensure a roof and shoes for their children, were shouting and singing about settling a score: the debt that society and the banks owed them.

In the banquet room, meanwhile, the bankers tried to recuperate from my invasion. They hurried through dessert amid frozen smiles. Then they descended elegant steps toward the hotel exit, as if walking toward gallows.

Outside we met them face-to-face. Neither the uniformed nor plainclothes police on site could have protected them. We shouted but, despite cowardly claims to the contrary by the bankers and their columnist friends, we didn't attack or even insult them. We are humane, and we know that social change comes not from hate or violence, but from hope and creativity.

MORE AK PRESS TITLES

Queering Anarchism

Addressing and Undressing Power and Desire
Edited by C.B. Daring, J. Rogue, Deric Shannon, and Abbey Volcano
$19.95 | £14.00 • paperback
AK Press
9781849351201

What does it mean to "queer" the world around us? How does the radical refusal of the mainstream codification of GLBT identity as a new gender norm come into focus in the context of anarchist theory and practice? How do our notions of orientation inform our politics—and vice versa? *Queering Anarchism* brings together a diverse set of writings, ranging from the deeply theoretical to the playfully personal, that explore the possibilities of the concept of "queering," turning the dominant, and largely heteronormative, structures of belief and identity entirely inside out. Ranging in topic from the economy to disability, politics, social structures, sexual practice, interpersonal relationships, and beyond, the authors here suggest that queering might be more than a set of personal preferences—pointing toward the possibility of an entirely new way of viewing the world.

Captive Genders

Trans Embodiment and the Prison Industrial Complex
Edited by Eric A. Stanley and Nat Smith
$21.95 | £18.00 • paperback
AK Press
9781849350709

Pathologized, terrorized, and confined, trans/gender non-conforming and queer folks have always struggled against the enormity of the prison industrial complex. The first collection of its kind, Eric A. Stanley and Nat Smith bring together current and former prisoners, activists, and academics to offer new ways for understanding how race, gender, ability, and sexuality are lived under the crushing weight of captivity. Through a politic of gender self-determination, this collection argues that trans/queer liberation and prison abolition must be grown together. From rioting against police violence and critiquing hate crimes legislation to prisoners demanding access to HIV medications, and far beyond, *Captive Genders* is a challenge for us all to join the struggle.

Sister of the Road

The Autobiography of Boxcar Bertha
Ben Reitman
$15.00 | £12.00 • paperback
AK Press/Nabat
9781902593036

Hobo jungles, bughouses, whorehouses, Chicago's main stem, IWW meeting halls, skid rows and open freight cars—these were the haunts of Bertha Thompson. This vivid autobiography recounts one hell of a rugged woman's hard-living depression-era saga of misadventures with pimps, hopheads, murderers, yeggs, wobblies and anarchists. *Boxcar Bertha*, as told to Dr. Ben Reitman, himself notorious as a whorehouse physician, Hobo King, lover and colleague of Emma Goldman, is fascinating history written from the bottom, the sort that the stultifying fairytales used in classrooms always cut out. A strong dose of the real thing. Kathy Acker contributes an introduction to this underground classic.

SCUM Manifesto

Valerie Solanas
$8.00 | £3.50 • paperback
AK Press
9781873176443

"Life in this society being, at best, an utter bore and no aspect of society being at all relevant to women, there remains to civic-minded, responsible, thrill-seeking females only to overthrow the government, eliminate the money system, institute complete automation and destroy the male sex."
This is the definitive edition of the *SCUM Manifesto* with an afterword detailing the life and death of Valerie Solanas. The manifesto is also available in audio cassette format at £7.50 from AK.

Tales From The Clit

A Female Experience of Pornography
Edited by Cherie Matrix & Feminists Against Censorship
$13.95 | £7.95 • paperback
AK Press
9781873176092

True stories by some of the world's most pro-sex feminists. These women have provided intimate, anti-censorship essays to reestablish the idea that equality of the sexes doesn't have to mean no sex. From sexual experiences and physical perception through to the academic arena, this groundbreaking volume documents women's POSITIVE thoughts, uses and desires for, with and about pornography. Essays include such diverse topics as how the authors discovered porn, what it means to a blind and deaf woman, running a sex magazine, starting a sex shop and what the contributors would actually LIKE to see. Compiled by Feminists Against Censorship, *Tales From The Clit* is erotically and intellectually arousing.

Prisons on Fire

Angela Davis and David Hilliard, et. al.
$14.98 | £10.00 • CD
AK Press Audio
9781902593524

Thirty years ago, prisons across the US burned. Here's how, why and what happened. Who were the Attica Brothers? Why did they seize control of the prisons? Who was George Jackson? Why was he murdered by a prison administration? What do these 'lost' histories tell us about prison repression and the struggle for freedom today? 30 years on, through archive audio, music and interviews, the voices of the Attica Brothers, Jonathan Jackson Jr., Angela Davis, Ruchell Magee, David Hilliard and more introduce and grapple with this legacy. *50 mins*

Pussycat Fever

Kathy Acker
$10.95 | £4.95 • paperback
AK Press
9781873176634

"If one day, a bad girl named Dante met a mean dyke called Hieronymous Bosch, this is the book they'd make"—Jenny Livingstone, director *Paris Burning*. "Scarified sensibility, subversive intellect, and predatory wit make her a writer like no other"—*The New York Times Book Review*. Kathy Acker holds a unique place among American novelists as a writer who constantly pushes at the frontiers of modern fiction, with each new work advancing further into unchartered territory. Pussycat Fever is a hallucinatory amalgam of emotion and desire. Join Pussycat and the anonymous narrator on a journey filled with sex and dangerous liasons. Coming of age was never like this! Kathy's words are complemented by the artwork of Diane DiMassa, best known for her long running comic book series *Hothead Paisan*, and the intriguing collages of famed artist Freddie Baer.

Beneath the Paving Stones...

Situationists and the Street, May 1968
Dark Star Collective
$15.00 | £9.00 • paperback
AK Press
9781902593388

This anthology comprises three pamphlets—*The Poverty of Student Life; Totality for Kids* and *The Decline and Fall of the Spectacular Commodity Economy* plus eyewitness accounts of the Paris May '68 events. For those people in the late 60's who were not involved in the "inner circle of situationist radicalism" or whose French was non-existent but had a growing awareness of radical politics, the chances are their knowledge of Situationist theory would have been based on these three pamphlets. The collection provides an accessible introduction to the main aspects of the Situationist Project in much more comprehensible language than that used by Debord in *Society of the Spectacle*.

Illustrated throughout by photographs of the May events and the graffiti that played such an integral part of the uprising, set alongside dramatic eyewitness accounts, the whole book gives a real sense of the spirit of revolution prevalent at the time.

An Anarchist FAQ

Volumes 1 and 2
Edited by Iain McKay
$25.00 | £20.00 • paperback
AK Press
9781902593906

This exhaustive 2-volume set seeks to provide answers for the curious and critical about anarchist theory, history, and practice. More a reference volume than a primer, *An Anarchist FAQ* eschews curt answers and engages with questions in a thorough, matter-of-fact style. Having been an internet staple for over a decade, we are proud to offer this solicitously edited print version. AFAQ's oversized and affordable format (topping out at over 700 pages per volume) will ensure it a place on every shelf, where it will be referenced again and again.

Anarchism and Its Aspirations

Cindy Milstein
$12.00 | £9.00 • paperback
AK Press
9781849350013

From nineteenth-century newspaper publishers to the participants in the "battle of Seattle" and the recent Greek uprising, anarchists have been inspired by the ideal of a free society of free individuals-a world without hierarchy or domination. But what exactly would that look like, and how can we get there? *Anarchism and Its Aspirations* provides an accessible overview of an often-misunderstood political philosophy, highlighting its principles and practices as well as its reconstructive vision of a liberatory society.

Partisanas

Women in the Armed Resistance to Fascism and German Occupation (1936–1945)
Ingrid Strobl
$21.95 | £13.00 • paperback
AK Press
9781904859697

Common stereotypes of women during wartime relegate them to the sidelines of history—to supporting roles like dutiful munitions factory workers or devoted wives waiting for their men to return home. The truth is that much of the armed resistance to fascism, before and during World War II, can be chalked up to women about whom official accounts have little or nothing to say. Through years of intrepid research and numerous interviews with the participants themselves, Ingrid Strobl excavates the history of the women who shouldered guns, planned assassinations, planted bombs, and were among the era's most active antifascist fighters. Strobl's commitment to and respect for her subjects has resulted in a work of both scholarly rigor and emotional depth. Weaving moving personal narratives into the broader history of the European resistance, *Partisanas* is both a detailed historical account and an investigation into what compelled women to reject their traditional roles to take up arms in a fight for a better world.This first English-language edition was translated by Paul Sharkey.

Arm the Spirit

A Woman's Journey Underground and Back
Diana Block
$19.95 | £15.00 • paperback
AK Press
9781904859871

In June 1985, Diana Block, her two-week-old son, and five companions fled Los Angeles after finding a surveillance device in their car. Facing the possibility of arrest because of her militant activities in the struggle for Puerto Rican independence, Diana spent the next decade living underground: on the run from the FBI, raising two children, and juggling security, solidarity, and motherhood. In a perfect demonstration that the personal is political, Diana's memoir offers insights into efforts to build homegrown clandestine resistance to US imperialism. With emotional depth and a poetic style, the book brings a woman's perspective to a subject typically dominated by heroic, male discourse.

Friends of AK Press

In the last 12 months AK Press has published tons of great new titles. We aim to continue this output of radical material, along with reprints of existing work. However, not only are we financially constrained as to what (and how much) we can publish, we already have a huge backlog of excellent material we would like to publish sooner rather than later. If we had the money, we could easily publish over thirty titles in the next 12 months...

Friends of AK Press is a way in which you can directly help us to try to realise many more such projects, much faster. Friends pay a minimum of £15 per month/$25 in the USA (of course we have no objection to larger sums!). In return as a Friend you will receive one copy FREE of EVERY new AK Press title. You are also entitled to a discount off EVERYTHING featured in the current AK Distribution catalogue on any and every order. (When ordering please indicate that you are a Friend.) We also run a scheme where groups or individuals can sponsor a whole book.

Please contact us for more details and to receive an order form

In the UK: **telephone** 0131 555 5165 or **e-mail** ak@akedin.demon.co.uk
In the USA: **telephone** 510 208 1700 or **e-mail** info@akpress.org
http://www.akpress.org/friends.html

www.ingramcontent.com/pod-product-compliance
Lightning Source LLC
Jackson TN
JSHW052008131224
75386JS00036B/1233

9781849351034